DATA MODELING

FOR INFORMATION PROFESSIONALS

ISBN 0-13-080450-9

90000

DATA MODELING
FOR INFORMATION PROFESSIONALS

BOB SCHMIDT | Edited by David Warren, Ph.D.

Prentice Hall PTR
Upper Saddle River, NJ 07458
http://www.phptr.com

Library of Congress Cataloging-in-Publication Data

Schmidt, Bob
    Data modeling for information professionals / Bob Schmidt; edited
by David Warren.
         p.   cm.
    Includes index.
    ISBN 0-13-080450-9 (alk. paper)
    1. Database design. 2. Data structures (Computer science)
I. Warren, David, Ph.D. II. Title.
QA76.9.D3S289   1998   98-18833
005.7--DC21   CIP

Editorial/production supervision: *Jane Bonnell*
Cover design director: *Jerry Votta*
Cover design: *Anthony Gemmellaro*
Cover/interior photo: *Tim McCandless*
  (courtesy of agpw, inc.)
Interior design and composition: *Gail Cocker-Bogusz*

Manufacturing manager: *Alexis R. Heydt*
Acquisitions editor: *John Anderson*
Editorial assistant: *Linda Ramagnano*
Marketing manager: *Miles Williams*

© 1999 by Prentice Hall PTR
Prentice-Hall, Inc.
A Simon & Schuster Company
Upper Saddle River, New Jersey 07458

Prentice Hall books are widely used by corporations and government agencies for training, marketing, and resale.
The publisher offers discounts on this book when ordered in bulk quantities. For more information, contact Corporate Sales Department, Phone: 800-382-3419; FAX: 201- 236-7141;
E-mail: corpsales@prenhall.com
Or write: Prentice Hall PTR, Corporate Sales Dept., One Lake Street, Upper Saddle River, NJ 07458.

Illustrations in this book were developed on SILVERRUN Relational Data Modeler (RDM) and are used herein with the permission of SILVERRUN Technologies, Inc. RDM is included on the CD; further inquiries should be directed to SILVERRUN at 201-391-6500 (US), or if you are dialing from the US or Canada, at 800-537-4262.

Data Modeling for Information Professionals revises and extends previous works by the author. Those works largely consist of computer-based training courses sold under the names CASE Essence, DataMaster (name dropped by agreement with DataMasters), and Infostructor®. Use of this material is governed by agreement between agpw, incorporated, and Prentice-Hall, Inc. Inquiries regarding electronic versions of these earlier works should be directed to agpw at 314-361-5224 (US), or if you are dialing from the US or Canada, at 800-795-7953.

Product and company names mentioned herein are the trademarks or registered trademarks of their respective owners.

Printed in the United States of America
10 9 8 7 6 5 4 3 2 1

ISBN 0-13-080450-9

Prentice-Hall International (UK) Limited, *London*
Prentice-Hall of Australia Pty. Limited, *Sydney*
Prentice-Hall Canada Inc., *Toronto*
Prentice-Hall Hispanoamericana, S.A., *Mexico*
Prentice-Hall of India Private Limited, *New Delhi*
Prentice-Hall of Japan, Inc., *Tokyo*
Simon & Schuster Asia Pte. Ltd., *Singapore*
Editora Prentice-Hall do Brasil, Ltda., *Rio de Janeiro*

This book is my contribution to the profession: for all the challenges it has presented me, for all the wonderful people it has introduced me to, for turning me toward a fascinating exploration of the way we structure data.

To my family, to my friends I dedicate myself—from now on, I promise.

—B. S.

To Rhona: *"the dews of your melody scatter/ Delight."*

—D. W.

Contents

Part **Two**

Sets of Predicates   **62**

Concept **4**

Entities 65

Concept **9**

Attributes...197

Part **Five**

Conclusion   **218**

You Could Do Everything Right...
but Still Make a Mess..221

Editor's Preface

Most information systems professionals think they already know all they need to know about Data Modeling. They believe they have the ability to think clearly about data. Yet the gap between what these folks say they know and what they actually know remains huge. One CASE vendor contracted specialists to develop a formal evaluation instrument. During trials, 1/3 of the questions apparently were too easy; 1/3 of the questions were too hard. As to the last 1/3, the experts could not agree on what the right answer should have been. Our own testing shows that information professionals score about 50 out of 100, and of those choosing alternative answers, little agreement exists as to what the right answer should be.

In addition, most information systems owners—the management that's paying the very large sums of money—rarely understand the importance of solid data analysis. How could thinking clearly about data *not* be a part of anyone's job?

Put these two scary facts together, and you can easily understand why projects keep coming in way over budget or just plain failing. I know of one Fortune 100 company where for the last five years (at least) they have followed the same roller-coaster pattern: when they are on a project, they declare themselves "too busy to breathe" (a very telling metaphor, wouldn't you say?) and so too busy to learn anything about Data Modeling; when everything falls apart and management declares a reorganization, they insist they must not do anything until "we know what our jobs are" and so can see no value in learning how to sharpen their abilities to analyze; when the reorganization finally concludes, the same old patterns take off all over again.

The waste we all know exists in the information systems world rivals that of the proverbial "government waste"—unless you are thinking of the money the government wastes on computer systems.

In the Spring of 1992, Bob Schmidt asked me to edit the text for the alpha version of a computer-based education he had created "for people who develop computer systems." As an academic who had recently developed a serious interest in hypertext, I decided I would be imprudent to turn down an opportunity to examine a real-world application of electronic writing space (and to supplement my university wages)—but I expected it to be dull. The topic sounded technical, and every technical treatise I had ever encountered had been a snoozer.

As I began to read the work, I found myself laughing and developing a strong admiration for the clarity of the style and for the wit that permeated the work. I remember picking up the phone and calling Bob to tell him how much I liked what I was reading, but also to give him my (ignorant) opinion that "computer people" just weren't going to appreciate what he was doing here. Bob told me not to worry. I took his advice and kept enjoying myself.

Working with Bob was so enjoyable that I eventually joined the start-up he founded—agpw, inc. (as in, "a great place to work")—to publish and market the interactive education in Data Modeling. Very quickly we discovered that my concern had been ill-founded: the vast majority of information professionals who studied the product were thrilled to have this topic explained in a way that was intelligible without losing its intelligence. Veterans of systems development told us that Bob's "electric book" was the only technical material they actually looked forward to reading.

While the fact that these technical professionals needed education that also managed to entertain was rapidly becoming clear, the key praise for Bob's work was for its depth. Members of the data profession were not only enjoying the course but also learning a lot. Indeed, apparently the longer someone had been involved with systems development, the more highly he or she regarded Bob's discussion. I have since concluded that this phenomenon is the result of the abundance of real project history that Bob has incorporated into his work. The more experienced data professionals have so much more to relate to in Bob's assessment of Data Modeling.

This unanticipated acclaim found its way into print in the January 1996 issue of *Database Programming & Design,* in which Terry Moriarty published a review of the then-current version of the product. Even Terry, who was and remains one of the outstanding information analysts on the planet, declared she had profited from reading Bob's course on Data Modeling. Towards the end of her review, Terry warned she believed "[t]here's a real danger that the modeling community may overlook the value of the insights found in [Bob's work] due to the impression that the class is for beginners. If Bob Schmidt had his ideas published in a book format, we would be heralding it as one of the outstanding works on information analysis."

So, Terry, here it is.

Preface

Have you ever thought to yourself as you were finishing a project, "I ought to write down everything I learned from this experience and…"? I finally did. Then I thought, "Gee, somebody might buy this and…"

Included on the enclosed CD as "Travl_DM.rdm" you will find the data model from a top-to-bottom and front-to-back business process redesign of a world-wide tour operator. You also get RDM.exe, the SILVERRUN CASE tool you need to bowse it. Reviewing a data model can be about as interesting as looking at the blueprints for Uncle Bert's vacation home. So we built an entire curriculum around the real experiences of this expansive CASE project. The static images found in the text expand and link to each other in SILVERRUN'S repository. The interactive data model, the SILVERRUN software, and the structured curriculum work together to demystify data modeling.

The techniques in this book resolve real problems. Too often we are lulled into believing that analysis is simple because we are fed simplistic examples which were conjured to prove the value of a technique. The twisted circumstances of the real world confound simplistic approaches. In this book you will find techniques to resolve everything that this tour operator could throw at my project from questionnaire processing to currency futures trading. I bet there is a technique in here to resolve your circumstance too. On the other hand, there are no "pet" techniques looking for an application. As a practitioner, you appreciate that there is simply not time for neat ideas that don't help you get the job done. There isn't one technique in this book that doesn't deliver value to your effort, either making it easier to document a requirement or to develop software or both.

This exposition of data modeling techniques first became available as computer-based training under various trade names depending on the company distributing it. I sell it as CASE Essence or Infostructor, IBM as Modelmaster, and Sybase sells it as Data Modeling for DataArchitect. A sampler of the original work is included on the CD; look for the CBT_Demo folder and Infos.exe. So, as I write, I have had the advantage of suffering a relatively constant critique of my ideas since they were first made public in December 1992. Because the first version of my work was self-published and rather expensive, I had the opportunity to engage in dialogue with many hundreds of evaluators. I am most proud of the more than half-dozen written reviews—a batting average of 1.000. In translating the material from the interactive work to the printed page, I have tried to make all the improvements I have wanted to make but could never find the time, and yet keep the loose spirit of the original that had won so much praise.

I would like to comment on a few aspects of the material. First of all, it is not about computers. Second, it is not elegant. Third, it is not about me.

You cannot use the word you mean to define in your definition. I cannot say, "A home is a home where I live." I cannot define the structures used in developing software in terms of software structures. So this book is not about software, precisely because its intent is to help you define software. My approach is to ask you to inspect your human language to explore the way we organize data. I have been greatly influenced by a few computer science classics such as *Essential Systems Analysis* by McMenamin and Palmer,[1] but most of my studies have been organized by Arthur Andersen, Ernst & Young, and Apple Computer. When I wanted to learn more, I found more inspiration in Ray Jackendoff and Ludwig Wittgenstein than in the usual literature. I am sure that these writers have influenced my use of dialogue and an inspection of common language to understand information.

Most of what I really know I have learned by doing. If you wonder, *what has this guy really done?* I can say that I have seen projects through from Planning to Construction at least four times over the last 15 years. If my approaches seem practical, the reason is that I have greeted too many Denny's waitresses at three in the morning to take software construction as anything more glamorous than a 90s version of the ditch-digger my father always warned me about.

This book is not as elegant as it is long. The introduction and the conclusion both contain a short summary of my model of data. Were I to practice strict economy of argument, this text might have fit on the back of a box of Shredded Wheat; it might also have been as impenetrable as the *Tractatus*. Perhaps real understanding is not so linear as the written word. Rather, to approach real understanding, we have to observe it from every possible perspective. Only after we have numerous experiences can we start to integrate them into a clear picture.

---

1. *Prentice Hall, 1984, ISBN 0-13-287905-0.*

The general approach to this exposition is to use a large number of examples to help you understand the underlying structure to the data with which you work. The examples are plausible versions of actual project issues; you will be tempted to react to them by asking, *But what if...?* The answer is, if the example is changed, then the answer will change. If the example seems abbreviated or somewhat contrived, it is only so in an attempt to highlight some one aspect of some one concept. I am amazed that as I study some examples, they continue to unfold their complexity; it turns out that even the simplest statement can exemplify not one but many of the concepts we are trying to teach. Pursuing all the issues presented by each example allows me to explain concepts from many different directions.

To help the reader distinguish the concepts one from another as they appear in various parts of the text, I have adopted something of a set of presentation standards, as follows. Any concept that you should master is capitalized, e.g., Domain. Domains and Classes, as you will learn, are kinds of lists. When referring to the list as a whole, I present the name of a Domain in SMALL CAPS. The items that comprise the Domain are between quotes. When referring to the name of a Class, I present the name in CAPITALS. An example of a Predicate, whether it be a Relationship or an Attribute, is underscored. I confess that when one tries to use standards such as these, one finds many confusing exceptions, such as what if you are asking the reader, "Is CUSTOMER a Class?"? I decided in these cases not to capitalize. What if the word was a Class but was not being used in the context of a data model as in, "People just don't think that way"? People is a Class, but if we capitalized every time we used a class word, the text would look like a paste-up ransom note.

One last note: I have tried to keep the text lively. Incredibly, many (and I mean quite a few) readers have told me they actually enjoy this course. As a matter of fact, only about 3% of readers say they are annoyed by the flip, corny, sometimes antagonizing style. (Three percent is down a bit from a high around 5% before I replaced "damn" with "darn" as in "darn" funny how people will react.) One way I have kept things interesting is to avoid equivocation. Rather than saying "almost always," I just get out there and say "always." Rather than saying "Be careful not to," I say "You will never work in this industry again." I'm sure I could get to 2% if I lightened up, but darn the quibblers.

To keep winning readers, I have eliminated any phony "we" references. I am not going to try and make you believe that there is a grand think tank at work here. When I say "I," I mean literally me. The text just reads better. I want you to know that everything I know, I learned from you. I am fully aware that I knew nothing about Data Modeling when I started, that a number of people have given me direction and insights, and that really I can add nothing new to all the valuable material that already exists. My contribution has been to pull together the pieces that seem to help explain how we organize data and try to explain them in a way that is, well, lively.

Acknowledgments

No one person has had a more supportive role in producing this work than my wife, Jen. I literally could not have done it without her. I probably would not have done it except I needed to support our children, Nicolas, Jacob, Justin, and a last one who is yet nameless.

David Warren has stood by me for six years through hope and disappointment. Without his constant praise and encouragement, I would probably be adding digits to dates in some dank COBOL factory.

I have learned from so many people that I am afraid to begin to list them, for fear I will omit someone. Some of the most significant teachers were students in classes whose names now escape me but whose crazy questions often sent me on fruitful re-examination of what I had been taught. I flatter myself that some of the people I have worked with over the years will pick this book up and recognize me. Anyone who, as I have, struggles honestly, with great passion and little sleep toward better Analysis is going to leave a trail of people with varying opinions as to their character. I want to say to everyone that I am deeply appreciative of your patience and would love to reacquaint. In any case, thanks to all of you.

Many other authors have allowed me to quote the wonderful things they have said about my work. I have been influenced and encouraged to pursue my ideas by Peter Coad, Clive Finkelstein, David Hay, Dan Kara, Terry Moriarty, Aric Rosenbaum, David Wendelken, and John Zachman.

Finally, I would be remiss if I didn't mention by name some people whose faith made it economically possible to spend the thousands of hours I have spent on various aspects of this book. Unbeknownst to many of these people, their business snatched me from the jaws of financial ruin. With apologies for all the changing employment, in reverse chronological order I would like to thank Mary Barnes and Tony DeTaranto of SILVER-RUN Technologies; Mark Taub of Prentice Hall; David Lepley of AMP; Doug Little, Mary Schmitz, and Bill Tingle of Enterprise Rent-a-Car; Cathy Owen, Marge Ulsomer, Davide Vieira, and Pete Williams of IBM; Todd Boes, Steve

Curtin, and Barbara Ludinsky of Sybase; Carolyn Benenati of Computer Task Group; Jim Armstrong, Becky Berry, and Mike Sweda of McDonnell Douglas; Jo Meador of Boeing; Tom Mayer of Anheuser-Busch; and David Brown, Susan Garber, and David Stuhr of Lotus Development.

The illustrations in this book are developed in SILVERRUN from SILVER-RUN Technologies, Inc. (www.silverrun.com). I am grateful for the company's support on this most important project. I could not have presented the ideas in this book without a CASE tool with SILVERRUN's capabilities. I encourage my readers to take advantage of the included data model and explore the features of SILVERRUN made available here.

About the Author and Editor

Bob Schmidt founded agpw, inc.—his first start-up venture—where he authored and marketed comprehensive education in Data Modeling. agpw titles include *CASE Essence, Infostructor, Data Modeling with PowerDesigner DataArchitect,* and *ModelMaster for VisualAge DataAtlas.* Bob has also served as Chairman of the Board in family ventures in the construction industry. Bob previously served as a consultant for the firms of Arthur Andersen & Co. and Ernst & Young, where he evaluated, designed, and implemented large-scale business systems. At E&Y, Bob was among the first to earn the title of Master Analyst. His insights into systems analysis are drawn from project experiences with such companies as Coca-Cola Foods, Michelin Tire, Exxon, Shell International, Service Corporation International, Southwestern Bell Telephone, and Chiquita Brands. Bob is currently promoting a better understanding of systems analysis through various speaking and writing opportunities. Bob can be reached at schmidt@agpw.com.

David Warren holds a Ph.D. in nineteenth-century British Literature. After more than a decade of university-level teaching, during which time he developed expertise in hypertext and multimedia instructional computing, he joined agpw, inc., in 1992 as one of the principals. His responsibilities have included being part of the design team for computer-based education on the structure of Information. His work has contributed to the training of information professionals in the United States, Canada, Europe, and the Middle East. David can be reached at warren@agpw.com.

Introduction

This book has been written for individuals who find themselves helping to create an information system, especially a computerized information system. No one can be computer-free these days. For most of us, the computer is something inflicted upon us. It may be the friendly telephone voice that keeps us from talking to anyone. It may be the efficient billing agent informing us we are a day late on our payment. It may be the vague notion that "out there" competitors are using computers to our disadvantage. The computer age is upon us all.

A very great number of us, millions of us in fact, are responsible for the creation of these modern marvels. You might be surprised if I said I have never met a programmer who ever wrote anything except marvelous software. This text is written for system developers who through painful experience are now hungry for perspectives and ideas that may make their next system better than their last. If it turns out that but one very prolific but ignorant programmer is responsible for all the bad systems, then I will be very disappointed to have gone on so long when I could simply have sat on the person's hand until he or she agreed to desist from writing any more bad software.

Among the millions responsible for all the software are a number of specialists: database administrators who hate the data administrators who are at odds with the programmers who aspire to be analysts. If you hold any or all of these titles, then you should work your way through the entire text of this book.

Project managers are persons who, having done well at what they used to do, have been asked to do something for which they are entirely unprepared. If you fit this description, then you should be spending your time learning to manage people and projects, but if you are unfamiliar with the concepts of Data Modeling, a quick read of this book will help you appreciate what the people you are managing should be doing. You may find a few helpful tips along the way.

You may have none of these titles and still be hooked into helping to create an information system. They may have told you that you were a Subject Matter Expert (SME) which sounds suspiciously close to *Schmo*. I am sure that They told you what an exciting opportunity this is for you. This text will help you when your old co-workers won't talk to you any more and the systems people disappear at lunch time. Announce loudly, "I am not going to lunch today. I am studying to find out what we are really supposed to be doing." Suddenly, you will have many people inviting you to lunch, if only to keep you fat and happy. SMEs should study each topic in detail at least through the discussion of "Sets of Entities." After that topic, the material is of a more technical nature.

This text makes Data Modeling concepts accessible to everyone on a project team, especially the people who ultimately will benefit from the use of the computer software. This text creates a structured and common language between those who pay the bills and those who build the software. Those reasons alone make this book something worth studying. Maybe this would be a good time to take comments from the audience.

I do not have time for this

You need to take time for this because computer software is very expensive. Recouping the investment becomes impossible if the ongoing maintenance of the finished product is more costly than the original construction. Ultimately, software proves to have a very short life-span; probably the project you are working on will replace software already in use. When software has no moving parts and is completely modifiable, why does it wear out? The answers to this question are many, but surely a major factor is the way each programmer has to build more and more knowledge of the business into the higher level languages. The software gets top-heavy and impossible to modify further.

The tenets of Data Modeling seek to improve the quality of the original software, to make it easier to change, and ultimately to extend the life of that software. The business knowledge is encoded into the lower levels of the application hence creating a lasting foundation. By improving quality, reducing maintenance cost, and extending the viable life of software, Data Modeling tries to improve the return on your investment in software.

But I need practical information

Nothing is more practical than understanding instead of rote learning. Nothing more is impractical than going out to design a complex information system without a real working understanding of Data Modeling. Would you hire a plumber if you were not comfortable that he or she really knew the trade?

How much do you really need to know about Data Modeling to make a database? I hope your answer is the same as mine: "All you can know." This book does not stop at simple examples such as <u>Invoice has Invoice line</u> because I know that your real responsibilities are more complex than that. The discussion does not stop at rote learning because I am not interested that you memorize, for example, my definition of an Entity. I would prefer that you be able to come up with your own definition and argue it with me!

My goal is to get the dedicated student to a level above "That's not the way this text said to do it." Rather, I want that student to declare, "I know that's not the way this text does it. This situation is different, and for these reasons I am doing it differently." You can reach such a level only when you understand the underlying concepts of Data Modeling. "Practical information" is often a misnomer for disjointed examples and simplistic rules that never seem to apply in any actual situation. Nothing is more impractical than trying to apply some overly simplified rule to some enormously important and complex situation.

But we're a Wang Shop

This text teaches some very basic concepts. It doesn't matter if you are developing software for personal, workstation, mini, mainframe, or super computers. The way you describe your needs is the same.

You may be using any methodology, Method/1, Navigator, Datarun.... Each methodology may develop systems in a different order or with different terms. However, they all deal with data in the same way: "Build ye the data model." Nor does it matter what Computer-Assisted Software Engineering (CASE) tool you use—PowerDesigner, DataAtlas, SILVERRUN.... To succeed with any of these tools, you must understand at least Domains, Names, and Predicates. To tell you the truth, I don't care if you are putting together a paper-based system or even just trying to organize a legal document. Thinking clearly about data can't hurt; being unable to think clearly about data is like sleepwalking in a burning house.

Understanding the material in this text is as critical as knowing arithmetic. Arithmetic is essential to everything you may do with numbers. This text is essential to everything you may do with information.

But I'm a user

Only one other industry calls its customers "users." Regardless of how appropriate this term may be, this text prefers the term "owners." You as owner need to understand Data Modeling more than anyone else—because you are paying for it.

Imagine buying a home. The architect shows you three hundred pages of memos and revisions, and then blithely declares, "Everything is in order. Just sign here, and we'll start building your house." You'd go ballistic; you want to visualize your new home.

Now imagine your new architect asserts, "Everything is in order. Just review these diagrams, and sign off. One small thing: instead of blueprints we are now using a state-of-the-art design tool. A little outfit in Greece came up with it. You couldn't possibly understand it, but we'd be happy to drag you through it by your eyelids at $150 an hour until you sign." You'd probably pass yourself coming down on your way up.

At a bare-bones minimum, you the owner need to communicate with your systems builder in a language that you both understand. In the construction industry, they use blueprints; in the information industry, data and process models are becoming the standard. You have to understand these models to take responsibility for the design. Do not trust the information systems group to get it right without your review. You should be able to understand your own needs in terms of the information with which you work. This understanding will ensure that you get what you want with the least frustration. You will likely find that Data Modeling will help you in unexpected ways, even before information systems professionals (and their big bills) get involved.

But I'm not technically inclined

Good, because this text is not technical information. The f symbol appears but just once or twice, and you can close your eyes when we get to that part. This course teaches you a way to describe your job to computer people so that they can build software to help you. It is more like learning a new language than learning computer science.

True, you already know a language; true, the onus to understand your needs lies with the system builders. But have a little heart: these poor people are killing themselves to understand in weeks processes you are still learning and devising. Knowledge of Data Modeling will give you the language you need to understand your own processes better; to communicate them succinctly, completely, and coherently to systems builders; and to verify that they have built a system as you had directed it be built.

So no technical ability required—just find the right words to describe what you already know.

But I don't want to learn this

You already know too much. The first (and still best) information system is language. This is not just a silly analogy; by any definition, the language you speak qualifies as an information system. However, you know your language so well you may find thinking about it difficult. It is like asking, "How do you walk?" Easier done than said.

If you had some Tinker-Toys and tried to build a model of walking, you would soon realize that walking is a pretty amazing feat. How could something so easy to do be so difficult to explain?! The same is true for trying to describe how we communicate. This text describes for you some of how we communicate; since you are an expert in communicating, you need only to follow along and see if you agree. Although the process may not be easy, you may find the discovery fun, something like seeing the back of your head for the first time in a mirror.

If I learn this, what's in it for me?

This book instructs you in certain modes of thinking that are very helpful when working with complex systems or in teams with other developers. The knowledge you gain here will not become obsolete with the newest operating system or programming language. You can take it with you from project to project, regardless of the challenges that new project poses.

You might ask, *helpful? How could I need more help? My development software increased my productivity 300%; my methodology increased my productivity 250%; and my quality team increased my productivity 1,000%. I am so productive, I can't stand it!* Careful study of this book will help you to develop systems that

- are simpler to use
- act more intelligently
- are simpler to maintain and extend
- contain fewer errors
- integrate in a meaningful way to other applications
- share data across an enterprise
- encourage reusability
- facilitate team problem solving

Some of these benefits are bound to improve productivity—I'd say about 437%. You'll be so wildly productive, you won't care if it's really only 400% or so. Write me a letter and tell me what you are doing with all your new-found free time. (Editor's note: your productivity gain may vary.)

Does a Thing Called Data Modeling Exist?

People often say, "No one right way to model data exists." Yet what we see during contentious modeling sessions is one person holding fast to his right way and another person holding fast to her right way. What they mean when they say "No one right way to model data exists" is that they cannot resolve their differences. Rarely does anyone stand up and say, "You could do it this way or that; it doesn't really matter." Nor are analysts going to start saying that, because that would give the impression that there is no reason to model at all.

One right way of expressing information system requirements in a data model must exist; otherwise nothing exists to argue, study, write, or teach. Data Modeling has been developed because we need common principles to guide our efforts to build information systems. Arguments do not arise because no right answer is available; we argue because we are dealing with different facts, we weigh the facts differently, or we are working from different principles. What makes one argument constructive and another destructive? Human factors aside, if we are arguing from different principles, then our arguments are likely to end badly. If we are arguing with the same understanding of the principles, then we are likely to discover the source of our disagreements and at least come to respect each other's position.

Consider how we behave if you and I come up with different answers to an arithmetic problem. We would probably work through the problem out loud until one of us saw how we had deviated from the rules of arithmetic. This scenario is an example of two people working with the same principles. Remember the last political argument you had. Did you agree with the other person's principles? The fact that analysts often refer to battles over information systems requirements gathering as "religious wars" is telling. For analysts to be able to work through an understanding of information systems requirements together, or to understand requirements gathered before, or to expect their requirements to be understood later or by another department, then they must share a common understanding of a single set of Data Modeling principles. For us to work together to analyze information systems then, these principles have to be as accepted as are the arithmetic axioms.

But do such axioms exist for Data Modeling?[1]

Rather than answer this question directly, allow me to pose a different question: why can English be translated into Greek? An English text can be translated into Greek in such a way that the Greek reader and the English reader can both understand the author of the text in the same way. We can infer from this fact that a thing called meaning can be attained apart from the language used to communicate it.

School children can tell you that a sentence can be broken down into parts such as subjects and verbs. Do we know as much about the structure of meaning? One argument supposes that the structure of meaning parallels the structure of language—but which language, and is the structure of language as we suppose it to be?

Languages are tools whereby people express their meanings. As with any tool, some are more well-suited to a particular task than others. (And some practitioners are better than others.) By way of analogy, a crescent wrench is a good all-around wrench, but a monkey-wrench is better for pipes. Natural languages such as Greek and English are suited for a broad range of ideas from technical exposition to artistic expression. Even as many natural languages are being extinguished, new designer languages are being invented. As with the monkey wrench, these designer languages are well-suited to a particular task. I am speaking now of the languages such as those that accountants and engineers use. These professions have a jargon, syntactical rules, and symbols that constitute a language, one that simplifies exchanging their meanings with their colleagues. Data Modeling is a language designed for expressing ideas about the things for which people want to record data.

Like all languages, the language of Data Modeling needs to conform to the inherent structures of meaning. True, language can be understood even when there is no awareness of the underlying structure of meaning, but how much more effectively can a language be used when one does understand the fundamentals! Data processing systems have to organize data in a manner compatible with the way the people organize data. So data processing professionals have a lot to gain from the study of Data Modeling.

Professional languages are inventions that evolve over many generations. Initially, many different approaches to the syntax, symbolism, and semantics of a language will be tried, but as each language matures, it will converge on one best approach. The computer itself is hardly a generation old, and so the languages we are developing seem forced and imperfect. The evolution is relatively fast, and we are still confronted with many dif-

---

1. *Portions of this section first appeared in* DM Review, *"The Language of Data Modeling" by Richard K. Fisher, Introduction by Bob Schmidt (April 1998).*

ferent approaches that have not yet converged. But already we can see that the various Data Modeling languages can be translated one into another. A diagram developed in the Merise notation can be translated into a diagram in the Information Engineering notation without difficulty. The fact that each of these Data Modeling notations are translatable one into another demonstrates that the underlying principles of semantics are now more uniform than disparate.

That one language can be translated into another proves that one underlying structure exists to information that we can learn and use to express information systems requirements. This one structure is comprised of the principles we need to be able to work together to design information systems. Cognitive scientists and linguists refer to this structure as the Universal Language; analysts call it the meta-model. Data Modeling applies an understanding of the properties of data and its uses to the development of data processing systems.

About This Text

Among data analysts, surprising consensus exists as to what that structure called the meta-model might be. This text attempts to explain the meta-model through many examples from systems analysis experience. It takes a lot of words to set up examples, give solutions, and explain the underlying principles. I would have made my discussion shorter if I had only known how to explain the meta-model without reference to actual application. Had I merely laid out the basic structure, the book would have resembled the next few paragraphs.

Putting aside many of the finer points of cognition (elements that escape computers), we can say that people create their picture of the world with just three concepts: what we can discover, the things themselves, and what we want to know about those things. These concepts are discussed in turn under the rubric "Basic Parts," which covers the concepts of Domains, Names, and Predicates.

From these three concepts, people finish their mental pictures in the same way they might pick out shapes in clouds or organs in a sonogram. We create the other concepts by connecting Predicates. An Entity is the one set of all Predicates that describe the same thing. A State is some subset of an Entity's Predicates necessary for some process. We can create sets of States to show how States sometimes interact.

Once we have connected Predicates into Entities and States, we can group Entities into Classes. A Class is the one set of all Entities that have the same Predicates. A Superclass is the set of all Entities that share certain

Predicates as may be needed for a particular process. A selection is a set of all Entities based on the values of the Predicates, not the Predicates themselves. The following table might help to summarize these concepts. For instance, the first row reads, "The concept Entity is a group of Predicates based on having the same argument which results in each Predicate pertaining to one and only one Entity. The concept is implemented as a record."

Concept	is a group of	based on having	which results in	Concept becomes a
Entity	Predicates	the same argument	each Predicate pertaining to one and only one Entity.	record
State	Predicates	the same argument and relevance to a process	any Predicate pertaining to any number of States.	projection of some fields of a record. Software encapsulates validation rules.
Class	Entities	the same set of Predicates	each Entity pertaining to one and only one Class.	table
Superclass	Entities	the same Predicates and relevance to a process	any Entity pertaining to any number of Superclasses.	projection of some fields and a union of records having those fields
Selection	Entities	the same value in some Predicate(s) and relevance to a process	any Entity pertaining to any number of selections.	select statement

The organization of this text is based on the progression from basic parts to the various ways those parts can be aggregated. These few basic parts of the model are exercised by people in such ingenious ways that the underlying simplicity is obscured in much the same way a Bach fugue would seem impossible to score with just twelve tones. And, truthfully, the model is imperfect, just as I would also be truthful in saying musicians use tones that do not strictly conform to the twelve of the musical score.

This text provides an education in the essential concepts that are the foundations of all information systems. Terms such as Entity or Superclass may be nothing but words to you right now, or you may have used them differently from the way I will use them in this text. The objective of this text is not that you should be facile with a particular set of labels but rather that we should all come to understand a rational model for structuring information. Once we share one perspective, we will work together more effectively.

The model that describes the structure of information is not a prescription. It is a reflection of the natural ways we all structure the information we work with day in and day out. Studying the way we make sense of information is like studying the way we walk or breathe. Although we are experts at walking, breathing, and thinking, we may find it rather confusing to describe exactly how we do them.

Usually courses on computers are about how you do something. Generally, you are shown some tool—whether a word processor, a CASE tool, a programming language—and then you learn how to use it. This course will not teach you how to use any tool. This text disassembles information in the same way that a chemist breaks down a compound. You will come to see how the atoms of language (Domains, Names, and Predicates) combine according to a few simple rules to make all the complex structures of data.

Information was not invented when the computer was created any more than transportation was conceived when the first automobile was built. The structure of information is older than our own species. *So?* you might ask. Artificial information processing is better when it follows our natural ways of thinking. We have difficulty imitating natural processes when we don't have a good idea of how the natural process works. Think of this course as stepping back from the specifics of a single system and looking deeply into the roots of all information systems. If you change your perspective on information itself, you change the way you look at everything from computer applications to legal documents.

Tip for System Analysts

If you have studied Data Modeling before, you might be surprised by this text. Most other courses on data modeling teach the principles in the following order:

- Classes
- Attributes
- Relationships

Such a lesson plan has CASE tool use in mind. You will probably use a CASE tool, but CASE tools are helpful only if you have a high degree of knowledge about Data Modeling.

CASE tools did not spontaneously create themselves. Nor is it any coincidence that CASE tools are fundamentally similar. CASE tools have been designed to facilitate Data Modeling in the same way CAD tools are designed to facilitate drawing blueprints. To really know how to use a CASE tool, you cannot just learn what the menus do—you must understand Data Modeling.

This text teaches you Data Modeling first and keeps CASE in its place as a tool. So don't mind that the flow of the course is different. The greater purpose of this text is to establish a common ground where the technician and the Subject Matter Expert can meet and exchange data requirements. To get to this common ground, technicians have to travel a long way from their comfortable discussions of megabytes and indexing schemes. Subject Matter Experts have a long road as well in that they have to qualify and quantify things that they never had to before.

Arriving at this new territory, both camps have the opportunity to see things as if seeing them for the first time, but they must have a language with which to begin a new dialogue.

Data Modeling Overview

Now might be a good time to reinforce distinctions among Data Modeling the discipline, methodologies that require Data Modeling, and CASE tools that facilitate it.

Data Modeling the discipline says that, for example, Entities exist in the world of the owner. A methodology might have a step like, A.2.2.2 "Develop the Data Model." (Easier enumerated than done.) A CASE tool is software in which you can easily document the data model. CASE is to a project team as a General Ledger is to the accounting department. Once you understand the discipline, you can explain to your project manager why step A.2.2.2 is going to take 50% of the project budget. Once you understand the discipline, you will be able to master any CASE tool easily and use not only the standard Entity-Relationship diagrams but also create other reports as you need them.

Data Modeling applies an understanding of the properties of data and its uses to the development of data processing systems. A data model is what you get when you document the Predicates, Classes, and Superclasses of the information system. A data model is simply a representation of the information needed to carry out some activity. A data model is to an information system as an architectural drawing is to a building or as a wiring diagram is to a circuit. This is not a new idea. Who can argue with the idea of working something out on paper before you build it? Nevertheless, many information systems have been hammered together without a data model. This could explain why there never seems to be an end to rewriting old systems.

Figure I-1 is meant to make you familiar with the Entity-Relationship diagram (ERD). This particular ERD focuses on the Class called Reservation; that is to say, all of the Relationships between Reservation and other Classes are shown. I chose a moderately complex part of the overall data model not because I want to intimidate anybody but because I do not want to give you the impression that real models are either small or simple. As in the case of learning any language, it will seem foreign at first. As you progress, you will find the diagram very easy to read and extremely useful.

If you are already using Data Modeling, then you might notice there are differences between the diagrams with which you are familiar and that shown. The underlying ideas are unchanged. Once you have fully understood what a Relationship is and what a Class is, you will be able to effectively use data models regardless of how they might be drawn.

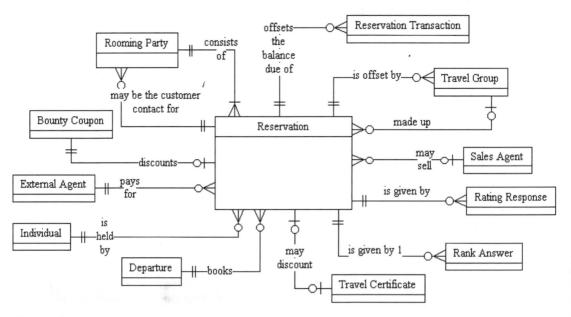

Figure I-1

Why all the jargon? Why all these new symbols?
Is this another Masonic conspiracy?

Just as in Architecture or in Electrical Engineering, Data Modeling uses a specialized language. Note the similarities among the three languages:

- Mix graphics and text
- Require rigorous syntax
- Specialize for a limited scope of use
- Facilitate construction of some end product
- Resist casual mastery

Note that the jobs of the analyst and the architect are similar in that their primary role is to translate the language of the people paying the bills into the language of the folks doing the construction. The diagramming conventions and specialized language are not obfuscations. For you to effectively engineer information, you must be fluent in the language of Data Modeling.

Why develop a model? I know what I need to do. There ain't
nobody crying at my door for any models.

Architects make drawings and build models for a number of reasons:

- To try it on paper first
- To estimate the cost of construction
- To present their ideas to the owners
- To direct the construction

Architects can use their models to test stress on key building elements and to simulate energy and lighting requirements. They can use their drawings to count palettes of bricks, yards of concrete, panes of glass, and other elements necessary to estimate construction costs. These important functions require that their drawings be detailed and accurate. The elements of the drawings must be standard and used consistently.

Data models fulfill these same functions of experimentation and budgeting, and have the same requirements for consistency. Data models reduce the endless meetings, hallway conversations, incomprehensible memos, and overbearing proclamations into the essential elements of an information system. The development of a data model may be bone-breaking, but the data model is as malleable as Silly-Putty when compared to a completed or even a prototypical computer system. In this way, the data model allows the project team to try out their scheme on paper before spending more of your money on design. Despite their protests, systems builders do appreciate having a blueprint. Nothing is more disheartening than to see good work wasted because of changing directions and priorities.

Data Modeling allows project managers to introduce a degree of objectivity into their estimation of the cost and duration of software development projects. While the ability to count the various parts of the data model creates an impression of objectivity, the fact that the system has been worked out on paper first gives a real degree of predictability to software projects.

Owners can become familiar enough with the models to contribute in a real way during the approval process. They should be at least as familiar with the conventions and jargon of the data modelers as they are with the blueprints for their own home. Who would build a house without blueprints? Why are so many multi-million dollar systems built without proper models?

Imagine a map that showed everything you could ever want to know about U.S. highways. It would include city streets, gas stations, motels, tourist information centers, and so forth. Such a map would be useless because it would be so full of useful stuff. The more you put on the map, the more it would resemble the reality in which you were lost. Real maps are more focused and less detailed.

Consider highway maps and city street maps. They both show the same kinds of information, only the latter are more detailed than the former. In the same way, data models may contract and explode detail to help keep perspective. Consider the difference between a city map and a tourist map. The city map will have more streets but will omit important sites such as "The Thing From 200,000 BC!" The tourist map focuses on a particular need. In the same way, data models will focus on distinct parts of the business. Data models focus on one critical concern: what data a business works with when it does what it does. Data models do not document how a business processes data.

We don't put everything we know about a place on a map, and we don't put everything we know about an information system on a data model. We must be consistent about the kinds of things we include. First of all, a data model is about data.

In the beginning, there was only process. We were always asking what people did. We flowed, and documented, and structured, and it was only sorta OK. But the rulers of the land of Getitdone called for more analysts and more programmers, and after great suffering, the pyramids rose from the shifting sand. Some who had built the pyramids saw in them a sign. At first, just a murmur, but soon a crusade for Data Modeling began. Many analysts have been eaten by the lions of Getitdone in the name of Data Modeling. Early persecution has driven data modelers into their own form of bigotry. These data bigots have forgotten that data comes from processing needs and ultimately serves some process.

However, a basic tenet of Data Modeling is the separation of data and process. You might recall from some other introduction to Data Modeling the ubiquitous mandala of the pyramid in which one side is data, and the other, process. The data model tries to decouple data from process for good reason. First, business knowledge properly captured in the database can radiate consistency throughout the applications that rely on it. The knowledge is recorded one time and used in many programs. Second, the structure of data changes less frequently than processes change. True, the reason for including data in a model is that it is needed for some process, whether the process is automated or manual. Nevertheless, we can clearly benefit from making the distinction between process and data. For example, a customer is a customer is a customer, but hire a new marketing manager, and all of your processes and reports dealing with customers may change. The data is constant; the way the data is used changes. To the extent that data can be distilled from process, the information system can be made more long-lasting.

That data is stable and process is flimsy is best witnessed during software conversion. So often, one can easily map the data of the old system into the data of the new system. Data structures remain unchanged despite numerous rewrites of systems.

Data models also omit any suggestion of how data might actually be stored, for the same basic reason they exclude process. How things are done in the system being studied is off-limits during the first steps of developing an information system. You must ignore how to do something until after you know everything that you want to do.

"How" might be interpreted to mean the steps of a process; they are definitely not a part of Data Modeling. There is a great temptation to describe how something is done or is going to be done. Those who want to reinvent everything every day and those who want to leave it like it is until retirement day drag us into discussions of "How" at every opportunity. There are two fundamental problems with jumping in and discussing how something should be done. First, it takes a lot of time. Second, the solution may depend on an understanding of the whole system.

Just as disastrously, we can get mired down in "How are we going to store this stuff?" By avoiding decisions about security, volumes, access speed, structures, and vendors, you save time and avoid rework. When all the requirements are in, then you can work creatively to satisfy them while balancing security, volumes, etc. Often what happens is you decide the whole system is too big and decide to defer parts of it—another good reason to have avoided talking bits and bytes.

In any case, the technical solution may depend on an understanding of the whole system. As you work on problem *b* you discover that you really need to rework something in problem *a*. Fine enough. When you get to problem *c* you realize you need to redesign parts of *a* and *b*. Problem *z*? Forget problem *z*. Imagine a process that seems very IO intensive. But the system owners decide that overnight processing is okay. So you make decisions about how the files should be structured. Then another team comes up with a requirement for the same data, but it has to be up-to-the-minute. This new requirement probably changes what you would do regarding the first requirement. Wouldn't it have been better if the Database Administrator had all the facts before deciding the particulars of database access?

As soon as somebody says, "It might be this way, or it might be that way," you can be sure that you have left the solid ground of What for the tar pit of How. You might as well stop struggling and wait for the wolves of project management to come and gnaw on your bones. You always have many ways to accomplish something, including ways yet to be discussed. However, there is only one What. Get the Whats described and leave the Hows for later. Then you stand a chance of getting finished.

Watch sign painters: they sketch in the letters first; then they do the fine work. You too should sketch and refine as you develop an understanding of an information system. Define what you want to do; then figure out how. As an exercise to achieve this goal, ask modelers to pretend that they are working with a "perfect computer," one that can store infinite amounts of data and access any of it in 0 nanoseconds at $0 cost. If you had such a computer, then you would not be concerned with how much history was kept or whether it was stored redundantly. This kind of mental exercise allows you to get to the bedrock, that is, "What" the system owners want you to track.

Tip for System Analysts

If, when you strip away all the nanos and teras, you find yourself in a state of mindlessness—a mental state without thoughts, a void—then you might find this state of mind a good way to relax. Practice this just ten minutes each day for a new you.

Tip for Project Managers

The fact is that your technical persons would rather discuss the 101 ways to store a piece of data than find out what a piece of data might mean. To know what something means is not a function of the database any more than a jar needs to knows what might be in it. So the technician reasons that the meaning of data is not something to be concerned about. Besides, finding out what something means would require talking to an owner. This alone should adequately explain why the technician would rather explore ways of shaving nanoseconds off read/write than finding out what we want to access.

You do not want them worrying with how to store something because it takes 101 times as much effort as finding out what should be stored. They should know that the next requirement that is discovered may invalidate all their earlier design. For this reason, we wait until all requirements are in before we decide how those requirements will be satisfied.

The following table will let you practice separating issues relevant to the conceptual data model from issues that should not be considered until the physical data model is built. You might want to cover the right-hand side of the table with your hand to see if you agree with the results.

Project Question or Issue	Resolve in the Data Model?
Has the appearance of new types of phones changed the business?	Data model
We will not have the storage capacity for all the customers.	Design phase
Who should have access to what data and what rights will they have?	Design phase
When an employee is a customer, do we treat them any differently?	Data model
What are the possible outcomes of the process?	Data model
Can a patient have more than one doctor?	Data model
What data should be placed on the server and what on the client?	Design phase

Data models specify only WHAT information the owner cares to store. Knowing what you are trying to achieve before you start working should be as instinctual as deciding where you want to go before you start driving. Maybe because computer programming began in an era when it was cool to put the top down and just drive in endless circles around the central business district, programmers decided it wasn't cool to have a destination in mind. You have to figure out what to do and you should stop there because the people paying didn't even give you enough time to do that.

DATA MODELING
FOR INFORMATION PROFESSIONALS

Part ONE

Basic Parts

Worms cannot tell the difference between dirt and food. So, they consume everything in their path and let their intestines sort things out. At the other end of the evolutionary scale, we may joke about dogs chasing cars, but I trust that Fido knows the difference between cars and carrion. A teenager can consume a hot dog out of a baseball glove leaving glove and fingers intact. Somewhere along the evolutionary path, animals developed the ability to use their senses to improve their diets. It is not really a conscious thing with the kid or the worm. I could not stop discriminating objects any more than the worm could "get with the program." And frankly, I find the ability to discriminate things to be useful to me in a lot of areas in my life beyond the kitchen.

Walk into a room. What do you see, a kaleidoscope of color? What do you hear, a hubbub of sound? Unless you have just walked in on a screening of avant-garde film shorts from the Czech Republic, you could probably make out individual objects and sounds. The ability to literally know what is up, or to reach out and pick a toy off a table, is so basic that it would seem silly to dig into it.

Nobody had to delve much into the idea of apples falling off trees when we were an agricultural society. Great cathedrals were raised by people who hadn't a clue of the gravitational constant. When Newton asked the

ridiculous question "Why do apples fall down?" he changed the world around farmers and masons. John Glenn took his glove off to show that space did not change our basic reality—his hand was still distinct from the glove. Down below, programmers were evolving their trade and discovering that things humans took for granted in physical space had to be explicitly programmed in cyberspace.

As an experiment, plug a video camera into a computer and leave it recording your dinner. Like the worm, it will take in everything in its path through the lens. Unlike the worm, it has no intestine that allows it to take out the truly useful bits. The stuff just comes out the same way it went in. A word processor takes a stream of data and spits it back out in the same way. Without any discriminating ability, and no sure way of elimination, huge stores of mulch build up (the WWW comes to mind). Devices, such as the video camera or the keyboard, can sense but they are not sentient. I could seat the computer at a screening of avant-garde films, and it wouldn't know enough to look for the concession stand.

If we are to make computers useful to us as computers rather than passive recording devices, then we have to perform those basic transformations on the raw input as we ourselves do automatically. We make three interpretations of the data. First, we categorize the input based on what is being sensed, for instance whether it is auditory or sensate; and we measure the sensation relative to prior experience. "Hot!" Second, we name the thing that is the apparent source of the sensation. The name may be as simplistic as "Hot, that!" or as sophisticated as "Fido." Finally, we associate the sensation to the object and we give it some relevance. "Fido feels hot." Granted, a certain amount of uncertainty remains to be resolved based on cultural norms and the context of the statement: do you take Fido to the doctor or do you eat him?

There is no getting around having a human involved in plucking only the relevant data from the masses of input around us at every moment. Only you can select, measure, attribute, and note the relevance of it. The "basic parts" you will study are Domains, Names, and Predicates—which correspond to these three instinctual transformations of data. When you have a better understanding of how you yourself deal with the data, then you will be better able to create a system of organizing the useful bits so that data can be arithmetically combined, sorted, and digested. ∎

Domains

Why Should I Study Domains?

Thag pursed his lips to suck from the boiling soup. His matted hair hung down on either side of his face and dangled in the crock. Beads of sweat on his face reflected the fire light; he bent lower and lower towards the churning surface...

Our story will continue after this useful information...

Neanderthals did not understand their new tool called fire. Had someone invented language, they could have said, "Look at Thag! He's going to stick his head in the hot soup!" We still use our inventions with only a superficial understanding of how they work. This statement could apply to fire, or language, or computers. Sometimes we get burned.

To make my stew hot, I don't need to know much about fire. But if I were to build a stove, then I would need to know a lot about fire. To use my word processor, I don't need to know much about information. For example, a lot of people can write well enough to describe where they killed the

Mastodon. But few people know anything about the way language works. However, if I were to build a machine to plot where the last five mastodons were killed, then I would I need to know a lot about information.

You can begin to understand how information works by dissecting language into fundamental elements. Take for example this simple pair of words, "hot" and "not hot." "Hot" and "not hot" might have been the opposites that made up the first Domain. We can create other Domains by replacing the polar opposites with a scale, i.e., "Hot, Warm, Cool, Cold." With a kitchen thermometer we could increase the precision by replacing fuzzy terms with numbers, e.g., "180 degrees Fahrenheit."

The above discussion provides just a few examples of the way one can gauge temperature. Temperature is one of a surprisingly short list of things that we can gauge. For example, Neanderthals were probably gauging distance and salinity at about the same time they were gauging temperature. Thag: "It's too far and too hot to go to that salty lake. Let's stay home and watch the game." (Editor's note: the author doesn't really know which Domain was first.)

So why should you care? Because everything we know is based on sensing the differences between two things—gauging one thing relative to another. All the decisions we make are based on where we put things on a gauge. Any system of information will have at its core Domains.

Our story continues...

There, around a primitive campsite, the information age was born. Though other Neanderthals could hardly see Thag through the clouds of smoke hovering overhead, they did hear Thag's muffled cry of "HOT!" Then, as if the steamy clouds had condensed on the cold surface of their nascent consciousness, thoughts formed within the onlookers. They had not burned their own mouths, yet they knew not to do as Thag had done.

Cautious cavemen thought, "I'll wait until soup not hot." Some thought, "I told them not to make a stupid soup in the first place. We should have just eaten the thing where we killed it." My own very-great-grandfather thought, "Doggone, if I don't eat it now, Thag's going to get it all, like last time!"

Domains and Computer Systems

The term Domain is often used to describe any set of values from which a response to a question may be selected. So if you were to ask, *Just how hot will it be in Peshawar?* you would expect an answer such as "25 degrees Celsius." What if you had gotten the answer "a burning telephone book"? A nonsense response like this from a Pakistani tour guide might be the result of a poor Pakistani-English dictionary and would make for a good laugh around the hookah later that evening. In matters such as this, a computer has all the good humor of a traffic cop. The data entry screen in Figure 1-1 asks you to enter a temperature for cities such as Peshawar. What would you expect the computer to do if you entered nonsense into the Daytime Temp field? The computer would reject nonsense because it is not one of the expected values. This distinction is the way Domains influence the way software works; the Domain establishes the set of reasonable values.

Figure 1-1

The values that the computer will allow comprise a list, but not just any list will do. This course teaches you to distinguish between Domains and another list, a list of things. You already make the distinction intuitively— remember we are learning about the way humans organize data. Prove to yourself that you already know this stuff; Figure 1-1 shows that the fields are computer implementations of three Domains and one list of things. Which of the fields is not like the other? That is, which of the four fields is not a Domain?

Pakistani City Name is different from the other fields in a number of ways. For one, the other fields describe the city. The city describes nothing. For another, the list of city names can be expanded or contracted at the discretion of the user. By contrast, temperature must be a number in a given range. Further, temperature, longitude, and latitude can have precision. Finally, Domains such as temperature, longitude, and latitude rely on a convention such as Celsius or degrees to be meaningful.

You can easily find Domains in such places as policy manuals under headings like "Approved Reasons for Absences." You can find Domains under the glass on the desk or on the walls of cubicles where they can be easily referenced. In computer systems, Domains are found in "lookup tables."

Interviewees will indicate the existence of a Domain with statements such as, "We assign it the thus-and-so code." Most systems have the "Codes Table," which has a layout such as

- Table ID
- Code
- Description

The Codes Table implements many Domains (one per Table ID). This way you need only one file for all those pesky tables. For example, the States may be table 2; Alabama would be code "01." So to find the state that corresponded to the code "01," you would use a key of "201" to get the result "Alabama."

The Codes Table was a good idea before we had databases and screen and report generators. It may still be relevant when you are concerned about performance when opening a lot of tables. However, putting all of the Domains in a single table makes using join statements more difficult and will frustrate end-user computing. You might consider replication of Domains into a single table to satisfy all needs.

Of What Are Domains Composed?

The words we use cannot be combined willy-nilly. Different types of words do a different part of the job of conveying information. Since I am writing of Domains, I want to direct your attention to those words that can be used only to describe things. For example, "hot" can describe a bowl of soup. Words like "hot" cannot themselves be described. You can quantify it: "100 degrees Celsius is hot." You can define it: "100 degrees Celsius is the temperature at which water boils." But you cannot add to your understanding of what it means to be "hot" by the use of other descriptors; you cannot tell me how tall "hot" is or how old "hot" is or how heavy "hot" is.

Come to think of it, I cannot tell you how hot "tall, old, or heavy" is either. What about these words makes them different from words such as Theresa, telephone, or terry cloth? → *Noun's*

With soup, you have stock and (at least) veggies. Information has distinct parts as well. The most important distinction you must make is between those words that we use to describe things and those words that represent things we want to describe. Of course, plenty of words exist outside these complementary opposites; but insofar as Data Modeling is concerned, the very most important words belong to one or the other of these groups. Before reviewing the following table, consider covering the right-hand column and testing yourself to see if you agree with the classification given.

98.7 degrees Fahrenheit	Used to describe
Exxon Corporation	May be described
Blue	Used to describe
US $100,000	Used to describe
Flight 100	May be described
Salty	Used to describe
Jennifer Colten	May be described
Asset Nbr 1444	May be described

Noun's

Tip for System Analysts

A blank on a form or computer record is confusing. Did the person completing the form intend for the space to be blank, or did the person forget to complete the question? For this reason, the best approach is not to allow blank as a value in a Domain. If "unknown" is a valid response, then the word "unknown" should be a value in the Domain.

Zero in a Domain is unavoidable but may lead to ambiguous information. Computers are nasty about zeros. If no value is supplied, the computer will assume zero. Requiring entry is no help when it comes to numbers. Don't even think about putting "unknown" in place of a zero; the computer expects a number.

Whether or not the value provided was intended or not is a kind of metadata that no current database system has features to support. In any case, an analyst can do nothing to prevent users from skipping data entry. When data is very sensitive to corruption by missing data, then analysts must work with the users to devise workable strategies.

Domains Measure

Terry Halpin once called Domains "The semantic glue that holds everything together." Although I may know how heavy someone is, I cannot make real use of that information unless I know how heavy someone else is. For example, if you tell a guy, "My wife just had a seven-pound baby," that guy is left with little to say but "That's nice." Hearing that the baby weighs seven pounds only leaves him feeling uneasy that he should think something of the statistic. If you tell a guy, "My son ran for 100 yards!" he does not say, "That's nice." He says, "Awesome, Earl Campbell never ran for 100 yards in a little league game!" So long as the same Domain is involved, the new data can be compared to other data. The Domain "distance" sort of duct-tapes the kid's run and Earl Campbell's childhood record together in the guy's brain.

Domains are like measuring sticks. (A measuring stick is an analog computer that calculates distance.) Our species has invented measuring sticks for nearly every experience. When our senses tell us how heavy something is, we put that experience on the measuring stick called "weight." When we judge the weight of one thing relative to another, we begin to reason. "Golly!" we might exclaim. "I've got a bowling ball heavier than your baby!" Truly, Domains are the beginning of wisdom.

Feet and ounces are not on the same measuring stick and so are not in the same Domain. Essentially, ounces and grams are the same because they measure the same experience. You can convert one into the other. I am not ready to say they are in the same Domain, however. Take for example this list of phrases: "really hot, day before yesterday, 100 degrees Celsius, yes, zero degrees Greenwich, 100 degrees West, tomorrow, no, today, yesterday, 98.7 degrees Fahrenheit, 98 degrees East." How many different kinds of measurements are implied? The following table may help:

Measurement	Example Measures
Temperature	really hot, 100 degrees Celsius, 98.7 degrees Fahrenheit
Time	day before yesterday, tomorrow, today, yesterday
State	yes, no
Position	zero degrees Greenwich, 100 degrees West, 98 degrees East

Each measurement is understood as a whole. We do not have to define each phrase; we understand all the phrases in relation to each other. We understand "yes" because we understand its relationship to "no." On the other hand, the set of all mammal names is defined by the criteria by which an animal may belong. Each element of the set of mammal names must itself be defined to be meaningful.

Consider the set of values "true or false." I am not qualified to give you a definition of what is truth, but by any definition, it is not false. With apologies to the philosophies, we understand that something that is false is the opposite of something that is true. In fact, we can't have a notion of "true" without a notion of "false." In a similar way, you cannot have a notion of "one meter" without implying that all distances are possible. On the other hand, consider a set of things like rhinoceroses. That you should encounter a rhinoceros does not imply that more rhinoceroses exist. (Sad but true.) The state of rhinoceros does not imply a state of not-rhino except in the sense of "Well, is he a rhino or isn't he?"—in which case, you are applying the "true or false" Domain from above. The fact of a rhinoceros does not imply an anti-rhinoceros.

Note that regardless of the way the information is phrased, the measurement always describes the same thing. For example, whether the vernacular such as "really hot" or the scientific such as "98.7 Degrees Fahrenheit" is used, all the phrases are used to measure temperature. The basic sense of each group is that they are used to denote a measurement.

These individual phrases are not Domains. The sets of phrases in the table above are not Domains. We are getting closer to the idea of a Domain. The phrases do describe, and the set of phrases measure something. However, for a set of descriptors to be a Domain, they must have a more exacting relationship to each other.

Naked Domain

Callous Neanderthals taunted Thag, "Hey! Was that soup hot or have you begun to molt?" Thag's cryptic retort "100" only convinced the tribe that Thag had in fact cooked his brains. Actually, Thag was toying with the notion that the numeric portion of a measurement was mere symbolism, devoid of meaning. Were the soup 100 degrees Fahrenheit, it would have been cool enough to eat; at 100 degrees Celsius, it made for a memorable dining experience.

A Domain is like a gauge. When you think of a gauge, you probably think of an instrument like a thermometer or a flood gauge. A Domain is a tool in the same way: a Domain is a linguistic tool used to measure something. *Merriam-Webster's Collegiate® Dictionary*[1] defines a gauge as a "measurement according to some standard or system." Their definition of a gauge is synonymous to that of a Domain; it does not make any mention of a particular device such as a thermometer. Think of a Domain not as the instrument itself but as the range of indications by which you read the instrument.

Gauges measure one thing in terms of something else, such as feet, pounds, or decibels. The thing we use to measure something is a standard or convention. For example, we may agree to use feet to measure property lines; "feet" is the convention.

Figure 1-2 is an example product catalog showing that we can select different conventions to measure the same thing, in this case, the diameter of a gasket.

Our Finest Gasket

actual size

	Centimeters	Inches
Inside Diameter	2.54	1
Outside Diameter	2.79	1.1
Outside - Inside	.25	.1

Figure   1-2

Be careful of Units.

The example also shows how selecting different Domains affects the processing of data. Two numbers of different Domains may not be arithmetically combined unless converted to be in the same Domain. In a similar way, you cannot make logical inferences when the things measured are of different types. Are twenty telephone books more than six sodas?

There are as many Domains as there are things to measure. They all require some kind of convention. Some of the special cases discussed below may provoke your thinking. Note that some conventions differ only in scale, such as feet vs. inches, but for practical purposes are still different Domains. Systems of conventions, such as the metric system, exist but we generally treat each individual measurement—such as centimeters, liters, grams—as its own Domain. One could make the argument that this dis-

---

1. *By permission from* Merriam-Webster's Collegiate® Dictionary, *Tenth Edition © 1997 by Merriam-Webster Incorporated.*

tinction was only a difference in precision, but at a certain point, we ought to just get on with it.

Some conventions are so commonplace you may forget that they are conventional. We take for granted that U.S. dollars is a way of measuring the value of something. But if I were buying a gold bar, I could pay in Pesos or Francs. I want value for my gold, regardless of how you denominate that value.

When considering a number of something, consider the something as a kind of convention. A count is meaningless without knowing what was counted. You can easily see that we need to know what a number is denominated in when we think of feet, but that need is equally true of a count of people or seats on an airplane. So "number of people" can be a kind of Domain. These conventions have some special properties as when I add apples to oranges to get a total number of fruit.

Conventions, and their associated Domains, can be combinations of other Domains—for example, dollars per hour or square feet. In these cases, you're better off not to lose sight of the component Domains and their relationship to each other. Oftentimes when you are trying to figure out complex calculations, keeping track of the combinations of Domains that are created is very helpful. If the resulting Domain is not a sensible one, then something is probably wrong with the formula.

One exception may be when the Domain drops out because of dividing a Domain by itself, as in the calculation of a percentage. Thus, if two people invest in a company, and one puts up $100 and the other puts up $300, then the first person owns 25%. The 25% is really $/$—or, algebraically, simply a number without reference to a Domain. Although we typically drop the Domain in these cases, it is still there helping us to interpret the number.

Non-numeric Domains

Some Domains, such as "number of inches" or "gender," are naturals. Their set of descriptors is established outside the information system and accepted as a standard. Many Domains, however, are contrived by the persons who own the information system. Common examples of contrived Domains include

- Chart of Accounts
- Product Classifications
- Sales Regions
- Table of Contents

The distinction is not all that stark. For example, Area Codes are pretty much outside the control of the information system—unless you happen to be the phone company, in which case you do pretty much as you please. The definition of an asset would seem fixed unless you stopped to think that the FASB (Financial Accounting Standards Board) changes that, too, every thousand years or so.

Contrived Domains are legitimate. But be careful not to confuse any list of things for Domains. For example, a list of States is a list of things that can be described as well as a list of things that describe where something may be located. Only in the second case is the list a Domain. Another common mistake is to confuse a list of types of things for a Domain. For example, your vendor file may include attorneys and utilities. Attorneys and utilities are not two values of a Domain but are names of two groups.

Tip for System Analysts

Readers who are already familiar with the techniques may wonder if these non-numeric Domains should be represented in the data model as Relationships. Figure 1-3 shows MARKET SUITABILITY and GOVERNMENT RATING drawn out as Classes.

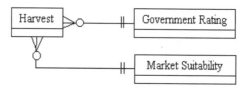

Figure   1-3

These kinds of Classes are characterized by the large number of Relationships in which they participate and a lack of Attributes of their own. Typically, these Classes will serve to further classify the Entities within the related Class. They are always a source of instability and trouble.

You can treat lists such as MARKET SUITABILITY and GOVERNMENT RATING on the data model in the same way you show Classes. They probably are Classes. However, Entity-Relationship Diagrams are confusing enough without adding dozens of classifications like these. Even though most CASE tools require that these Domains be set up as Classes in order to generate databases, I still advise deferring adding these classifications until just before the database is generated. Treating these kinds of Classes as if they were Domains makes your data modeling life easier. When treated as Domains, your model looks like Figure 1-4.

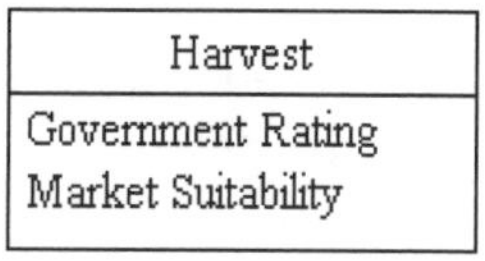

Harvest
Government Rating
Market Suitability

Figure 1-4

There is a tremendous temptation to let one Domain accommodate everyone. Without exaggeration, this is a most common and costly mistake. For instance, you might decide that only one Domain, PRODUCT TYPE, be established. Sales, Manufacturing, and other departments all agree to establish a uniform system to improve communication. Prices are established by TYPE; routing steps are set up by TYPE. Then six weeks after the system is in use, Sales wants to drop prices of all type A products except model #22. In order to effect this change, the VP of sales wants to put model #22 into a separate PRODUCT TYPE. The VP of Manufacturing says that he will not change the types because he would have to update all the routing information. Everybody is unhappy.

Often, a convergence of classification schemes seems advantageous to the organization. But the classification schemes are the way the departments organize their work; therefore, trying to take control away from one group is dangerous. Too often the compromise will fall apart at the eleventh hour, leaving the designers holding the bag.

Tip for Project Managers

Designating classification schemes as Domains rather than Classes will reduce the time analysts spend at the CASE tool and simplify Entity-Relationship diagrams.

If Domains have been set up as Classes, ignore them for estimating purposes. Assuming you are using some kind of code generator, the programming effort involved in generating screens and reports for these Classes will be insignificant.

Sets of Domains

A Domain is like a gauge in a broad sense. The indications on the gauge are not always numbers. They can be items on a list such as male/female, the settings on a switch such as on/off, or category headings as you would find in the Yellow Pages.

Very commonly, in systems, users want things to be described in some standard way. A Human Resources manager will want to know what skills an applicant has; an insurance reporting system will want to know what kind of damage a vehicle has sustained; and just about every business system will have a Chart of Accounts used to describe financial transactions. The following is a real story; it is proof that the Domains have everything to do with reasoning and only affect computers after the fact. No computer can fix the problem with the Chart of Accounts given below.

Description of Expense	Charge to Account
Labor	6555
Maintenance & Repair	7222
Unplanned Expenditures	8333
Worker Safety Related Expense	9444

Imagine you are an oil well drilling supervisor. You have approved an invoice for contract labor associated with welding repairs to a ladder that unexpectedly failed on a drilling rig. For accounting, you must select an expense category from the Chart of Accounts above.

Any, or better yet all, of the descriptors in the Domain could apply to the invoice. You are stuck with a situation such that whichever code you choose, you are right once and wrong three times.

How·do you think the drilling supervisor in this example coded the invoice?

    a.   Randomly
    b.   To his/her customary account
    c.   To the account with the biggest budget

How do you think the accountants should take this information?

    a.   With a grain of salt
    b.   With a poker face

A fix would be to allow the supervisor to select more than one item from the list. That supervisor would note that the expense was labor, maintenance, unplanned, and safety-related. This answer would also imply that it was not any other expense description. But this solution is a problem because it does not prevent the supervisor from selecting just one or two valid categories and unintentionally implying that the invoice is not related to the other categories on the list. Further, the later addition to the Chart of Accounts of some new expense category could mean that all transactions prior to the addition of the expense category were not that category. For instance, if after this transaction had been coded, the accountants add the category "Contract costs," then this transaction would be interpreted as not having been contract. Do you think that the supervisor and the accountant would get better information with a checklist format?

Circle either Yes or No.		
Contract Labor?	Yes	No
Maintenance & Repair?	Yes	No
Unplanned Expenditure?	Yes	No
Safety Related?	Yes	No

Both solutions carry the same information; the differences are largely a question of how users will react to different presentations.

A supposed Chart of Accounts is actually a series of shorter Domains with all their values intermingled. The account "labor" should be in a separate Domain along with other values that contrast with "labor." This Domain might consist of "labor, materials, interest expenses." Likewise, "maintenance" should be contrasted with a description such as "new purchases."

The analyst must get to the bottom of the question "What does accounting want to know?" If they want to know how much is spent in contracted work, that is a separate question from whether or not the expense was planned. These two aspects of the invoice must be kept separate, and the possible responses should be kept in separate Domains. Of course, you could get your Domain exactly right and still have an impossible situation, as is illustrated in the following story from the same corporation.

In order to encourage the domestic production of oil and gas, Congress passed laws giving tax breaks for exploration activity. The IRS elaborated the regulations, defining what kind of activity was "exploratory" as opposed to "developmental." Drilling might be "exploratory," but a pipeline to carry oil to market would be "developmental." Of course, they could argue about a good deal of stuff in the middle.

The tax attorneys required accounting to distinguish expenses related to exploration from developmental work. Of course, only a judge could decide how an expense should have been classified. So the accounting department hired a judge to classify all of the expenses. No, not really; actually they hired data entry clerks and paid them based on the number of expenses they could classify in a day. Then the accountants totaled up the "exploratory" expenses and the "developmental" expenses and gave the numbers to the tax attorneys. The grateful, indemnified tax attorneys would sign and file the income tax returns.

Spot the error. The persons who described the expenses as "developmental or exploratory" (the Domain) could not know what either value meant. The moral of the story is that Domains are more easily created than put to use. In this case, the Domain is legitimate since it is what it is; essentially it is a "yes/no" type Domain. The rules that cause one value to be applied instead of the other were simply not articulated.

So Where Are We?

A Domain is a system of values used to measure a quality of an object or experience. The two most fundamental elements of any information system are

- the things we know

- what we know about those things

The things we know about we call Entities. Entities are explained in Concept 4 of this book. What we know about Entities, we know by putting the Entity on some scale and giving it some value. This one is blue; that one is red; this one is light; that one is heavy; and so forth. The Domain is the scale. No Domain, no information.

Tip for Project Managers

Your project may not have a work step for "Define Domains." This work is often buried in the "Define Attributes" step. Systems use relatively few Domains. Analysts associate these Domains with Attributes over and over again. Identifying Domains separately from Attributes will speed up Attribute specification. Ultimately, separately defined Domains will save time in user interface design and lead to greater consistency.

I suggest that you develop a list of Domains as a part of current state assessment. If no current state assessment is to be done, then very many Domains can be identified early in analysis in a short brainstorming session. That list can be expanded as the data model is elaborated. Note that many of the columns in the existing database will contain values that do not conform to the standards for a Domain. Fix this problem.

Here's what you should have learned from reading about the concept of Domains:

- Domains are essential for the development of information systems.
- Domains are composed of words used to describe but which cannot themselves be described.
- These descriptors that make up Domains are related to each other, such that for any single measurement, they constitute a mutually exclusive set of choices.
- A Domain is a system of values used to measure a quality of an object or experience.
- Because Domains measure, a Domain is like a gauge.
- Domains don't have to be numeric.
- Domains may be natural, such as gender, or contrived, such as a Chart of Accounts
- Contrived Domains may in fact be a set of simpler Domains.

Names

Why Should I Care a Whit About a Nit Like Names?

Names are pervasive. I have one; you have one. Dodge names their cars things like "Caravan." When we tire of naming things, we assign them a number. If you look under the furniture in your office, you might find that some naming fairy has marked each piece with an asset identification number. For that matter, the Social Security Administration has christened me 123-45-6789. Like it? It suits. Anyway, my SS# is at least as telling of my character as is "Bob." At least it is not as misdirecting; any Bob who has perused the Bob literature will tell you that he is not like the Bob authors like to deride. I assure you that knowing my Name is Bob tells you nothing about me. We do sometimes invent descriptive Names. I always liked the Moon's "Sea of Tranquillity." Across the street from NASA, a muddy slough is called "Clear Lake," so named to draw desperate urbanites out to see the latest subdivision. These are what we call descriptive Names. Someday, I suppose, we'll all get a call to the effect of "You have already won beach-front property on the Sea of Tranquillity. All you have to do is ...." I suppose some nitwit, dreaming of his Ponderosa, will be listening. When a part of language such as naming things is so widely accepted and used, then the practice deserves a little study.

"What's in a name?" How often have we forgotten someone's Name and started probing around, "You know, he was Kojak on TV, bald guy ...." How often have you heard the expression "I'm really bad with names." It is always followed by an assurance that "I remember the face" or "I can remember everything about the person." You won't often meet someone who says they are bad about Names, faces, and can't remember a thing about anybody. Nor can I recall anyone stopping me in the street, "Oh Bob! Isn't that funny? I remember your name, but I can't think of another thing about you." Whether due to the wiring in the brain or some kind of socialization at work, we clearly subordinate Names to the knowledge of people's characteristics or circumstances. That my Name is Bob or Mital is not so important to you; you just hope I know what I am talking about.

Names and Computer Systems

So why are computers so number-happy if numbers and Names are just different ways to effect identification of things? The reason is because computers have the initiative of the beach sand from whence they came. If you said, "Update Mr. Rogers's record," the computer would not know that you are talking about THE Mr. Rogers, our best client who always stops by when he is in the neighborhood. Computers crave certainty. The computer wants everyone to have a unique Name.

The number of something, and sometimes its human-given Name, are used to get to data about that named thing (see Figure 2-1). Give the computer the Name, and it can remember everything about the person—even his or her face. I once heard the computer referred to as a prosthesis for the mind; this is a great example of how our friend the computer is good where we are bad and vice versa. Give a computer a Name and bingo, a face. Give a computer a face and—well, programmers are working on that.

The unique Name the computer uses to access data about some thing is called the key. Key is a very apt metaphor. Just as the keys on your ring allow you to get at the data in your desk drawer, the key to a file gives you access to the data in that file. A descriptive term used for the unique Name of something is the unique identifier or, less redundantly, identifier. In some graphical user interfaces, designers are using a tab as a metaphor. This is an improvement since tabs let me thumb through a file to get the record I want, whereas I use my keys to lock up my lunch from the local Neanderthals.

Figure 2-1

Computers can also keep non-unique Names, such as my own, and other unique (or practically unique) numbers for me, such as my SS#. These are sometimes called alternate keys, although this term has more meaning to the database software than to the owners of the system.

You need to know that the number you use in a computer to identify something gets sprayed into every nook and cranny of the database and even beyond. You get Names others have set up shoved into your system. Examples include UPC codes, product serial numbers, and telephone numbers. How did you like the Post Office lengthening the zip code or the phone company splitting your area code? Maybe your numbers are showing up in other systems, too. You do not want to change a Name once you have established it. This goal is the most practical reason not to use descriptive Names. If you were to have used the unique Name Southwestern Bell Corporation as your key to that company in your files, you would have been very put out when they changed their Name to SBC. If you set up a troublesome customer as Nitwit, what a pain it will be when he turns out to have been right. Even a number can actually contain a description. Wily system owners will encode descriptions into the Names. For instance, a type of vehicle you might rent has been given the innocent-seeming Name ECAR, which translates into "E = economy, C = car, A = automatic transmission, R = with air conditioning." Who needs encryption when you have this kind of hidden data? Even numbers, such as 2001, turn out to be partly descriptive, as in "2xxx are liabilities, 20xx are current liabilities." Neither your Name nor your number when it acts like a Name should signify anything.

Tip for System Analysts

You have the option to give things meaningless Names that system owners need never see. We sometimes refer to these things as tokens. For instance, each packet sent TCP/ IP is tied to all the other related packets by a token. No addressee would ever see that token. Of course you must also store meaningful Names, such as the account code given above. You can make system owners think this meaningful Name is the key, but it isn't the primary key that is being pushed into other files as a foreign key. The rigorous rules about modifiability and optionality do not apply to alternate or secondary keys. You will note that this approach does entail extra programming steps and reduced performance.

What Is a Name?

Names stand for individual things in the real world. To be more precise, I should say Proper Names, since words like "sea" stand for things in real worlds, too. "Sea" and "lake" are class Names; we use those words to describe not an individual thing but a whole lot of things that fit some general, sometimes very general, description. When we are searching for a class word, we say, "What do you call those things; they are big and you can put a boat on them?" Class Names are also important, but this chapter is about Proper Names.

Names and Domains

To a system analyst, a list of Names and a Domain are very similar. The Domain "smoking, non-smoking" is a list of words just as is "Chicken Little, Henny Penny." This kind of myopia is an occupational hazard caused by sitting too close to computers. Whether a person prefers smoking or non-smoking describes that person. Henny Penny does not describe anything, and neither M. Little nor M. Penny are to be trusted to gauge anything. Analysts will sometimes refer to Names as "a Designed Attribute." They are not Attributes or even Predicates, two terms that will be defined later.

Names are arbitrary symbols signifying nothing; they are labels intended to distinguish one thing from all other things. Their utility to an information system depends on their remaining meaningless and unique. Domains cannot be described, but they certainly have meaning. One

Name has no inherent relationship to another Name so that the list "Bob, Jen" contains no more information than "Jen, Bob." A Name is neither a Domain nor even an element within a Domain; they are two distinct basic linguistic elements from which we can build information systems.

Doing Without Names

What if we had to do without Names? "My oldest son, go tell that gal to whom I am married that dinner is ready." The world would be different, but we could get by. The trick is to use enough descriptive information such that the listener can figure out whom you are addressing. This book isn't long enough for the infamous "Shaggy Dog Story," but to paraphrase: Pat in New York City loses a shaggy dog with one blue eye and one brown, and a white Star of David on his chest, with a tail bent to the right, missing his left ear, and who can only walk backwards. A bum in the Bowery finds a dog matching that description exactly and goes through harrowing experiences to return the dog. (Editor's note: If you have young children, you can make this run for a week.) When at long last Pat sees the dog, he exclaims, "Not that shaggy!" The moral of the story: sometimes you just can't tag enough descriptors to a thing to make it completely identifiable. So, instead, we say, "Nick, go get Mommy," or "Go to the kennel and grab mutt number 456," or "Go to the parts room and count part number 123."

What if you wanted to check the price on a product at your grocer? You say, "Could you tell me the price on _____?" You could fill in that blank a number of ways.

You could ask for "UPC code 73056 00300." If you happened to have the can of soup in your hands, giving the UPC code would be a very effective way of getting information.

Leaving aside the incredible shame one should feel at replacing the art of human language with the soulless newspeak of computers, what if you didn't have the UPC code for the soup? Then you would have to describe it. The UPC code is an example of a numeric key, an abbreviation for other data that may or may not be available for that thing. You should note that by itself the UPC code is worthless; its only value is that it allows you to get to other information. The UPC I gave you was as made up as the SS# I gave you before. There is no way for you to look at a code and know what it is. If the computer were not working at that moment, then the UPC code would be less helpful than just looking at the shelf in front of you.

You could say "this soup," while waving the can overhead. "Soup" is a description of the item. However, "soup" does not give the grocer enough information to know the price. There may be different prices for different

sizes and brands of soup. "Soup" does not adequately identify the item to
determine its price. You need to search for a Name that, like the UPC code,
narrows the number of things you are looking at until there is only one
answer to your question. (Or you could act normally and hand the can of
soup over to the nice grocer.)

You could say, "Could you tell me the price on a 32-oz. can of Thag's
Red-Hot Chili soup?" In that case, you would have chosen to describe the
item so that the grocer could tell you the price. Your description included
the

- name of the food
- size of the can
- brand name

This description constitutes a unique identifier for the soup. Note that if
you changed the value of any one of these items, you could expect that the
price might be different. Not that it necessarily would be different, but it
might.

What is the relationship between this unique identifier and the UPC
code, also a unique identifier? The UPC code literally means "a 32-oz. can
of Thag's Red-Hot Chili soup"; it is shorthand designed for the convenience of computers.

Finally, what if you had asked about "a 32-oz. can of Thag's Red-Hot
Chili soup on aisle G"? This time you would have gone too far. When you
asked about just the "soup," you didn't provide enough description. Now
you are providing too much. Would you expect that the soup on aisle G
would be priced differently from soup on any other aisle? Of course, the
grocer doesn't care if you also told him the Names of your three sons; he or
she can figure out what is the relevant part of your question. Computers,
on the other hand, hate to get too much of a key; it's just not normal.

When Names Won't Do

The notion is counter-intuitive, but coming up with just the right descriptors for a plain can of soup in order to determine some fact like its price is
a far easier problem to solve than to come up with the Name of somebody
or some object that is clearly unique.

"Where is Schmedlap's file?" I might ask.
"In the cabinet."

"Oh great. Which cabinet?"
"The blue one, by the wall."
"Okay, I have two blue ones by walls."
"Isn't there a vase of lilies on one of them?"
"What, these little pink flowers?"
"I'll get it for you."

Silly? How could something that happens twenty-five times a day not be an important insight into the way we organize information? How is the file cabinet example different from the soup example? Trick question! We weren't looking for soup; we were trying to find out a price. It was a fairly simple task to determine which characteristics of soup determine price. If you had just asked for a can of soup, it could have turned into a shaggy dog story like Schmedlap's file. So why is it so hard to find just the right dog, or can, or file? Because nobody was here when the world was created to stamp everything with some Name. The real world is messy; our neat little made-up world of prices is very orderly. Oh, we try to go back now and label everything we can put our hands on, but it really doesn't work so well.

What if someone who claims to be Jerome Schmedlap calls to inquire about the balance due on his account? You may not want anybody but Jerome getting that information; often businesses worry more about spouses than the less commonly occurring con artist. Do you ask, "May I have your account number please?" You can ask, but many of us are not so organized that we have every account number for every vendor readily available. Probably the second thing anybody tries is, "What is the name on your account?" This, of course, is not foolproof. There may be duplicate Names, or the Name may have been entered not exactly as Jerome would have had it.

You could ask, "What is your phone number?" Any descriptive information about the person can be used to find him or her. You could ask for the person's address or the mother's maiden name. A phone number is a great way to try to find someone in a database. Unlike a Name, it leaves little room for interpretation. Still, I may have more than one phone, or the number may change.

Any of the above questions are legitimate. Each solution has a different set of drawbacks. There is no perfect solution, but progressively narrowing the number of possible matches usually solves the problem. In the case of people, no unique identifier exists. In fact, real things such as a person, a product, or a place don't come equipped with identifiers. In order to keep track of them, we give them Names or numbers. If the serial number is ground off or the fingerprints are scarred, then we lose the identification of the thing.

Of course, none of these lines of questioning can assure us that Jerome is telling the truth. We cannot be sure that Jerome is in fact on the line or even in the line; and we cannot be sure that Jerome isn't actually both the J. Schmedlap with the lousy credit record and the Jerry Schmedlap with the excellent credit record.

Postscript

I have enjoyed writing this concept, but I am afraid that I have lulled you into thinking Names are simple. You have to grapple with one critical idea. The things we say we know about a real-world thing like Bob are about the flesh-and-blood person—not the Name Bob. The Name stands for, is shorthand for, all the things you know about a thing that would make it unique but would be impractical to list each time you wanted to refer to the thing. So the Name comes from the things we know about that thing. Now you cannot turn around and say that something you know about a thing depends on the Name. That would be circular logic. Beware the trap of thinking that a fact about me such as credit rating is determined somehow by my name.

One last dialogue:

> "Mr. Rappaport, I'm looking at my computer; your credit is terrible."
> "I'm not Rappaport."
> "But, Mr. Rappaport, you've been videotaped stealing lingerie."
> "I'm not Rappaport."
> "But, Mr. Rappaport, the police found stolen goods in your townhome."
> "I'm not Rappaport."
> "Well, Mr. Rappaport, so now you've changed your name!"

Here's what you should have learned from reading about the concept of Names:

- The concept of Names is a familiar way of describing the information system concept of a key or unique identifier.
- A unique identifier is an arbitrary symbol intended to distinguish one thing from all other things.

- Unique identifiers can be numbers and/or characters, but they should signify nothing about the things they label.
- Things can have any number of unique identifiers.
- In the absence of a single Name, a thing needs to be uniquely identifiable by reference to descriptive information about that thing. Computers normally require that this be a fixed set of descriptors.
- Names stand for facts; as a convenience, we use Names to get to facts, but facts do not depend on Names. Facts depend on actual things.

Predicates

Tip for Project Managers

If you get nothing out of analysis but an excellent inventory of well-understood Predicates, you could still be okay. If you had everything but the Predicates, or the Predicates were incorrect, no one could save you. The correct inventory of Predicates is the key deliverable of analysis and a critical success factor going into design.

Hold this thought: Predicates describe things. Now if you read something in this section that confuses that simple idea, ignore it. It is a simple idea, but description is the essence of an information system.

A friend came out of a lecture and proclaimed, "The speaker was okay, but I wish she could have come over and woken me up before she said things that were important." This is your wake-up call. If you master Predicates, then you will be financially secure, your co-workers will think you a

genius, and you will spend more time with your children so they don't ter-
rorize you in your old age.

Most courses study Predicates in two separate parts: Attributes and Relationships. The approach here is to study the common ground between Attributes and Relationships first, and then study each in turn.

Please note that system owners do not have to know the difference between an Attribute and a Relationship, and I suspect you will be able to
understand their needs without trying to explain the difference. However,
CASE tools work specifically with Attributes and Relationships rather than
generally with Predicates. You as an analyst must continue your study
through the discussions of Attributes and Relationships.

Consider this typical conversation:

> **Jaime:** So, what's he like?
>
> **Pat:** Well, he has blue eyes; he's tall; he owns a lot of cars;
> he works at the Astrodome selling beer....

In this description, which are the Relationships and which are the Attributes? The difference starts to matter only when you sit down to use
your CASE tool.

Say we have a Class, GUY. You could have a Class for EYE COLOR as well,
in which case the description of a guy would be accomplished by relating
a guy with an Entity in the EYE COLOR Class. Alternatively, you could simply have Pat choose an eye color from a fixed Domain or just make up an
eye color. We would say then that eye color was an Attribute. Whether an
Entity is described with a Relationship or an Attribute is not something of
interest to either Pat or Jaime.

Whether the situation calls for an Attribute or Relationship depends on
what else the system owners want to do with eye colors. Attributes and Relationships are interchangeable in many ways. You could always take
something initially identified as an Attribute and make a table out of it, effectively converting an Attribute to a Relationship. Or, going the other
way, you might decide to reduce a table to a Domain, effectively collapsing a Relationship into an Attribute.

Attributes and Relationships are similar in almost every way we think
about Data Modeling concepts. Both Attributes and Relationships attach
themselves to Entities following the rules of normalization. Both have an
essential relevance to their Entity. Both can be multi-valued; however, for
an Attribute we say it is "not in first normal form," but for a Relationship

we say it "has a cardinality of greater than one." Either an Attribute or a Relationship can be optional. They both can be part of what makes an Entity unique; although some Attributes shouldn't. Either an Attribute or Relationship can justify the existence of an Entity. Once the system is constructed, you can look at an unformatted record in a file, and the Attributes and Relationships are indistinguishable. If you were to write a text such as this one, you would find yourself explaining the same concepts twice, once for Attributes and again for Relationships. (You might do as I have done and explain them three times, including this first go 'round called Predicates.)

ATTRIBUTE and RELATIONSHIP are Classes of a Superclass called PREDICATE. Since Attributes and Relationships have so much in common, starting with Predicates to cover all the basic similarities is natural. Differences between the two kinds of Predicates are covered in their respective segments but only after all the concepts that a system owner like Pat would need to know. That way Pat can get back to more important pursuits while you drag yourself through more titillating discourse on the nature of information.

Predicates and Computer Systems

AWR Co.
Product Catalog

        Product: AB123
           Desc: Electro-Spandex Tummy Trimmer, XL
          Price: $49.95
       Ship Wt: 2.5 lbs.
         Colors: Red, White, Blue
    Accessories: Extra Battery AB234
       Warranty: Standard
      Comments: Money-Back Guarantee

When you complete the Analysis Phase, the first product of your work to be used will be the list of Predicates. They are the grist for the database designers and then the screen and report designers. There are a number of

Predicates evident in the above excerpt from a product catalog: <u>description</u>, <u>price</u>, <u>weight</u>, <u>color</u>, <u>related products</u>, and <u>type of warranty</u>. Not everything you see is a Predicate: "AB123" does not evidence a Predicate, and "Comments" may not be a Predicate.

<u>Predicates</u> are the most visible component of computer software. The <u>column headings on spreadsheets</u> are the <u>names of Predicates</u>, such as <u>budget</u> or <u>price</u>. Whenever you look at a computer screen that has <u>blanks</u> waiting for you to fill in, or <u>fields displaying data, these fields are Predicates</u>. A database is just a bunch of Predicates, because behind the scenes, Predicates become the fields in records. (Editor's note: Why do you think they call them fields? Is a field literally a magnetic field? Is that how these things work? Maybe they think those of us who work at computers are modern-day field hands. Typical. Or if the screen is a kind of cyber-wilderness, then the field is a plot in which field hands plant tiny magnetic impulses, hoping to have their questions fielded. It's an etymologist's field day.)

Predicates Describe Something

I start an exploration of Predicates by looking at some examples. The underlined phrases indicate Predicates:

> The <u>blue</u> car <u>is owned by</u> Dee.
>
> Tar-Mart Stores <u>has purchased</u> products <u>totaling $250K</u>.
>
> The patient <u>is scheduled to receive</u> chemotherapy <u>on Dec 3rd</u>.
>
> Winton <u>is the manager of this</u> booby-hatch <u>called the "AP Department."</u>

What can you tell about Predicates from these examples? Would you say that <u>Predicates are verbs</u>, that they capture the action in the sentence? You cannot connect a subject and an object without either an active or a being verb. All such connections have verbs, but the verb is not the essence of the Predicate. For example, whether I say "blue car" or "car is blue" the same information is conveyed. (I cannot resist an aside to point out that you cannot record action in a digital computer system; at best you can record transformations of data over time, sort of the way a movie camera does. If you wanted to get the idea of "kick" across to a robot, you would be left with describing a displacement of the robot's legs—again, just a description of some element at points in time.)

The essence of Predicates is the way they can describe something in some way. For example, we are told that Dee owns a blue car. Before we knew nothing of Dee; now the value of the Predicates has told us something about Dee. Predicates describe things.

Predicates Are What Can Be Known

Not only Predicates, but perhaps Predicates in particular, confuse people about the distinction between an idea and the kind of idea. In the case of Predicates, we must not confuse knowing something, and knowing what you can know. An example of knowing something could be "Dee's car is blue." You can only know that which is knowable; that which is knowable about something is what we call a Predicate. For example I might say I know that Dee's <u>car has color</u>. I could know just that much; that is, I can know what I can know. To repeat, what I can know is the <u>color of Dee's car</u>. That Dee's <u>car has a color</u> is a Predicate. When we say that we know something, we are saying that we know the value for some Predicate. When I said that I know that "Dee's car is blue," I have evaluated the Predicate Dee's <u>car's color</u> to blue. (Editor's note: I told the author this was confusing. He claims it's a riddle.)

Try a second example, "Deep Blue is the world's best Chess-playing computer." Or "Gary Kasparov is the world's best Chess player." These are statements of fact; that is, something I know. The idea of ranking Chess players is a Predicate; that is, anything that can play Chess can be ranked against anything else that plays Chess. The following table summarizes this confusing discourse.

	What I Can Know	**What I Know**
Data Modeling Term	Predicate	Value of a Predicate or fact
Example	Dee's <u>car has color</u>.	Dee's car is blue.
Example	Kasparov's <u>rank among chess players</u>.	Kasparov is a top-ranked chess player.

You might want to cover with your hand the second column of the following table and test yourself to see if you can easily distinguish between the things you can know and the things you know.

Things You Can Know (Predicates)	Things You Might Know (Facts)
The maximum permissible level of (239)Plutonium in the body	0.04 microcurie
Title given position in Football team that used to call the plays	Quarterback
Title of the first collection of poems published by William Blake	*Poetical Sketches*
Color of David Bowie's hair on the *Ziggy Stardust* album	Orange
Direction in which you must go to win tug-of-war	Backwards
Season a salmon swims upstream	Spring
Point at which sound becomes painful	140 decibels
Uniform rate of acceleration for an object falling freely to the ground	9.8 meters per second^2
Electrical resistance of silicon	50k ohms per cubic centimeter
Capacity of a kiloliter	1.308 cubic yards
Fuel octane rating of regular gas	87 Octane
Year Columbus made a name for himself	1492
To whom President Lyndon Johnson was married	Lady Bird Johnson

Predicates Have Meaning

A large international manufacturer went to very great expense to build a worldwide network to integrate their data. They boasted the most advanced technical architecture that yielded the easiest, fastest access to data on any kind of machine they owned anywhere in the world. In the end, the whole effort was worthless.

When employees were allowed to grab data from these disparate databases, they discovered their computers still could not answer even the simplest questions. For example, "How much product did Lever Brothers buy last year?" Well, in Europe, Lever Brothers went by one name, in Africa by another, and in the United States by a third. Even when the name confusion was solved, the manufacturer discovered that certain services were considered "products" in the United States but not in Europe. In Africa, these services were rendered by a wholly-owned subsidiary. These kinds of inconsistencies thwarted the business at every turn.

Integration is primarily a question of knowing what data you have and what it means. The international manufacturer should have spent the effort standardizing the definition of a "product" or a "customer." Then even if they had to fax the information back-and-forth, they would have been better off.

How do well-meaning system developers work so hard for so long and yet go so wrong? Perhaps our fascination with technology blinds us to our more mundane goals. Even without the distraction of lots of cool electronics, the thousands of small decisions we make on projects can easily amount to a giant loss of direction. See the exchange between a concerned system-owner-to-be and a systems analyst.

Memo
To: Analyst Ed
From: Pat, Reservations Specialist

I was uneasy about some aspects of our conversation last Tuesday. In the example we worked together, I said, "The reservation was for Jack," meaning that we will send the invoice to Jack. When I said "The reservation is for Jane," I meant that Jane is the person who will be traveling on the ticket. One reservation, two people. Does this clarify at all?

No PROBLEMO PAT!
THERE WILL BE A PLACE
FOR YOU TO RECORD WHO
THE RESERVATION IS FOR.
— THANKS!

The easy question would be to ask if Pat is justly concerned, but what mistake is the analyst making? Does the analyst suffer from hearing loss? Truly, while the medical community is chasing red herrings such as carpal-tunnel syndrome and electromagnetic exposure, hearing loss among computer professionals rampages unchecked! However, Pat probably wouldn't have been heard even if she had been using Mick Jagger's amplifier.

Did the analyst fail to recognize that the Reservation "is for" more than one person? That is, should they create more than one place to record for whom the reservation was made? Perhaps Ed entirely missed the point of more than one person being involved; nevertheless, solely allowing a reservation to be for more than one person would not address Pat's concern since Pat has to distinguish one from the other for billing and reservations.

The key is that a Predicate must be more meaningful than "for." If we were to allow two persons to be "for" a reservation, then we would have recorded a bit of what is needed but would be short of having enough information to help Pat. Knowing that a reservation is "for" both Jack and Jane does not help Pat send out invoices or print tickets; you haven't indicated who gets what. If all you indicated was that the ticket is "for" Jack, do I send him an invoice or put him on a plane? You add meaning to Predicates by including a description of their purpose. For example, a reservation can be described as having someone to pay and someone who will travel. The result is two distinct Predicates, each supporting just one fact about the reservation.

A Predicate that does not in some way affect a decision somewhere is irrelevant; such a Predicate is trivia. You must keep this need for meaning in the forefront of your mind as you determine what the Predicates are in the context of the information system you are building. For example, does your system require a customer's daytime phone number, or does your system really need number where you can be reached during office hours. In the first instance, I am talking about a fact, something true about a customer, but this fact might not do what I want it to do. In the case of number where you can be reached I get straight to the fact that is essential to my business. The difference is slight but important. Consider also the example of bill-to address versus ship-to address.

The principle is that data has to have real meaning. Plato once said something to the effect, "What is a bed? A bed is where I sleep." Joan, the AP supervisor with whom I worked, never asked me, "What does this field mean?" (which as a data bigot I wanted her to ask); no, Joan always asked, "What does this field do? What will happen if I put (whatever) in there?" A wonderful illustration of the essential principle that data has to have real meaning is Howard Benbrook's example about audio-visual equipment.

What if you were developing a system to coordinate schedules for both meeting rooms and employees? The system should integrate room reservations and personal schedules to better coordinate meetings. You might find that you had a Predicate of people and rooms such that people are found in rooms from time to time. (Editor's note: the author assures me he wanted it worded just that way.) Later, you are demonstrating the nearly finished application. Your software displays where a person has meetings, who is meeting in which rooms, and a message if you overbook a person or a room. In short, it is a thing of beauty. The owners say, "Wonderful. Can you build in the capability to schedule audio-visual equipment?" Now you lie: "That will be Phase II."

Here's the quiz; don't peek ahead! What do the owners do when they get their hands on your software that was so beautifully built to emulate the way real things work in the real world? They hire Mr. Overhead Projector—needs a little help getting around but real bright. Owners have an intuitive grasp that data is what data does. Data derives its meaning from what it does to our process or decision-making. Incidentally, M. Projector works great until you try and integrate the payroll system with the scheduling system.

What Is a Predicate?

A Predicate is any relevant property, quality, or characteristic ascribed to a thing.

Of course, if the concept were as easy as the definition implies, then information systems might write themselves. It is that simple for humans; our big brains handle Predicates so adroitly that our consciousness need hardly be bothered with them. Our human information systems do write themselves. But although even your brother-in-law may have no difficulty understanding Predicates, our biggest computers can't tell a Predicate from their rear access panels. We have to hand-hold them every step of the way.

Predicates describe things, but how does one describe? Think of description as consisting of these five essential parts:

1. What do you want to know?
2. What do you want to know about?
3. How many answers do you expect?
4. Do you need to know more than just the current answer?
5. What kind of answer do you want?

I explore each of these five items in turn. Actually, I've already spent a good deal of time talking about number one and number two. What you want to know are those things that have meaning to you. What you want to know about are the things Predicates describe. These first two items are the essence of a Predicate. At risk of being redundant, we are going to start over at number one and march through all five parts—first once quickly and then again with a flood of examples in a desperate attempt to overwhelm any remaining doubt.

This first step, *what do you want to know,* is deceptively difficult. Many software projects derail before they get started because the sponsors of the project don't know what they want to know and are vaguely hoping the computer will come and tell them. For instance, you start your interview of the new Southside branch manager by asking, "What can I help you with?" He responds, "We're okay, just working hard, doing what we're asked. You know, getting along and all that." This is a worst case. Even if you might know what they want to know, your insightful computer reports might end up as oversized coffee-cup coasters.

The Northside manager has a different style: "You wanna buy something? I got time for customers, and I got time for stocking. When I'm not with a customer, I'm stocking and trying to figure out why I ain't with a customer. And when a customer wants something I ain't got, then I'm trying to figure out why that." At least this manager knows in broad terms what he or she wants to know—how to get more customers and how to have what they want. You can work with this manager; this is why they pay you.

What if that interview had gone something like this: "I need a three-month rolling average of sales figures in units sold for each product trended for 12 months." In that case, you really wouldn't have much to do. It would have been very clear what the Northside manager wanted to know. Although we rarely start with such explicit information requirements, we always have to end up with just this kind of detail.

What do you want to know about? Every Predicate describes something. The following dialogue with your boss, Mr. Wattle, shows that he was less specific than the Northside manager about his need for sales figures.

You:	Here are the sales figures!
Mr. Wattle:	Sales figures for what?
You:	For the NE division. We were up all night. You wanted them ASAP.
Mr. Wattle:	Of course. For what products?
You:	The Electro-Tummy Waist Reducer. You said it was our make-or-break item.
Mr. Wattle:	Of course. What period do these figures cover?
You:	Spring quarter.
Mr. Wattle:	Spring! I needed Summer!

Mr. Wattle wanted to know about sales. However, it is meaningless to talk about sales without talking about sales for what. In this case, the what, Tummy Trimmer Sales, was not specific enough. You had to specify not only sales of what and where those sales took place but also when they took place. Is it correct to say the sales figures describe Tummy Trimmers? The sales figures describe Tummy Trimmer Sales in the NE division in Spring, not Tummy Trimmers in general.

How many answers do you expect? In the above example, Wattle is expecting a single number. To other questions, he might expect more than one answer. For example, when you ask the question "What credit cards do we accept?" you expect to receive one or many responses. Consider another similar example, "What customers are in the NE region?"

Do you need to know more than just the current answer? Mr. Wattle may want to work on the number a little bit. Surely, you knew that managers work on their number a little bit? But once Mr. Wattle gives his number to the Security and Exchange Commission, Mr. Wattle will have to live with that number. Some Predicates, especially financial information, should not be changed once established. Does Wattle want a history of changes? Does Wattle want a what-if number alongside his real number? Does Mr. Wattle give a different number to the IRS? Does Mr. Wattle give another number to the profit-sharing directors? This Mr. Wattle, he sure is good with numbers!

The last part of any description is: *what kind of answer do you want?* Knowing what kind of answer you want is particularly important when dumb-as-a-box-of-rocks computers are involved. Every question so far as silica is concerned is a multiple-choice question. For instance, you may decide that the answer must be rounded to thousands, or denominated in French Francs, or in numbers of units sold.

You can restate these five parts of a description as steps you would follow to develop a full understanding of a Predicate:

1. Find out what you want to know

2. Find out what the parameters are that identify what you want to know about

3. Find out how many answers you expect

4. Find out whether just knowing the current answer is enough

5. Find out what kind of answer you expect

Please do not go out and design a form to capture this data. Your CASE tool is designed to make documentation of this kind of analysis easy.

(Editor's note: Believe it or not, the last few pages were the promised "quick run-through" of the five parts of a Predicate. Now you are really going to get the detailed explanation.)

How to Know What to Know

Predicates are the raw materials and the end products of information systems. In manufacturing, the end product and the manufacturing process dictate the raw materials required. For example, if you make cars, you need steel and welding flux. In the same way, the information you use dictates the Predicates you need. If you are going to produce a cash receipts schedule, you need to know the value of the outstanding invoices and the date they are due.

It is pretty easy to look at a car and see what materials went into it. How do you find out what you want to know? Let's look at three examples. Notice that all three examples start with some end point and work backwards. When you know what you want to do, you can determine what information you need to do it—which is quite different from taking apart a car, but I hope you get my drift.

Example one: if you wanted to calculate the amount to be paid an hourly worker, then you would want to know <u>hours worked</u> as well as <u>employee wage</u>. <u>Hours worked</u> and <u>employee wage</u> are Predicates that you should include in your data model.

Example two: you determine that the reservation specialists assign cabins starting with the most desirable to the least desirable cabins. In doing so, he or she considers the <u>lifetime receipts from a customer</u>; any memos from the boss; and, oh yes, the <u>customer's preferences</u>. The <u>degree of desirability of the cabin</u>, <u>lifetime receipts</u>, <u>VIP status</u>, and <u>customer cabin preference</u> are all Predicates.

Example three: if the surgeon suggests that the surgical order contain certain descriptive notes about the patient such as eye and skin color, then you should include <u>eye color</u> and <u>skin color</u> as Predicates in your data model.

These three examples demonstrate three different ways that systems use Predicates:

- factors in mathematical operations
- arguments in logical operations (in the statement "if x then y," x is the argument)
- simply descriptors

Tip for Project Managers

Managers partition big jobs into smaller tasks and assign each to different persons or teams. When the tasks are serial, such as Analysis and Design, then it is genius. When managers try to divide duties that are parallel, such as data and process analysis, then it is foolhardy. Instead of a relay, they create a three-legged race. Data and process analysis are skills like reading and writing—they go hand-in-hand. Every analyst must be skilled in both and every time an analyst speaks to an owner they will learn something about both processes and data.

Some companies have set up data analysis teams. These teams cannot justify their actions on data except by reference to processes. Invariably they end up at odds with the process teams. Or sometimes it is suggested that the data model be completed before the process analysis begins. How do you know that the data model is correct until you have done the process model?

When you realize that the data is meaningless when it is divorced from some action or decision, and that the process is moot except as it acts on some data, then you understand the futility of separating the process model from the data model. You cannot study data without referring to the processes that use the data. Analysts must be trained to analyze both the data and process models simultaneously, and they must develop both data and process models from the same meetings with the system owners.

Do you know what you want to know? Generally, you know many of the things you want to know—it's the things you didn't think of that cause all the problems. For example, if you needed to prepare the Forecasted Receipts report shown below, what Predicates do you need to know to prepare the report?

Forecasted Receipts
Prepared: 12/31/97

Week	Receipts
1/4	$125,123
1/11	$230,578
1/18	$215,890
1/25	$255,890
2/1	$150,000
2/8	$125,000
2/15	$ 95,444
2/22	$ 33,900
3/1	$ 15,010
3/8	$ 10,000

The <u>amount</u> and the <u>due date</u> of all outstanding invoices are almost certainly required; however, you may need more than meets the eye. Perhaps these totals are (or should be) adjusted for anticipated return merchandise or uncollectible accounts. When you know everything you need to know, your data model is complete and you are on your way to a successful project.

What Is It About?

Predicates describe things. (Did we already cover this?) Predicates don't just describe; they describe some thing. Throughout this section, I will refer to things. Some of you who have already worked with data models may think that by a "thing" I mean Entity or Entity Occurrence. I might, but many of you will think of the computer record when you see the word Entity, and I mean for you to think of the actual thing itself. If I say that the customer is six feet tall, I mean that person, not customer number 456, and not the ones and zeros on the disk.

Precisely which thing is being described often gets confused. After all, in everyday conversation, no one would mistakenly attribute some fact to the wrong thing. I might say, "That bag is heavy," but you know intuitively that the bag itself is not heavy but that its contents must be. This knowledge of the world is precisely the kind that computers lack. If you were conversing with a computer, then you would have to be very explicit that the bag may have a weight but it is not important and that the thing in the bag has a separate weight. The computer has no way of knowing that the weight of the contents is relevant and that the weight of the bag is irrelevant. You might find it goofy that which thing is being described by a Predicate could be misunderstood. If this is the case, then do not let this discussion confuse you too; it is intended for those of us who have become befuddled by long association with computers, an occupational hazard.

Consider the example of a <u>home phone number</u>. Say, for instance, you are developing a membership list for a golf club. Is a member's home phone number a Predicate describing the member? No, not for standard phone equipment; a phone number belongs to a place, a member's home. Different members can share the same phone number, especially when they belong to the same family. Correctly identifying that <u>phone number</u> as a Predicate describing the home has important implications. Consider what happens when a family changes its phone number: do you have to change the number in your records just once, or one time for each member? Consider what happens when contacting members by phone: is a family contacted just once, or one time for each member? Although the world knowledge that allows people to correctly identify what is being described by a Predicate seems simple, it is so important that a high degree of accuracy is essential.

Tip for System Analysts

Determining what is being described by a Predicate is the essence of the second and third normal forms. I am going to explain the first three normal forms without referring to these terms, but I want to point out to analysts that the intent of this chapter is to give a full understanding of the first three normal forms. Actually, almost everything in this book could be interpreted as some permutation of the three normal forms, and so you may see them being explained in a dozen ways over the course of dozens of examples.

What follows are two examples of Predicates. Each example represents a different kind of challenge that information system builders face. In each case, you should be able to figure out what the Predicates describe. This first example suggests a way to deal with statistical data.

Memo to the Project Team:

In our discussions of the new marketing system's database, we forgot to mention one key item, Average Household Income. This statistic is provided by the census bureau for every census tract every ten years. We are interested only in the most current figure, honest.

Please be sure to include a place for us to record this data in the new design!

Is <u>average household income</u> a Predicate of a household, a census tract, or the census tract in the decade that the census was taken? Does any individual or any household earn this average income? Not necessarily. An average is based on a sum of a series divided by the number of items in the series. Although the statistic is based on an individual's or household's income, the resulting statistic, <u>average household income,</u> does not pertain to any single individual or household.

The census tract identifies which households the average is based on. Would the average be useful if you could not identify the region on which it was based? Certainly not. The census tract is not a number; the census tract is this region.

The <u>average</u> is a Predicate of the census tract itself. A number of different zones are used to capture statistical data: school districts, zip codes, counties.... Each zone represents a new set of households, and each would give a different answer to the question "What is the <u>average household income</u>?" Therefore, each would have this Predicate.

The last option, the idea that <u>average household income</u> describes the tract as it was at a point in time, is a good one; but the memo states that they are interested only in the current data. The Marketing Department is not being short-sighted; only they can tell analysts what is relevant. If they wanted to trend the data over the decades, then they would need to describe some thing called "Census/decade." For each decade, you would record the <u>average household income</u>. After a few decades, you could trend the data. Of course, by then you would be long gone.

The second example suggests a way to deal with approximate data.

Memo to the Project Team:
From: Marge N. Overa, Marketing Manager

We noted the omission of some marketing data about our customer base. As you know, we buy mailing lists from magazines. We want to know what magazine, or magazines, a customer has subscribed to. We feel this is an important clue as to the kinds of direct mail that will be of interest to these people. We understand that the name on the subscription is usually that of the person whose credit card was used to place the order. We can live with the occasions in which the person who has an interest is not the person who placed the order.

The Predicate is <u>magazines a customer subscribes to</u>. Is the thing described some John Buck, that is some individual; or is the thing described John Buck's house? Ideally, the marketing department would know which individual at that address received the copy of *Sports Illus-*

trated.   If the Predicate were <u>John Buck reads MAGAZINE</u>, then they could send a letter such as

---

Dear Mr. Buck:

Mr. Buck, we know you love SPORTS as much as we do. That's why, Mr. Buck, we have this special SPORTS offer for you....

But if the Marketing Department had its way, each of us would be hooked up to electrodes all the time. Barring the realization of that nightmare, we must accept the fact that the name on the subscription tells us only who actually ordered the magazine but not who reads it. Trying to associate the subscription with any one person at the residence could result in classic computer goofs. Maybe Mrs. Buck is interested in Sports while Mr. Buck mostly waits for the Victoria's Secret catalog.

When the data is fuzzy, you must be even more precise in your definition of Predicates. In this case, you have the Predicates <u>Buck residence subscribes to MAGAZINE</u> and <u>Mr. Buck appears in address line for MAGAZINE</u>. By recognizing as a Predicate only what you know and everything you know, then you are not misleading the owners of the system into thinking they know something they don't. With the two Predicates, I can still send a "Dear Mr. Buck" letter; however, I might pick up the cue and send a more general "To the sports fan at..." letter.

Predicates Can Describe Other Predicates

Predicates can be about other Predicates. For instance, what if you were to assign a probability to a number? It could be <u>how probable it is that Mr. Buck did use his credit card</u> or <u>how probable it is that Mr. Buck reads the magazine</u>. An expert system for emergency care might produce a report on Mr. Buck such that

> heart failure chances are 10/100
> exposure to noxious gas chances are 85/100
> aliens taking over body chances are 5/100

The simple Predicate is <u>patient has any number of diagnoses</u>. One Predicate of this Predicate is <u>each diagnosis has some probability of being correct</u>. The probabilities describe (modify our understanding of) the diagnosis.

The most common example of a Predicate describing another Predicate is the circumstance in which things are described in terms of other things. For example, the Data Mart project employs Pat and Jaime. Jaime works for the Data Mart and the Common Data project. In Data Modeling terms, I have the following facts:

> Jaime works on the Data Mart Project
> Pat works on the Data Mart Project
> Jaime works on the Common Data Project

These examples indicate the need for the Predicate <u>an employee works on PROJECT</u>. So far, there is no hint of Predicates about Predicates since these are all facts about things. But if I wanted to know when the employees began to work on projects, then I would need to describe the Predicate <u>employee works on PROJECT</u>. That Jaime started on the Data Mart Project on 12/1 tells me something about the event of starting work on a project. It does not exactly describe Jaime or the project.

Take this example further: consider the manager. Alone in her office, making the big decisions such as where to take the client to lunch or how to get a trip to London out of this project, she might be concerned that you are not spending as much time on her project as had been promised. Is <u>how much time you have spent on her project</u> a fact about a) her project, b) you, or c) neither <u>and</u> both a & b?

Is it a fact about her project? By way of comparison, consider the fact <u>total time on project</u>, the sum of all persons' time. Is that a fact about the project and only the project? It is not a fact about you or any other individual. Yes, <u>total time</u> is a fact about the project. What is different about the Predicates <u>total time</u> and <u>your time</u>? If you wanted to know how much time was spent on a project, what would you have to know? Just the Name of the project. If you wanted to know how much time a person spent on a project, then you would have to know the Name of the person and the Name of the project. The two facts are different because the data you have to provide in order to get the information you want is different. In Data Modeling, this is a key difference!

I dislike jargon, but I must stop this example to introduce a term, or we will both go crazy always trying to word around it. When you determined that you had to know "the Name of the person and the Name of the project" to determine <u>how much time a person spent on a project,</u> you put together a logical proposition. *I'd never do such a thing.* I'll prove it to you. Replace the first independent variable <u>Name of the person</u> with X, the second independent variable <u>Name of the project</u> with Y. Replace the Predicate <u>how much time a person spent on a project</u> with Z. Now restate as "Given X and Y then Z; or, $Z f(X,Y)$." This is important vocabulary:

- X and Y are called the argument.

- The Predicate Z is said to be "functionally dependent" on the argument.

You can review all the Predicates I have talked about and see how this analysis applies in the following table:

Predicate (if you want to know this)	Argument (all you need to know is this)
Time a person spent on a project	Name of the person and project
Total time on project	Name of the project
Projects an employee is working on	Name of the employee
Odds that diagnosis is true for patient	Name of diagnosis and victim
Magazines received	Residence of household
Name appearing on magazine label	Name of magazine, residence to which delivered
Average household income	Census tract
Member's phone number	Residence of member

You might have hoped that I had forgotten about the project example, but now we return to it. The time you have spent on a project is not a fact about a project. So is the time you have spent on a project a fact about you?

A fact is a fact about only one thing. How long you spent on a project is a fact that could just as easily be true of the project as of you. Therefore, it is a fact about neither you nor the project.

Knowing precisely what a fact is about is not just linguistic mumbo-jumbo. I love language, but the jobs are in computers. Good software design requires that you settle on a single thing to be the object of the fact because it is more efficient to record facts in just one place. Yes, you want to have to record or change it only once, but even more importantly, if it is recorded only once, then you know that it will be consistent. That is, you wouldn't want your records to show that you spent 200 hours on a project but for the project records to show only 50 hours. How can you structure your records so that the Predicate person's hours on a project is recorded only one time? And, very important, can you do it in a way that is consistent with the way we all have learned to process information since we were children?

How much time you spent on her project is <u>not</u> a fact about you. The answer to the question "How much time did you spend on her project?" depends on both the project and the person. "Project" and "person" together are the argument to the Predicate <u>time spent on project by employee</u>. You might have in mind a simple report like the following:

Person	Project	Hours
William	Data Whse	50
William	Accts Rec	40
Patricia	Data Whse	40

Depending on whom you are talking about or what project you are talking about, the answer changes. The answer (for example, 40) is meaningless without both the Person and the Project. The Predicate <u>how much time a person spends on a project</u> is not about either persons or projects. It is about the Predicate <u>person works on a project</u>.

The Predicate gives us (partial) information about both projects and persons, so the answer "neither <u>and</u> both" is appropriate. The challenge was to structure the records so that the Predicate <u>person's hours on a project</u> is recorded only one time. It was so long ago that you may have forgotten, but I ran through this from the perspective of the project and determined that <u>how much time a person spent on project</u> was a Predicate with the argument "the name of the person and the name of the project." Do I now have a second Predicate, <u>time spent on project by employee</u>? No, clearly they mean the same thing; you would never expect a different answer for one question from the other, given the same values for the argument. Two things that have the same argument are in fact the same thing. The order of the independent variables that make up the argument is irrelevant. This does not mean that two Predicates that have the same argument are the same Predicate. Predicates describe the argument, but don't forget that Predicates have an argument and a meaning. In this case, the Predicates have the same argument and the same meaning, and so we have but one Predicate. We just looked at the same Predicate from two perspectives.

That a Predicate can describe another Predicate is not an unnecessary elaboration on Data Modeling; it is an example of how Data Modeling tries to keep up with the linguistic gymnastics of your inventive mind. For the most part, you can use your intuition to figure out which thing a Predicate describes. Any approach that is not intuitive is probably wrong; but, on the other hand, an approach that cannot be described in terms of rules is not a real discipline. Rules give us something with which to resolve differences between your intuition and my intuition. This next example demonstrates a critical rule normally employed by analysts; call it the necessary and sufficient rule.

An Electro-Tummy Trimmer is a pretty simple thing because we can pick it up, disassemble it, sell it, or take it home with us. We could describe Tummy Trimmers as having a color; color is a Predicate of Tummy Trimmers. The color of a Tummy Trimmer doesn't change once it leaves the factory. Just having the Tummy Trimmer in hand is sufficient and all that is necessary for us to know the color.

The color of a Tummy Trimmer might not change, but the price might. Prices are set for Tummy Trimmers periodically. So if I were to return my Tummy Trimmer to your store, you couldn't refund my money until you figured out how much I paid for it. Just looking at the Tummy Trimmer, you can't tell how much it cost. However, you would know what you charged if you found out when I purchased it. Knowing what I bought and when I bought it is sufficient to find out what you were charging on that day. You don't need to know the color of the Tummy Trimmer—color is not necessary to determine price.

Given the sloppy way data is entered into computers, to determine the value of some Predicates, such as color, you best put the thing in your hand and look at it. On the other hand, the value of a Predicate such as price depends on other data, in this case the type of product and when it was purchased. So does the Predicate price describe Electro-Tummy Trimmers? No, it wouldn't be correct to say that this Electro-Tummy Trimmer costs $12.95—at least not in same way it is correct to say that this Electro-Tummy Trimmer is red.

Price describes the Tummy Trimmer as it was on a particular day. In fact, it doesn't describe any single Tummy Trimmer but all Tummy Trimmers on a particular day. Imagine this dialogue:

Customer:	What day is it?
You:	December 21, 1999.
Customer:	Got any Tummy-Trimmers?
You:	Yes, I have a dozen.
Customer:	What's your price?
You:	Manager's special today, just $12.95.
Customer:	You got any donuts?

Price doesn't describe any concrete thing. $12.95 describes a Tummy Trimmer as it was on 12/21/99. The price of something on a certain day is not so strange, really; we often talk about the dollars per hour we earn or the miles per hour we drive. All you need to understand is that price depends on the product and when it was sold (or to be sold). If, for every Predicate, you can identify the argument (factors that determine the value of that Predicate), then you are through—the rest is arithmetic. Ask yourself the question, "What do I need to know to know the value of the Predicate?" The "what you need to know to know" is the thing the Predicate describes. So imagine this dialogue:

Customer:	I want to bring back these donuts.
You:	Did you buy them here?
Customer:	Yes, I have the receipt right here.
You:	Ech! You dug this out of a dumpster!
Customer:	Yes, and so? It is a receipt from this store.
You:	I can't read the prices.
Customer:	So how much do you charge for those donuts? Refund me that.
You:	Okay, I see here the date was 12/21/99. We were running a New Year's special. Why are you returning them?
Customer:	You don't need to know that.
You:	I don't need to know that to determine the price, you are right. Take this.
Customer:	Sixty cents! You thief!
You:	I am not a thief. This store charged five cents a donut on that day.

You needed to know which store, which product, and which day to determine the value of the Predicate price. Store, product, and date are sufficient and all that is necessary to evaluate the Predicate. The argument to any proposition must be inclusive enough to determine the value of that Predicate. But it should be only sufficient; it should contain no more than what is necessary. The <u>reason for the return</u> may be another Predicate, but it is not necessary to determine <u>price</u>.

All is not lost if you don't want to visualize a price tag hanging off a donut floating in a four-dimensional time-space continuum. Nor is it lost if the above dialogue doesn't help with this aspect of Predicates. If you are mathematically-minded, just think of it as a function. Let x be the <u>price</u>. Let a be the store, b the product, and c the date. Then $x = f(a,b,c)$. I prefer the donut.

Tip for Project Managers

Here, deep in the jungle of this text, lies the essential thing you really need to understand to organize the information with which you work. If you know everything you want to know (the Predicates!), and if you can item-ize all of the necessary and only the sufficient factors that determine the value of each of these Predicates (the arguments!), then you have com-pleted your analysis.

If you got all the Predicates right during analysis, you got 90% of what you needed.

This next example will give you a chance to work with a Predicate of an abstraction, such as a thing at a point in time.

Memo to the Project Team:

This memo is to clarify our discussion of foreign currency exchange rates and how they are used in receipt processing. We allow our customers to pay in their local currency. We will quote an exchange rate for monies received by the next day. For example, if you were from Colombia and were paying in Col. Pesos, then we would quote costs converting from Dollars US to Col. Pesos at the exchange rate the Accounting Dept. had established for that day. If your payment is received before the close of the next business day, then we use that exchange rate, regardless of what had happened in the market overnight.

The exchange rate is a Predicate of what? Is the thing that is being described the currency, the currency as of a date, or the currency quoted the customer?

The exchange rate for a currency is changing all the time. Just knowing the currency is not enough to know the exchange rate. A business strategy could be developed that used the real-time exchange rate, but that is not the way the company does it. You would be wrong to assume that this real-time rate would be inherently better or that the daily rate could be derived from the instantaneous rate. Neither of these assumptions would be correct. The rate used is the "exchange rate the Accounting Dept. had established for that day." The Accounting Dept. sets a rate based on the market rate but also considers that the money may not be actually converted for up to two business days. A considerable degree of judgment on their part makes their rate both better and independent of the instantaneous rate.

The thing being described is the currency as it was established for that day. That is, the Predicate <u>exchange rate</u> depends on the argument that includes the name of the currency and the day for which the rate was effective. If you are on the phone to a customer inquiring about his or her account, you need to know the exchange rate for the day so that you can inform the customer of the payment due. If you have received a payment, you need to know yesterday's or today's rate to give proper credit for the payment. You need to know the exchange rate for a currency on a specific day.

What about letting the Predicate describe the quote to the customer? Strictly speaking, you do not need to know what was told each customer, since everyone who called that day would be given the same exchange rate. Adding the name of the customer to the argument would be more than is sufficient.

Tip for System Analysts

A careful analyst might follow up with the Accounting Dept. by asking, "What if you changed your mind in the middle of the day after some customers were already guaranteed a rate? What if you mistakenly gave an incorrect rate to a customer?" If the Accounting Dept. needed to be able to change the rate at any time but still honor the verbal agreement, then adding customer to the argument list for the Predicate <u>quoted exchange rate</u> might be necessary. In such a case, you clearly must have the Predicate <u>exchange rate the Accounting Dept. had established for that day</u>, but nothing prevents you from also having the <u>quoted exchange rate</u> as well.

I am amazed at the complex patterns you can create from the very few and simple ideas so far presented. All we have talked about are Domains,

Names, and some aspects of Predicates, and already we can express fairly complex information. I want to return to the project manager example to see how we can combine the idea of a Predicate to a Predicate and data that exists at a point in time. I'll bet you aren't as excited about this as I am, but your real work is even more complicated.

Consider the common example of project time reporting. A manager needs to know how much time each person is spending on which project. For example:

Person	Project	Hours
William	Data Whse	50
William	Accts Rec	40
Patricia	Data Whse	40

As you have already seen, the time a person spends on a project is a Predicate of the Predicate <u>person works on a project</u>. But the example is still a bit simplistic, isn't it? After all, project managers want to know how much time William has spent on the Data Warehouse project in September, not just since inception. Not to panic. If you made yourself comfortable with the person/project association, then you can also get comfortable with the person/project/month association. It is the same idea carried one step further. In the end, all we are going to do is add an independent variable to the argument. This is why mathematically-minded people seem so calm. They just trust that there is no limit to the number of variables they can add, and every problem becomes trivial.

For example, William worked 50 hours on the Data Warehouse Project. That 50 hours is the sum of the 20 hours he worked in September and the 30 hours he worked in October. The table from above now looks like the following:

Person	Project	Month	Hours
William	Data Whse	Sept	20
William	Accts Rec	Sept	40
Patricia	Data Whse	Sept	40
William	Data Whse	Oct	30

The level of detail required by the manager pushes the design to keep a Predicate whose value can be known only if you know the Name of the person, the project worked on, and the month worked. The Predicate depends on the argument made up of the person, the project, and the month. Turn that formula around and you can say that this new Predicate cannot be understood except in the context of a person, project, and month. That is, if I simply said "40," your natural response would be "Forty what?!" What is the 40 hours about? Is it about William? Yes, but does it make sense to say that William is 40 hours in the same way it makes sense to say William is 6 feet tall? Is it about September? Is it about Accts Rec? Forty hours is about William in September regarding the Data Warehouse; it cannot be understood without all of these pieces.

What Answers Do You Expect?

Tip for System Analysts

What I am talking about here is either Cardinality or 1st Normal form, depending on whether you mean to be talking about Relationships or Attributes.

A Predicate may expect a single answer, a specific number of answers, or any number of answers. To effectively set up an information system, you need to anticipate whether supplying more than one value to a single Predicate is rational.

For example, if you were the maître d' at some posh restaurant, then you could cope with a reservation specifying either the smoking or the non-smoking section. You could deal with a party that said "No preference": you would put these folks at the first available table. You could not cope, however, with a reservation requesting smoking and non-smoking; these people shouldn't be out together. The Predicate reservation's smoking preference must have a single value, or it is worthless.

Often, however, a Predicate must take on multiple values. For example, the Predicate "My favorite movies are _____" must be allowed to have more than one answer. Occasionally, a Predicate may have a specific limit to the number of values: "My favorite months of the year are _____."

Analysts will often forget the major principle that Predicates have meaning and confuse Predicates that have the same kind of response for the same Predicate. The most common example is that of Customer Address. One might make the mistake of thinking that a Predicate <u>customer address</u> can have many values. The error here is that address is not meaningful enough. To be able to use a customer's address, you need to know whether it is the shipping address or the billing address or any one of a bazillion other addresses those pesky customers might have. What you really have are a number of meaningful Predicates with names like <u>shipping address</u> and <u>billing address</u>.

Modifiable Predicates

Your analysis needs to remain objective. If you are loyal to the principles of Data Modeling, you can move the masses towards superior design without raising your voice. Without reason, you can add cysts of the vocal chords to the other occupational hazards, such as carpal-tunnel syndrome and hearing loss. That said, Predicates can be subjunctive.

Can the value of the Predicate be changed once that value has been established? Actually, most Predicates are modifiable. If the <u>patient's current weight</u> is 285 lbs, then that weight can still fluctuate. Sometimes, a modifiable Predicate becomes fixed when we consider time. For example, the <u>patient's weight on his last visit</u> was 300 lbs; that Predicate can't be changed.

But should such a Predicate be modifiable in the event of an error? What if someone erroneously recorded the <u>patient's weight</u> as 2,850 lbs? The usual answer: it has to be modifiable. But the data model does not reflect modifiability in the case of error. In some cases, even errors are not modifiable. A check made out for $2,850 to pay a bill for $28.50 remains a $2,850 check. Entries to the General Ledger behave this way: a mistake is corrected by a second transaction that reverses the effect of the error rather than changing the transaction that was in error. As you define what a Predicate means, you need to understand what the system owners expect insofar as audit and security is concerned.

Owners seem to want more and more from their computer systems. The most basic database will hold the current value of a Predicate, the value as of the last time it was updated. You may need to show both the current value and an as-was value, the value the field had at the time it was used in some way, such as when it was posted to some report or ledger. This allowance can be necessary in unexpected Predicates, for example the Name of a customer like AT&T Bell Labs. If we were to write a refund for this customer, we might have to put the new Name of the company, Lucent Technologies, on the check. But what if a payables clerk changed the Name to something like "Aunt Millie" instead? At the least, you would want it recorded that the check cashed in Rio was in fact written to Aunt Millie, not just customer number 123, Lucent Technologies.

Some owners would like to track an as-was, an as-is, and an as-should-have-been—this last category being what they should have had in the system at some previous time but for some reason didn't. The should-have-been would be used to restate the report without affecting accounting history. If there is a reorganization (when there are numerous reorganizations?), the new managers would like to see history for their accounts as if they had always been in their care so that they can show how effective they are at their jobs, as if they stood a chance of holding them long enough to actually have a track record. Some owners would like to track the entire history of changes for a record. As you can see, there will be plenty of work for computer people for a very long time despite our own track record.

Tip for System Analysts

You can add all the date fields to accomplish the future, present, past, subjunctive, and past imperfect. Just don't get tense, and don't forget that each date has a particular meaning, just like the earlier examples of knowing for whom a reservation has been made or knowing for what an address is used. Do not simply allow multiple dates on a record; each date is its own Predicate and must be analyzed and justified separately.

Where Will You Get Your Answers?

In everyday speech, we don't concern ourselves with the kind of response we get from an inquiry. For example, if we ask, "What's it like outside?" we might be satisfied with "Hot" or "It's 95°." If, however, we track temperatures to study a region or to know when to declare a heat emergency, then we need to be specific about the kind of answer we require; for example, all measurements are to be in CELSIUS TO THE TENTH OF A DEGREE. Systems of information always need a specific answer, the value taken on by the Predicate, and that answer must be derived from a particular set of choices.

A Predicate may be associated with a particular Domain. For example, the Predicate <u>customer's smoking preference</u> will be associated with the Domain consisting of the values "non-smoking, smoking, indifferent." A Predicate may also be associated with a set of things. For instance, the Predicate <u>customer buys car</u> is associated with a list of cars for sale. The customer is a thing, and so is the car he or she bought. Every Predicate must be associated with either a Domain or a set of things.

You might think of the Predicate as a question and the fact as the response. So you can think of the Predicate as a fill-in-the-blank question, "The color of Dee's car is _____." Notice that if you try to make a question of the fact, you get a different Predicate: "Is Dee's car blue? (Yes or No)." Any time you ask a question, you are implying a Predicate.

The following table shows how Predicates expect responses from Domains or sets of things:

Questions You Can Ask (Predicates)	DOMAIN or Set of Things
The maximum permissible level of (239)Plutonium in the body	microcuries
Football position that often hands off to a fullback	titles of football positions
Title of the first collection of poems published by William Blake	list of publications by William Blake
Color of David Bowie's hair on the *Ziggy Stardust* album	hair color or just colors
Season a salmon swims upstream	seasons of the year
Volume level for the threshold of pain	decibels
Uniform rate of acceleration for an object falling freely to the ground	meters per second^2
Electrical resistance of silicon	ohms per cubic centimeter
Capacity of a kiloliter	meters cubed
Fuel octane rating of regular gas	octane rating
Year Columbus made a name for himself	date/time
To whom President Lyndon Johnson was married	persons

This is a good point to leave Predicates. I have mentioned "a set of things" or what we term a "Class," and so I owe you an explanation of what that is all about. You will have to wait until I explain what a thing is, which is Concept 4. If the question a Predicate poses is answered by drawing a value from a Domain, we call that Predicate an Attribute. If the question a Predicate poses is answered by referring to another thing, we call that Predicate a Relationship. Since you don't really need to make this distinction to do very complete analysis, I have put the discussions of Relationships and Attributes after the section on Classes. These later discussions will give you lots of practice with the Predicates, as well as teach you the specifics of Attributes and Relationships. Also note that CASE tools generally require you to distinguish between these two types of Predicate, and so if you intend—as you should—to use a CASE tool, then you will need to study these two sections.

Here's what you should have learned from studying the concept of Predicates:

- Predicates describe things.

- Description is the essence of an information system.

- A Predicate is any property, quality, or characteristic ascribed to a thing.

- That thing is identified by the argument of the Predicate.

- Predicates can describe other Predicates.

- Find Predicates by asking "What do you want to know?" and "What do you want to know about?"

- The full specification of a Predicate includes how many answers you expect, whether you need to know more than just the current answer, and what kind of answer you want.

- A thing may have one or many values for a Predicate.

- Most Predicates are modifiable.

- The Predicate is evaluated by a Domain or set of things.

■ If you know everything you want to know (the Predicates!), and if you can itemize all the necessary and only the sufficient factors that determine the value of each of these Predicates (the arguments!), then you have completed your analysis.

Part TWO

Sets of Predicates

robably the most powerful and least understood capability of the mind is its ability to discern patterns. Superficially, I can see that the suit is a print or a plaid. More profoundly, I can see through the suitor and understand that he is a prince or a cad. Pattern, pattern everywhere, making me stop to think—briefly, I assure you, and then we'll get back to the commercial portion of our program.

Pattern recognition is a distinct capability from the kind of logical inference that a computer is capable of automating. For this reason, humans will have to do most of the pattern matching for computers. Your Data Modeling skills are not going to become obsolete.

Consider the Kasparov versus Deep Blue chess match. Kasparov, the current chess champion, is observing the pattern of the chess pieces. He is getting a sense of the ebb and flow of strategic control of the board, perhaps in the same way a meteorologist reads highs and lows on a weather map. Meanwhile, Deep Blue is cranking out move after move by rating each move against every other move just like the programmers told it to. Irrespective of the fact that the programmers were able to develop a rating scheme that is comprehensive enough to beat everybody all of the time and even beat one Grand Master most of the time, the point remains that the approach to the problems are inherently different. Kasparov is manipulating whole patterns of high and low control with his moves; Deep Blue is

reducing moves to a score. (On a personal note, I'd like to see Kasparov take Mr. Blue apart in a game of checkers.)

What if we directly experienced the world; that is, what if the light and sound and smells of the world entered our consciousness unfiltered and unassembled? They would be useless. I suppose the experience would be like sticking a telephone wire in your mouth and trying to speak, or like watching the static on the TV. We know that we do a great deal of filtering, as in "What was that, dear? Were you speaking to me?" Filtering tends to work against us when we are trying to understand the needs of a system owner-to-be. But the other amazing mental process is the assembly of all this sensation into discrete objects. We are all familiar with the visual trickery in which a vase may seem like two faces or vice-versa. Or take an example from everyday life: "I'm sorry. I must have thought that was junk mail and thrown it away." Pattern recognition allows us to see shapes in clouds, to discern the fates in our lives, and to take the eggs out of the refrigerator.

We not only recognize patterns in data, but we also generalize those patterns. While a child can see a horsey, a meteorologist (after certain cognitive abilities have been removed by the educational system) looks right at the horse and mumbles "cumulo-nimbus." (Editor's note: The author's disparaging remarks regarding the educational system are not shared by this publisher nor its parent company. Clearly the meteorologist is greatly benefited by building on his knowledge of cumulo-nimbus to know enough not to go out into the rain. In any case, anyone who could look right past a really good horsey has no reason to go out in the rain.) The horsey is a one-of-a-kind; the cumulo-nimbus is a generalization.

Your native ability to create sets is so far advanced from what is needed in Data Modeling that it is a little like taking a rocket to the corner store. To data model, you will use pattern recognition and set creation that wouldn't tax your pet beagle. There are two major divisions in the set-making for Data Modeling: you make sets of Predicates; you make sets of things. Immediately, you are going to study the two ways you create sets of Predicates. Later in this book—once we have discussed what a thing is—you will study the three ways to make sets of things. In total, you use just five criteria to create sets in order to build data models. Granted you combine these different criteria to create beautifully complex sets.—What good is a rocket ship if you can't leave your beagle for the weekend?

Sets of Predicates

We make sets of all the Predicates that have the same arguments. Predicates are set together regardless of which process may be justifying the recognition of the Predicate. These sets are called Entities. Relevance is a function of process. We recognize that certain subsets of the Predicates of an Entity are related in the way they interact with some process; that is, they may need each other to be fully relevant. We call these subsets of Predicates States of an Entity.

I don't mean to be obtuse; one of the great paradoxes is that when language is very precise, it is hard to understand. (Look what happened to the legal profession.) What I am talking about are things, Entities—for example, people. To an information system, an employee is nothing but a set of facts about some person. That is all anything is to an information system. People, property, events, and concepts are all just the set of Predicates we associate to those things.

You don't have to work through the identification of Entities—such as people—or States—such as employees—laboriously pasting Predicates together. As I have said, you do this work naturally, and you will identify 99% of all the Entities and States with which you work without ever thinking of them in this way. Nevertheless, in a number of situations, what the Entity or State is might not be so clear; full knowledge of the way we form these concepts will therefore make you even more successful. ∎

Entities

This section, Entities, is about things—individual things, not the idea of things. In everyday speech, we are very accustomed to referring to either individual things or whole categories. For example, we might say, "How much did you pay for your car?" In this case, we are referring to a specific car. We might also say, "I need a car." In this second example, we are referring to a class of things. Figure 4-1 provides further examples. Forgive for a minute the limitations of a book; I have no practical way of folding a Chevrolet in between these pages. Pretend the pictures in the first column are in fact as tangible as this book in your hands. Imagine this conversation:

Popeye: How much is this car?

Wimpy: Oh, that's no car. That's a light truck; it has none of the safety features of a car.

Popeye: Okay, then, how much for this truck?

Wimpy: Not a truck, a light truck. Couldn't really haul anything in it.

Popeye: It is what it is! Whatever you call it, this thing right here. How much money?

Wimpy: Money?

Entity	Could belong to classes of Entities (list is not exhaustive)
	Vehicle, insured item, asset
	Home, insured item, asset
	Appliance, terminal, product
	Furnishing, product
	Vehicle, bicycle

Figure 4-1

Notice that the actual car (or truck or whatever) could be said to belong to a large number of classes. Although any argument among reasonable people about the nature of the car could be settled by inspecting the car, many brutal arguments arise about its inclusion in any class. An information system keeps data about individual things but almost always in the context of classes of things. Concept 4 deals with properly identifying the individual thing, what I will call the Entity. Properly defining the collective class is Concept 6.

Tip for System Analysts

Be careful how you read this section. Most texts on the subject of Data Modeling begin by discussing Entity Types, what I prefer to call Classes. In writing this text, however, I believed that one could not understand a Class unless one first understood Entity Occurrences, what I shorten to Entities. So, unlike those texts, I begin with an inspection of an individual Entity.

Entity is synonymous with what object-oriented texts would call a persistent object. As I use the term here I mean only those objects representative of the subject matter as opposed to system control. Use of the term Class is consistent with object-oriented approaches.

Further, one cannot understand Entities without an understanding of Attributes and Relationships. (Attributes and Relationships are referred to collectively as Predicates.) Hence, the organization of the curriculum: from Predicates to Entity instance and then to Classes. This is a subtle shift in thinking. Ask yourself the question, "Does an Entity instance have Attributes? Does the book in your hands have weight?" The answer has to be yes. Ask yourself, "Does a Class have Attributes?" This section is about Entity (Occurrences) and not Classes, so you will have to read on to get an answer to that question.

Why Should I Study Entities?

Basically, an Entity is a specific thing. Since an information system stores information about things, being able to represent them properly in the computer becomes very important.

Assume the owners wanted to answer these questions:

- What is the value of contract #1?
- What is the weight of the part A?
- Where is car 54 located?

The contract, the part, and the car are all things. As you study Entities, you may begin to wonder how the concept of a thing gets so involved. Don't let my explorations confuse you; I should not be able to distract you from the simple point that an Entity is a thing. Entities are so simple because you are so smart; your brain assembles them for you before you are aware of any thinking at work. (There is no homunculus inside your head watching the world projected for him on a screen. I know that because the popcorn would make your eyes water.) Reflecting on the essential structure of Entities and how effortlessly you work with them, you will begin to appreciate how stupid computers really are.

Entities and Computer Systems

If your computer were a chicken coop, Entities would be the chickens. If your computer were a grocery store, Entities would be the groceries. (Attorney's note: Be advised that this text in no way suggests that you put chickens, groceries, or any foreign substance in your computer without first consulting the manufacturer.)

Entities are the things for which we keep records. Examples are endless: people, places, things. The business card you keep is a record of a person. If you type the information from the business card into a computer program, there a computer record is created. For everything we want to track, we create a record. In the computer screen shown in Figure 4-2, Henry, David, and Melissa are all Entities.

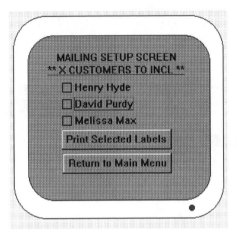

Figure   4-2

Consider another example, a pawn (a chess piece). You might record that the pawn was black, was worth one point, and was at position A1 after move 7. For a game of chess, the pawn and the move are both Entities. If you kept data about all the pieces and especially all the moves, then you could reconstruct a game of chess. Conceiving of a pawn as an Entity and keeping record of its movements will lead to a better information system than any other approach to record-keeping. We define the Entity, pawn, to have the relevant characteristics of the real chess piece, and so the record-keeping mirrors the real chess game. The better the mirror, the more likely it is to contain all the data the owners of the system will need to analyze the game.

Consider a business example, an air traffic control system. What is the first Entity that jumps to mind? If you said an aircraft, you are on track. What do we record about airplanes? We probably record their airline and their position at a point in time, to name just two characteristics. An air traffic control system deals with real things that have almost limitless descriptive possibility. Nonetheless, organizing records around the Entity, aircraft, is the best way to keep the data because it mirrors the real world and thus anticipates the needs of the system owners.

Granted, most of us work on mundane software used to keep track of chickens and cans of soup rather than chess pieces and aircraft. Nonetheless, if you learn to recognize Entities and let them mirror your business needs, then you will create simple-to-use and cheap-to-keep computer programs. The identification of Entities is a very intuitive and natural skill. "Bees do it, birds do it, even mouse-happy nerds do it...." Now let's do it. I'm talking about distinguishing things one from another.

What Is an Entity?

Excuse my geeky language, but how do we interface with our world? On the input side, we get stimuli of various kinds from all directions. Our brains organize this information into discrete things that we credit as the source of these sensations. Only brains can do this. A dog can find a duck in the woods, but it took millions of dollars to get a computer to find a "D" in the word "Dog." I take it as a given that we don't know how to get a computer to tell a duck from a dog or even a dog from a log.

The following is a list of Entities:

- Reservation #55
- My Plantation
- Your Opinion
- Our Contract
- Alberta
- Invoice Line #1
- The Airline Ticket
- Contract Revision #1
- His Accident Report
- Experiment
- Elvis Presley
- Vehicle TNJ171
- Stock Certificate #15Q73

The following is a list of words that cannot represent Entities:

- Blue
- 500°
- Finally
- Grow
- Sell
- Classify

- Decompose
- Loud
- Temperature
- Reserve
- Verbally
- Acrid
- Hire
- Revise

What can you infer about the nature of Entities from these two lists? Would you say that all nouns are Entities? All the Entities in the first list are nouns, but there are nouns in the non-Entity list as well; for example, temperature is a noun. Some approaches to Data Modeling tell you to find the nouns. This approach is okay as a first step in finding Entities, just as a journey of 1,000 miles begins with but one step. However, let's hope that your project plan is a good deal less detailed than 1 step in 1,000 miles!

Would you say that Entities are nouns? Entities are not verbs or adjectives. Entities are the way we refer to things, so yes, they are nouns. Entities become the subjects or objects of verbs: a customer makes a reservation; a person files an accident report. Entities are described by adjectives: the employee is "blue"; the accident report is "revised."

Basically, an Entity is a thing. If you are a high-priced consultant, you may feel uncomfortable calling an Entity "a thing." Try "phenomenon." In a bog of squishy words, phenomenon is a rock. Listen to *Merriam-Webster's Collegiate® Dictionary*[1]:

- "an observable fact or event"
- "an object or aspect known through the senses rather than by thought or intuition"

Phenomenon is a genuine high-dollar word, and its definition seems to really encompass everything that could be an Entity. (If phenomenon doesn't suit your style, try your thesaurus. You can select from: doodad, whatchamacallit, gizmo, whatzit ....) Just about anything that can be the subject or object of a sentence can be an Entity. For example, "The accident involved a single vehicle." The accident and the vehicle are Entities; note that the accident is an event, while the vehicle is an object.

Take a look at the following examples of Entities. In the sentence

---

1. *By permission from* Merriam-Webster's Collegiate® Dictionary, *Tenth Edition © 1997 by Merriam-Webster Incorporated.*

- "Big Jack Jumps," Jack is the Entity; Jumps is not.
- "Cancel the reservation," reservation is the Entity; Cancel is not.
- "The sales total is $1," sale is the only Entity.
- "Jamie bought a gallon of gas," Jamie and a quantity of gas are the only Entities.
- "Buy the large, hilly tract of land," tract of land is the Entity; neither large nor hilly can be Entities.

Entities can act or be acted upon. The action itself is not a part of the Entity in the way that the Entity can be said to be "big." To say that Jack, Mary, and Kim can all jump is to describe them. (To describe how to make Big Jack jump is a concern of object-oriented design and is outside the scope of this text.)

Entities Are Describable

Knowing that Entities are nouns is only a first step. Study this list of nouns, none of which would represent Entities:

- Age
- Sequence
- Temperature
- Color
- Description
- Amount
- Quantity
- Total
- Longitude
- Weight

This list draws out the key distinction between Entities and all other parts of an information system. The original list of Entities are all things that can be described; this last list are words that cannot themselves be described. You cannot say how heavy age is, not in the same way you can talk about how heavy Elvis was. You can say a customer, John Buck, is "satisfied, rich, a bad debt," or whatever. Try to use Color, or Sequence, or Temperature in the same sentence; try, for example, "Color is satisfied"!? Color,

Sequence, and the rest of the list are all words that describe. Entities are what these Domains describe.

Entities Are Elemental

So far, you have learned that an Entity must be a noun and must be describable. Let's look at another collection of nouns and understand why they cannot be Entities. Study the following examples, in which you will find adjectives in unexpected places:

- "The passenger" is not an Entity; but in the phrase "the person in seat 2a," the person and seat 2a are Entities.
- "The salesperson" is not an Entity; but in the phrase "the person who is selling," the person is an Entity.
- "The fist" is not an Entity; but in the phrase "the clenched hand," the hand is an Entity.
- "The bid" is not an Entity; but in the phrase "the bidding phase of our negotiation," our negotiation is an Entity.

At first, a noun like passenger would seem to indicate the existence of an Entity. But what is a passenger? The answer depends on who is answering. The operations executive says, "A passenger is someone on the flight manifest, someone on a plane." The lawyer says, "A passenger is someone who has flown on one of our flights." The reservationist says, "A passenger is someone who holds a reservation." Who's right? They all must be right since the information system is theirs. The project team can go gripe about how the owners can't even agree on a definition, but it is not the owners that are having difficulty doing their jobs. They do agree that a passenger is someone. The Entity is a person. Predicates are indicated as well; I'd assume something like has boarded a flight, has at some time boarded a flight, and intends to board a flight.

Data Modeling disassembles information into its parts. It not only breaks words out of a sentence, but it also breaks apart the words themselves to find that they too may be made up of distinct parts. Nouns can incorporate modifiers to form new and more meaningful nouns. Conversation is simplified when we use these nouns that are compounded with adjectives. For example, a fist is a clenched hand; clenched is the hidden modifier; hand is the base Entity. We don't say, "He hit me with his clenched hand" (as we might say, "He hit me with his cupped hand"); we say, "He hit me with his fist." Computers are just too stupid to hit; for them to understand the way we organize data, we must separate the modifiers from the base Entities.

The requirement that modifiers be stripped out of complex nouns is not just academic. It must be this way; otherwise, each time some new compound noun comes into use, the analysis on the old noun would become obsolete. Further, managing data that is transient (such as "passenger") is difficult. The simple noun "person" can get on and off a plane and remain a person. A passenger seems to disappear as he or she gets off the plane! Make a fist; open your hand. Where did the fist go?

Tip for System Analysts

I am formulating a definition of Entity that contributes to a stable data model. Passengers become non-passengers once their trip is complete. Salespeople become executives. So these terms are unstable, shifting due to other information or changing over time. By tearing the Predicate out of the Entity, the analyst quickly sees commonality between Entities that may not have been so apparent before. During Planning and Analysis, this commonality simplifies the models. During Design and Construction, this commonality will lead to more efficient systems. Imagine deleting a passenger record and then adding a customer record, deleting customer and adding passenger, and so on.

Tip for Project Managers

Management must support this kind of simplification from day one. It may seem contradictory to confront you with a lot of rules about how Entities are to be defined and then to tell you to keep them simple. When you are learning the rules, they seem complex. Once you and the people you work with understand the rules, then those rules make the job and the design itself simpler. Imagine playing cards when you don't know the rules.

Play by the rules, and have the analysts and the system owners work together to simplify Entities from compound things, such as "salesperson," to simpler Entities, such as "person," and Predicates, such as "sells."

The nature of analysts and programmers is to come charging into the project manager's office asking to be exempt from the rules. These rules are not for breaking; we are not talking about arbitrary standards. These rules are closer to the rules of arithmetic. Management must beware of those who will ignore the rules or, worse still, those who think they are following the rules but are not.

The nature of Project Managers is to come barreling out of their offices when analysis is almost complete and to beg analysts to reduce the number of Entities because they are driving up their cost estimates. Strictly enforcing the recognition of the base Entity from the outset will reduce the complexity of the model. The other common cause of "Barreling Managers" is the unhappy client.

When you strictly enforce the rules for Entity identification, the owners of the system may complain that "their" Entities are not being given full consideration in the model. If the owners do not understand the concept of stripping Entities clean of Predicates, they will feel as though you are not listening to them. If they don't see a box somewhere with the word "customer," they will speak poorly of you when you are not there. Before you throw out the rule book, remember that the rules reduce the number of Classes and untangle the model.

Cheat: use aliases; make up special presentations. The team knows it is a person, but the presentation to the system owners talks about customers. Document the different data requirements for persons and corporations, which both happen to be customers.

Could everyone understand these concepts well enough to work together in the way we might help each other solve an Algebra problem? First, everybody has to see that the rules of Data Modeling are akin to the rules of Algebra. The only way to get to a Nirvana with everyone analyzing a system from the same set of analysis principles is to stress training both the team and the owners. If you wait until the last minute to explain these concepts, then the owners will feel as though you are making the rules up as you go along—like someone who teaches you a new poker game as you play. You know how it feels to play a card only to be told, "No, No, No, not until the one-eyed jack has mated with the queen of hearts!" Keep the clients happy, keep the model simple, and minimize special presentations. Teach everybody to model and then play by the rules.

Entities Are Identifiable

So far you have learned that an Entity is a noun, that it can be described, and that it does not contain any hidden modifiers. One further important criterion is demonstrated by the following examples. Can you tell what is this last characteristic of an Entity?

■ A batch of ball bearings can be an Entity; ball bearings in the process of production (ball bearings work in process) can be an Entity; but an undifferentiated ball bearing cannot be an Entity.

- A truck load of gas can be an Entity; gas delivered to your home in December can be an Entity; gas under a lease can be an Entity; but an unbounded cubic meter of gas cannot be an Entity.
- A country can be an Entity; a tract of land can be an Entity; but ordinary dirt in your dustpan cannot be an Entity.

What can you learn from these examples? That things become Entities when they reach a certain level of significance? Some definitions of Entity include the phrase "particularly significant," but who is to say that Elvis Presley is significant? A quality of the rules of Data Modeling is objectivity. The goal in establishing these principles is to see any number of people arrive at a single data model for any given circumstance. You cannot objectively evaluate the significance of a thing.

What I want you to get from these examples is that each of the Entities can be identified. The essence of an Entity is its separation from other Entities. You must be able to gather information about an Entity for that Entity to have any purpose in your information system. Look what happens if we violate this identity principle. When I sell you a gallon of gas, do I sell you a particular gallon? Why would it be ridiculous to get an itemized bill at the gas station?

Gallon	$1.31
Gallon	$1.31
Gallon	$1.31
Total	$3.93

The obvious, and correct, answer is that they all have the same price. Why do they all have the same price? Because you cannot distinguish one gallon from the other. If you feel that you did not get three gallons of gas, it wasn't the first gallon or the second gallon that was shy; it was that the whole transaction was short. If you complain of water in your gas, you do not say "One of those gallons you sold me had water in it."

Tip for System Analysts

When dealing with things that cannot be uniquely identified or even bounded, such as gas, we measure off a bit and note the quantity. So, for instance, when I sell you 50,000 cubic meters of natural gas from my pipeline, you will get what I give you and assume that it has the same character as the rest of the gas in my pipeline. When gas passes through the meter, there is a sale; the sale itself is an Entity. Once the gas I sold you mixes with gas already in your tanks, it is again undifferentiated and loses its Entity-ness. The gas is now a part of some other Entity such as "Tank #7," which has a certain p.s.i. that describes how much gas it contains.

Some Entities Are Not Unique

You might be thinking that when you go to the grocer, you get a receipt that looks a lot like the gallon, gallon, gallon example because the clerk has figured out that it is quicker to scan the milk three times than to reach over and hit the quantity button on the register. You will have occasion to record facts about some thing or event that are identical to some other thing or event. That's okay. Some analysts try to force the things to be unique by, for instance, recording the date and time for each Entity and assuming this information makes each record unique. It probably does make it unique, but the uniqueness is trivial in that we still don't think of "gallon 12/22/2001 11:00:037789" as being any different. Time at which it is sold to the millionth second adds nothing to what we know of the milk. It is not important that things be unique; but later, in order to associate new data with the proper Entity, you will have to be able to uniquely iden-tify to which Entity this new data applies. I would have to stretch this example too far to imagine some data that you would later associate with just one of the gallons of milk. So, if like the clerk, you end up with a lot of data that is identical, then you can summarize all of the Entities into a sin-gle record and note the quantity. There would be no loss of information if the receipt had said "Gallon milk 3 @ $2.29."

What happens when one of the gallons is returned? You scratch off any one of the three from the receipt. Or you write a note on the receipt, "returned one gallon." The clerk, even if he or she has not read this text, knows that it just doesn't matter which is scratched. Even if it did matter, there is no way to know which was which, and certainly knowing the mil-lisecond that the milk was sold is still useless.

Some Entities Don't Start Out Unique

Entities don't have to start out having different data about them; however, the potential for collecting data particular to the Entity must exist. In the following dialogue, you will see how from the perspective of the customer, the Entity is not the individual item. From the perspective of the salesperson, the item is an Entity because the data about each Entity will become different once it is sold.

Customer:	Do you have any refrigerators left?
Salesperson:	Yes, we have two of them, but they are going fast!
Customer:	Great, I'll take one!
Salesperson:	You've made a good buy! Which do you want?
Customer:	What kind of refrigerators are they?
Salesperson:	They are both GB Model 100's.
Customer:	What color are they?
Salesperson:	They are both brown.
Customer:	Do either of them have any special features?
Salesperson:	Both are energy-efficient and come with extra racks.
Customer:	Wait a minute. These refrigerators seem identical. What's different about them?
Salesperson:	To you, they are identical; to me, I have paperwork.
Customer:	You twerp! Why should I care which refrigerator I buy?!
Salesperson:	Just pick one, you soggy waffle!
Customer:	That one.
Salesperson:	Thank you. Now read me the serial number off of it.
Customer:	What do you need that for? They are identical.
Salesperson:	They were until you bought one. Now you own that one—not this one.
Customer:	Next time I'll select a model from a catalog. Are we through?
Salesperson:	With every purchase, we are giving a gallon of milk. Which gallon would you like?

The thing with data that makes a difference to the buyer is the model, so to the customer, the model is an Entity. The salesperson, on the other hand, has to turn in a warranty card, and note on what day the item was sold, and on and on. The salesperson wants to know more about each refrigerator, and so to the salesperson the refrigerator is also an Entity.

An Entity Is Something About Which We Keep Data

One good and representative definition of Entity is "an item of particular significance and interest to the organization about which it needs to keep information." This could be interpreted as simply a statement of project scope. That is, if you are not interested in any data about something, then why bother? True enough. You can look at it in a second, more profound way: how can you know of the existence of something if you know nothing about that thing? From a practical standpoint, if I have no Predicates, I have no thing. What this statement means is that the Predicate precedes the Entity into the data model. The Predicate is the cornerstone of your analysis, not the Entity. So an Entity is not only theoretically describable, but it is something for which we actually have a description, a Predicate. That Entity must be included in the scope of the project, but the scope of the project should be established by the systems owner's questions. Those questions, or Predicates, determine what Entities are in scope.

Remember I said that I would have to stretch to create a situation in which data was kept about a particular gallon of milk? This situation is eggs, not milk, but we will bring into our information system something that is not unique and make it unique. Between the customer and the salesperson, the same thing was either an Entity or not, depending on perspective. In this case, some of the very same things can become Entities or not, depending on circumstances. You are up early, and you hear from the next room, "Careful when you make your breakfast; Suzy has injected some of those dozen eggs I bought yesterday for her science experiment." Terrorized by being ill-informed, you reach for the Shredded Wheat. Ruminating, you jot down suggestions for future science projects.

What should Suzy have done? Should she have numbered each egg and made notes on a page regarding those eggs that were a part of an experiment? Numbering things in this way is very common practice—for example, customer numbers, serial numbers, and marketing codes. But is this always the right thing to do? When might numbering each thing not be productive?

Let's review what we know, slowly—after all it is morning. You have a mental file on the basket of eggs: you know that a certain number were purchased and that they were purchased yesterday. All you can know about the eggs applies equally to all the eggs. For example, you know all the eggs were purchased yesterday. You could write on each egg "purchased yesterday," but that would be tiresome. You also know you have twelve eggs, but on which egg should you write "twelve eggs"? No single egg is twelve eggs, just as no single egg is the twelfth egg. This data, date of purchase and quantity, are facts that apply to the Entity basket of eggs. Tear off a piece of the cereal box and write "Twelve eggs, purchased yesterday" and put it on top of the basket of eggs. Don't forget to close the refrigerator door.

Let's assume that the uninjected eggs were to be consumed in the usual fashion; that is, nobody should keep a file on the eggs we eat. Our tendency is to think of each egg as an Entity; after all, I can put each one in my hand. But unless we intend that each egg may have different data about it, then we should not think of individual eggs as separate Entities. Numbering the uninjected eggs would be useless.

Should Suzy have numbered the injected eggs? Insofar as the injected eggs go, the date purchased and the quantity of eggs would also be descriptions of the entire batch. Additionally, Suzy will keep other data about each of her experimental eggs. Maybe she wants to know how much botulin was injected in each egg, or the precise weight of each egg. For the experimental eggs, we have data about both the batch of eggs and about each individual egg. Therefore, Suzy must cause the injected eggs to be identifiable by numbering them in addition to identifying their source. Both the batch and each egg are Entities.

Should Daddy stick with the Shredded Wheat? You bet, but should Suzy keep all her eggs in one basket? The moral of the story is that you can keep data only about something you can identify, and you should identify only those things about which you keep data. As you have seen with both the milk and the eggs, you may keep data about a quantity of things as well as you can about an individual thing.

An Entity Is a Set of Predicates

Daddy, who is fine by the way, goes around the office all morning asking people to feel his forehead. "Do I feel a little hot to you?" Finally, Daddy's boss sends Daddy to the nurse.

Nurse:	We don't use thermometers much any more. This gadget in the ear, press a button and voilà, I see that your temperature is perfectly normal.
Daddy:	I just really want to be absolutely sure I'm okay. Would you just put a good old thermometer in my mouth and double check?
Nurse:	Okay, it's been two minutes. Let's see. Well, the technology works. You're perfectly normal.
Daddy:	You're sure?
Nurse:	Look, I could …

Daddy: No, that's not necessary. My ear is normal; my mouth is normal …

Nurse: Why don't we just put on your file that you have a normal temperature at this time? Come back in an hour if you still think you are dying.

The two temperatures are each Predicates of a complete medical report. What is the Entity, the ear? the mouth? the Daddy? Strictly speaking, the temperature is of Daddy's ear, but we do not see relevance at that level of information. We are not worried that the ear, or any other part of the anatomy, might be sick. "Is Daddy sick?" is the question we are trying to answer. Although we measure the ear, we say that the person has the temperature; hence Daddy is the Entity.

From the evidence, we presume two Predicates, ear temperature and mouth temperature. What is the argument for the Predicate ear temperature? Ear temperature depends on whose temperature we take, Daddy in this case, and what time we take it.

The nurse keeps very good records. Here is Daddy's record for ear temperature on that day:

Patient Name	Date & Time	Temperature, Ear
Daddy	7/8/99 8:45 am	98.6
Daddy	7/8/99 9:22 am	98.6
Daddy	7/8/99 10:44 am	98.6
Daddy	7/8/99 11:38 am	98.6

What is the argument for the Predicate temperature by mouth? Again, an oral temperature depends on whose temperature we take, and what time we take it. To help visualize this, look at Daddy's record for temperature by mouth on that day:

Patient Name	Date & Time	Temperature, Mouth
Daddy	7/8/99 8:45 am	98.6
Daddy	7/8/99 9:22 am	98.6
Daddy	7/8/99 10:44 am	98.6
Daddy	7/8/99 11:38 am	98.6

Who's crazy, Daddy or the nurse? Daddy will eventually realize that he is not dying. Without emergency Data Modeling, the Nurse will never realize that his record-keeping may be the reason administrative costs are out of hand. Don't you think that the nurse would be grateful if we showed him this alternative way of keeping track of a patient's temperatures?

Patient Name	Date & Time	Temperature, Mouth	Temperature, Ear
Daddy	7/8/99 8:45 am	98.6	98.6
Daddy	7/8/99 9:22 am	98.6	98.6
Daddy	7/8/99 10:44 am	98.6	98.6
Daddy	7/8/99 11:38 am	98.6	98.6

"Well, I just don't know about that. I've been keeping records like I've been doing for a long time now and ...." Why do I always do this to myself? Why do I always think that I'm going to show somebody something great and they are going to just eat it up?

Well, nonetheless, it only makes sense that since the two temperatures have the same argument, they describe the same Entity. Or look at it another way, the Entity is the argument. If I hadn't the need to keep track of temperatures over time, then there would be no Entity, Daddy/ time. In fact, there are two temperatures that I need to track over time; either Predicate is enough to justify the Entity. But we do not create two Entities; the Entity is the set of all Predicates that have the same arguments.

Tip for System Analysts

Some modelers would say that the Predicate is temperature and the argument is not just who and when but also where. Where would have the values of "oral, aural, or whatever." Taking the names off of some Predicate and making those names into values in a table is a common technique but one that can lead to trouble. In the last section of this book an example is made of customer address; reading that, you will appreciate some of the pitfalls of this technique.

If there were no temperature, there would be no Daddy. This is a silly play on words, but it is worth pushing the example a bit further. If our application were being developed for the nurse's station, then surely some Predicate, temperature or weight or something, would justify a need for a type of Entity such as patient. When you start working on information systems, you don't usually drag yourself through the exercise of finding all Predicates, documenting their arguments, and then creating sets. You start right out assuming there is something called a patient. But, for sake of argument, let's say that you did find a Predicate called <u>height</u>, which they assured you for purposes of this project was recorded one time about the patient and never changed. The argument for the Predicate <u>height</u> is just the individual patient, Daddy, just as Daddy is the first part of the argument that I noted in the previous discussion on temperature. Many Predicates have just the barest argument, the thing in question itself. Nonetheless, the rule holds; the Entity is the set of all Predicates that have the same argument.

The following situation could apply to any process manufacturer. The intent is to show how we can construct an Entity to suit our information-gathering needs. This example also shows how the same thing can be an Entity in one context but not another. What if you were to receive the following memo?

12/22/99
To: The World
From: Analyst Ed
Re: Meeting w/ Ms. Smith of Production Control

Spoke w/ Ms. Smith. Confirmed that each bottle of Billy Bob's Hair Tonic is manufactured to extremely tight tolerances and that each bottle of any given size is identical. Finished and inspected bottles are packed on pallets of 5,000 bottles. Once bottles arrive at the dealer, no further reporting is done.

Smith confirmed that a number of lawsuits claim failure to produce follicles. Ms. Smith has no way to determine the age or the lot number for any of the implicated bottles. I quote, "Which bottle failed to grow hair and why—that's what I want to know." There is a real need to begin comprehensive tracking of each bottle. I want to involve scores of executives and analysts in a huge, day-long meeting to hash this out. Can I please? Can I? Can I?

In response to Analyst Ed, would you: a) complain about the size of the database, b) tell Ed he was nuts, or c) ensure that the bottle-numbering scheme was non-significant and would fit on the bottle.

Insofar as the size of the database is concerned, you have enough to worry about without taking on database design as well. At this stage, just figure out what they want and tell 'em what it costs later. Skip b. Insofar as c goes, what if we were able to ascertain that bottle 1,111,111,111 failed?

We wouldn't do anything differently if bottle 1,111,111,112 failed. Data that doesn't confirm or change our course of action is just trivia.

You know which bottle failed anyway; it is in the little bag marked "Exhibit #444." From the perspective of the court proceeding, it is an Entity. It might be described by the day it was entered into evidence, who owns it, and other data that pertains to that individual bottle.

Knowing which individual bottle failed does Ms. Smith no good unless it leads her to know what made that bottle different. For instance, if she could know from which production lot it came, then she could see what was different about that lot, recall other bottles in that lot, produce production data about that lot, and so on. What's a lot? In manufacturing, lot means all the product that is the result of some set of inputs. Since lots vary, and since Billy Bob has reason to keep track of data about a lot, then a lot is an Entity. On the other hand, since bottles within a lot are all the same, knowing which bottle within a lot failed adds nothing to Billy Bob's understanding.

What if all Ms. Smith does is watch workers dump a variety of vegetable matter into vats periodically, ferment them, and sluice the result into bottles? When does one lot end and the other begin? This problem points out the way the Entity is, well, fluid. That is, an Entity is what you need it to be. I did NOT just say that you can make stuff up. To resolve the problem, you must ask Ms. Smith (and others) what they reasonably need to know about a lot. It is a legal/bio-engineering/business question; it has nothing to do with computers.

What if it is determined after an all-day session with scores of executives and analysts that the only thing that could possibly cause Billy Bob's Hair Tonic not to encourage follicle growth is the high and low temperature of the tank during fermentation? Then, so long as the values for the high and low temperature remained the same, you would gain nothing by declaring one lot finished and another begun. On the other hand, every time the values changed for the bottles you were filling, you would also need to change the lot identifier so that the bottles of that lot could be properly distinguished from bottles that were made under different conditions.

I cannot possibly discuss all of the ways to analyze process manufacturing. But what if during this grueling session, the engineers said that the tonic was very sensitive to the quantity as well as vat temperatures? What if the lawyers said that they needed to know who made the ingredients? What if the business people wanted to know who was working when the lot was created? What if they each said that they wanted the data to be clear—in other words, they wanted only one set of conditions, one vendor to have provided any ingredient, and one shift of workers? Then when any one of these factors changed, the simplest thing to do would be to assign a number to a lot and start another.

The major theme of this story is that an Entity is an invention that serves to collect relevant data about itself. When you consider the example of the eggs and even the gasoline, you get the impression that those really are things that we know about. The example of the lot starts to shake well that world view. The definition of a lot depends on what is determined to be relevant and can change as the understanding of the process changes. In fact, in order to get the data about a lot, the engineers might have to change the process.

The bottle is not an Entity to us, but it is to the courts, revealing that what constitutes an Entity depends on the perspective of the person who is determining the relevance of the data. So answer b was correct, so long as Analyst Ed does not go to work for the courts.

Finding a Level of Relevance

In the example of Billy Bob's Hair Tonic, we say that we can actually construct the Entity to suit our data-gathering need. This next case is a variety of that same theme; it comes from experience with agri-business, but the idea of finding the level at which data is relevant is universal. What if I were in the ball-bearing business: do I need to track every bearing? every box? boxcar? What if I told you I'm an international trader? What if I told you I'm a materials engineer? Does my job affect how granular I want my data to be?

Juan Amarillo grows bananas. He has three small plantations along the sides of an active volcano in Costa Rica. He sells his bananas to larger growers like Yellow Banana and Whole Banana on the banana market, promising so many pounds on such-and-such a date.

Juan has good relations with his buyers; they never see the bananas. The buyers operate the packing houses. They provide the boxes and the labels. Once Juan delivers the bananas to the packing house, he has no further responsibility. The boxes are shipped to Limón by rail and loaded on boats for the market.

In order to maintain these good relations, Juan carefully monitors the sweetness, size, and degree of ripeness of the harvest. A good harvest is the result of careful control and timely application of fertilizer and insecticide. Boxes are marked with a harvest number, so that if there were any subsequent problems they could be traced and unsold bananas could be recalled.

Juan wants an information system, but what is the Entity about which he wants to collect information? Is it the banana, the box, the boatload, or the harvest?

Juan would go bananas if he tried to keep track of every one. He sells by the pound, he ships by the boatload, and he tracks quality harvest to harvest. Banana is far too low a level of detail. Box is a good idea, but the boxes are incidental. Juan can't tell one box from another and doesn't seem to care. He doesn't do anything with boxes. Juan doesn't do anything with the boats, either; he is not in the reefer business. What constitutes a boatload or what goes on a boat is of no interest to him. Harvest meets all the criteria you have identified to make it an Entity. Harvest is a noun that can be described. Data about harvests is relevant.

Does it surprise you that the relevant Entity is so large and so abstract? It shouldn't; size and degree of abstraction are not issues when defining the Entity.

Entities That Group

Often, we try to group Entities and then to gather data about the group. A host may ask, "How many in your party? Will you want smoking or non-smoking?" This is another way in which we can invent Entities in order to collect data. On a grander scale, we invent a census tract and then figure out the average household income for that area. When we create groups such as these, we have to trust that the constitution of the group does not change; otherwise, the data becomes irrelevant. For instance, if the government were constantly changing the boundaries of census tracts, what would that do to the trending of data? If Tract #121 was made smaller in 1995, and you learned that there were fewer people in Tract #121 in 2000 than in 1990, then what? Did the people leave the tract, or did the tract leave the people?

What about groups we make up, such as an area code? To rely on area codes for trending demographics would be problematic, because that is not why the area codes were set up. When there are more than 9,999,999 phone numbers in an area code, the phone company cannot do much but redefine the area. Companies are always making up groups: groups of inventory, groups of employees, groups of customers, and so on. They may group inventory in different and sometimes conflicting ways. What happens when two departments each want to group the same Entities? Consider the following situation, as illustrated by a series of memos:

Memo to the Files
From Analyst Stallone

I had to twist some arms, but the VP of Sales and the VP of Marketing have agreed to standardize their regions as follows:
   All customers will be assigned to one of two regions, East or West. Mel will be responsible for sales in the East; Sal will be responsible for marketing in same. In the West, Jamie will sell, and Pat will market.
   To summarize, I offer this fine table:

	Sales	**Marketing**
East	Mel	Sal
West	Jamie	Pat

   Of course it's all table-driven, so if they want to add new regions or change assignments, they can. No problem. Incidentally, those signatures are not red ink—it's real blood. This time we're covered if these folks come blubbering to us later that they want some change.

Memo to Stallone
From Project Manager

I am pleased that you are pleased about your progress on the Regions issue. However, I would like to ask you the first of three questions I have for you. First, if the VP of Sales were to decide that Mel was too busy and then hired Tracy to take over a new region called Central, could you accommodate this change?

Memo to Project Manager
From Analyst Stallone

You could tell the VP of Sales to split the East region and assign half to the new person and leave half with Mel. So now you have three regions:

	Sales	Marketing
East	Mel	Sal
Central	Tracy	???
West	Jamie	Pat

But what does the Marketing VP do now? Maybe put Sal in both the East and Central slots in this way:

> East - Sal
> Central - Sal
> West - Pat

You can almost hear the gates of data hell groaning open.

Best case, Sal has to look at both the East and the Central reports. More likely it would redefine Sal's and Pat's jobs. As each department grows or changes, the VPs will have to refight the battle of how the country should be subdivided. Each VP will have to make compromises, either assigning persons to span divisions or share divisions or work in divisions that do not make sense for their organizations.

Memo to Stallone
From Project Manager

Now here's my second question: can the VP of Marketing decide that Ohio should be moved into the West region because Sal is overloaded?

Memo to Project Manager
From Analyst Stallone

What's with all the memos? Why don't you come over here and ask me? This is the whole point of making the regions uniform. The two VPs ought to get together and decide where Ohio goes and get on with it. From the outside, it might seem crazy that managers spend so much time on these schemes, but they have big impacts. When we created the Central region, what did that do to Mel's job? He had a harder time getting the same commissions because he had fewer customers. Changes to the Regions can be made only if both the VPs agree to the change. Mel, the East Region salesperson, would be pretty hot if suddenly sales in Ohio started showing up in the Sales Report for the West Region.

Each department must be free to define its regions and to assign its personnel based on the department's differing needs. A regionalization scheme must be based on some one purpose. Stallone is arguing as the Sales VP would, ignoring the Marketing VP's needs. Marketing and Sales need a data-divorce because the one grouping scheme has put them at cross purposes.

Memo to Stallone
From Project Manager

On the other hand, a common set of codes would make comparisons between Marketing and Sales possible.

	Marketing Expense	Sales $	% Return on Marketing
East	$1,450	$23,945	1651
West	$945	$15,440	1633
Total	$2,395	$39,385	1644

(cont)
A report like this one would be meaningless if the marketing investments were not made in the same areas in which the sales were generated. This solution seems to be a difficult trade-off. On the one hand, a common set of regions is unworkable because the VPs use the regions for their own purposes. On the other hand, if the regions are not common, comparisons between regions would be meaningless.

Now for my third question: what if you set up three different Region codes? 1) Sales Region and 2) Marketing Region as were described before. And 3) a Unified Reporting Region, used for reporting long-term trends and for matching marketing efforts to sales results. The values could be

- North–North of latitude 40 degrees N
- South–South of latitude 40 degrees N

Each customer could be classified in any of three ways. For instance, Acme Co. in Columbus, OH, would be classified as

- Sales Region: Central
- Marketing Region: East
- Reporting Region: North

What do you think? Will this approach work?

Memo to Project Manager
From Analyst Stallone

Now you are starting to tell me how to do my business, aren't you? No, I don't think this would work. Not that you couldn't do it. You can do anything with a computer. It won't work because the "unified reporting region" is an arbitrary assignment. No one is assigned responsibility, and the assignment is not based on anything real such as the media market or customers. So the assignment of customers to some arbitrary region is a waste of time.

(cont)
Since the grouping is meaningless, any summarization of data by that grouping is also meaningless.

You don't need any unified whatever. Give the Marketing Department one set of codes and give the Sales Department another set of codes. Let them do what they want to their own codes. Marketing assigns customers to their codes; Sales assigns customers to their codes. Same customers, so we have sales by customer. Then you can total sales for those customers within a particular marketing region to get the very report you suggest. Just like I said in the first place.

The moral of this story is get up out of your chair and go talk to each other. All this memoing is nonsense. Also, you will define many groups and gather data about each group. Every group must have some defining purpose such as rate setting or trend analysis or work assignment. If you have purposes that may be in conflict, then get different groups. Different groups of the same Entities can be reconciled one to the other so long as data is gathered for each individual Entity.

Here's what you should have learned from studying the concept of Entities:

- An Entity is an elemental and unique thing or record of an event.
- An Entity is the set of all Predicates that have the same identifier.
- An Entity must be able to be the subject or object of a sentence. That is, an Entity must be able to be described and uniquely identified.
- An Entity must not contain hidden Predicates.
- An Entity may be a group of other Entities.
- If an Entity is a group of other Entities, then some defining reason for that group must exist.

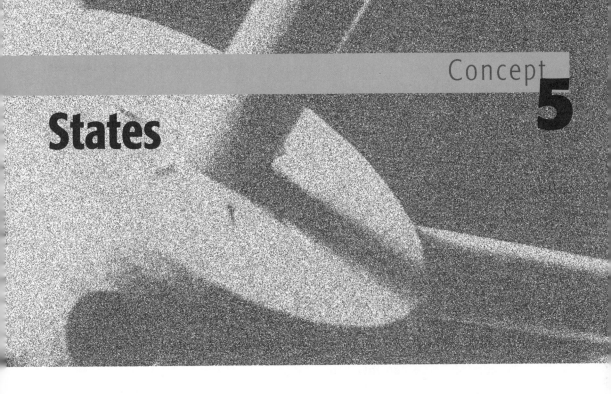

States

Why Should I Care About States?

A seriously injured teenage boy enters an emergency room in a very bad state. A moment ago, he was just one of the neighborhood boys; many of the nurses and doctors knew him because he had been in many times before with less serious wounds.

My editor has cautioned me to stick to technical writing: "I've read that story," he tells me. So our cities are burning, but I'm not supposed to write about it. Too bad, I'm stuck writing about writing about it. My last social commentary then is this: to the horror of absolutists, everything is a matter of perspective, at least insofar as Data Modeling is concerned.

The boy in the story was a customer of the hospital even before he was admitted this last time. He still is a customer, but now he is also a patient. He may also be an organ donor. The administrator is banding him while rifling his pockets in search of proof of insurance. The doctor on call is looking into vital signs. The transplant specialist is getting ready to speak to the parents. Each team member needs some of the same but also some different data: name of insurer, name of insured, pulse, respiration, age, condition of heart, and so forth. The data they are gathering may be different, but the customer, patient, and donor are all the same person.

Well, no duh. Patient number 787878 died of heart failure, and his heart was not suitable for transplant because it had a bullet-hole in it. Merely coincidence? Patient number 787878 had no insurance and did not receive a transplant. Again, a coincidence? Medical ethics aside, anybody whose capacities are not too seriously affected by over-exposure to software development practices can see that there is only one Entity on the gurney—patient 787878.

Believe it or not, this issue is tremendously contentious in the world of software development. The hospital administrators approach the computer people and say, "We need a system to keep track of patients because we are losing money." The doctors approach the computer people and say, "We need a system to track transplant recipients and match them with donors because we are losing patients." Then the computer people build a system for the administrators because it costs money to write software, and the administrators control the money.

Some time later, maybe the same computer people get the go-ahead to develop the transplant tracking system. Now the last thing they want to do is fool with the accounting system. They would have to look at unfamiliar files and programs. They would have to acquaint themselves with some of the issues of the previous project. They would have to meet with other people. So they would rather not ask, "Gee, is the patient record in the accounting system related in some distant way to the dead guy?" They would rather just start fresh.

Consequently, the hospital finds itself with two, three, or even more places to look to get the complete picture of the patient. Sooner or later, the hospital wants to carry data over from customers to patients, from patients to customers, and from either to donors. Discrepancies begin to appear. A patient turns out to be O positive in the donor file but B negative in the customer records. The software development process and the poor results are a natural outcome of the workplace. Sometimes, things just don't evolve into optimal states. I hope that after reading this chapter, you can make the choice to disintegrate your patients with full knowledge of the consequences.

What is unconscionable is for software developers to excuse silly databases by suggesting that the customer, patient, and donor are somehow different Entities. Reading this scenario, you cannot escape the intuitive sense that the accountant, the doctor, and the specialist are all looking at the same cadaver. But you do not have to rely on intuition alone. When you consider a Predicate of that cadaver, such as <u>description of the wound</u>, you see that both the doctor and the specialist are looking at the very same bit of data. If you suggest that somehow they are not, that somehow the

Predicate <u>description of the wound</u> is functionally dependent on more than one thing, you are proposing to disintegrate the data. Since <u>description of the wound</u> is just one Predicate, it follows that I have just one Entity. (It also follows that if they are the same thing, then they are also the same type of thing.)

Properly identifying what Entity a Predicate describes is central to Data Modeling. Recognizing a State transition and avoiding the trap of seeing more than one Entity when there is in fact only one is crucial to integration of data.

States and Computer Systems

Although an Entity may have many States, it is still just one Entity. Consequently, everything that has been said about Entities and computer systems applies to States. The general rule for Entities is that for all Predicates with the same argument, you will have just one record layout. As always, the data model is an idealized view of the things with which the business concerns itself. The database is an implementation of that ideal given all other constraints.

That system owners need one table that unites States of an Entity does not mean that they have to see everything at once or even be aware that the States unite in a single table. The presentation of the data should speak the language of the person using the computer. Returning to the example of the hospital, the Accounts Receivable Department will see all customers. The Transplant Specialist will see donors, only those patients for whom additional data and consents have been gathered.

The Entity must have all the required data (evaluated Predicates) for the State, but every Predicate does not need to be evaluated at all times. Predicates that may be required for a State the Entity has not yet reached will not yet be evaluated; that is, they may be left blank.

Tip for System Analysts

Because some data may be required for one State that is not required for another, you will find that an Entity may have many Predicates that are left blank. Analysts gag when they see how many blanks can be in the database when systems are designed to have one record for an Entity regardless of what State it is in. Often, some records are mostly blank during their entire useful life. Database designers have many options, including simply living with the blanks. Database design is a separate skill that takes into consideration a number of parameters before determining how the data model is to be transformed into a database. The total number of records, the percentage of records in each State, the length of time a record stays in a State, the cost of disk storage, the cost of programming resources, and the project timetable are all relevant to the decision of whether all States should be contained in a single table. But the point of Data Modeling is to put these issues out of mind for now.

We may also learn from the owners that there is a defined path from State to State or that some Entities cannot be in some States at the same time.

These other characteristics of States, such as validation requirements that vary between States, rules about which States might be mutually exclusive, and rules about the path that an Entity may take between States, are beyond the scope of what has traditionally been called a database. For instance, databases with which I am familiar do not have the ability to support more than one correct State for a single record. A record either requires that a field be evaluated or not, irrespective of any State. Regardless of whether your database can accommodate these requirements or whether you have to write code outside the database, you will want to encapsulate these requirements for each State and make these modules work for all accesses to the data.

To the extent that the database can be built to mirror a single, complete Entity, that system will have a higher degree of integrity, perform better, require less storage, and cost less to construct. Some circumstances may require compromises; however, the database designer needs to justify deviations from the one-type-of-Entity-becomes-one-table rule.

State Analysis Can Lead to Business Process Improvement

One of the best examples of an Entity that has many States is a purchase. There are a zillion variations of this process, but for the sake of example, assume the following scenario. A company sends out a purchase order, a PO, to a vendor. The PO specifies the items to be purchased and may specify a delivery date, price, and payment terms, among other things. The vendor responds with an acknowledgment confirming the same. The receiving dock vouches the receipt of the items in good condition. The vendor mails an invoice. The accounts payable department verifies that the invoice is accurate per the PO and the receipt vouchers. If all is in order, they pay it.

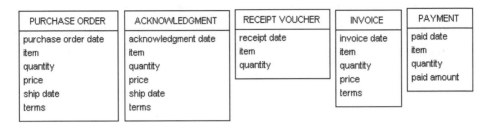

Figure   5-1

One might see the purchase process as being made up of a series of discrete Entities (see Figure 5-1):

- Purchase Order
- Acknowledgment
- Receipt Voucher
- Invoice
- Payment

Alternatively, one could see the process as a single Entity—call it a negotiation—that progresses through States from PO to check acknowledgment (see Figure 5-2).

Figure   5-2

The way we understand a process or the Entities that are involved can profoundly affect our ability to improve that process. Case in point: many companies, including Ford and Mazda, are not accepting invoices from many of their vendors; they see them as redundant. Eliminating invoices is saving millions of dollars. What do you think? Are invoices unnecessary, or are invoices an essential control? The following analysis may clarify the Predicates used at each step of the purchasing process.

Predicate	Purchase Order	Acknowledgment	Receipt Voucher	Invoice	Payment
PO Date	Create	Read	Read	Read	Read
Acknowledge Date		Create			
Received Date			Create	Read	Read
Pay Date					Create
Item	Create	Read	Read	Read	
Quantity	Create	Update	Read	Read	Read
Price	Create	Update		Read	Read
Ship Date	Create	Update	Read		
Terms	Create	Update		Read	Read

The table intersections, the cells, show whether the process creates, reads, or updates the Predicates. You can easily see that the invoice adds no new information to the process. The transition from a receipt voucher to invoice does not change what the buyer and seller had agreed to when they signed the PO—it can't. In fact, the whole point of matching PO, receiver, and invoice is to be sure that the invoice is unchanged! The matching process does nothing other than prove that the vendor's invoice program works correctly.

This business process improvement, elimination of the invoice, is not the result of computerization; in fact, most off-the-shelf Accounts Payable applications merely recreate the manual process of matching receipts, purchase orders, and invoices. When analysts see the process as a series of distinct documents, they make the mistake of simply automating a worthless procedure. When you call an invoice an Entity, you mistake an artificial contrivance for something real. The negotiation is real: it happens, and no matter what you call it, any information system will have to deal with it. The invoice is the way some long-dead analyst decided to deal with a negotiation before anyone had computers and modern management. When you make an invoice an Entity, you have built part of the way the dead analyst did things into the model of what you do today, thus limiting your options in the future. To see opportunities such as the total elimination of long-standing practices, new approaches to analysis such as those suggested here are required.

You also need either visionary or desperate management. Now is my chance to tell you that the easy part of the job is the Data Modeling. The hard part is getting the executives to buy into new practices.

Would your company benefit from the elimination of invoices? Probably it would. You can find any number of Entities with various States. You are very lucky if you find a way to eliminate one of them. Properly identifying these life-cycles is one of the two or three most powerful contributions of the Data Modeling discipline.

What Is a State?

Consider a car rental agency in which cars are purchased for rental and then later sold. An analyst is to set up a database of cars; for our purposes, assume that he or she is told that the scope of the project does not allow investigation of any other Entities. (You may want to make notes as you read these requirements.) The analyst interviews the car buyers and learns that what they need to know includes how much they are paying for a car, when it is scheduled to arrive, and whether the car has electric windows. The analyst interviews the rental managers and discovers that, among other things, these folks want to know how much the home office is going to charge each day for them to hold a car, when the car is scheduled to arrive on their individual lots, the date the car is due back on a lot, and the most recent odometer reading. The analyst finally interviews the used-car salespersons. Naturally, the salespersons have to talk to their managers before they can tell the analyst anything. Eventually, the analyst learns that their requirements include the asking price, whether the car has manual windows, the original price paid for the car, and the number of miles driven. Immediately the analyst decides there must be three Entities because there are different Predicates.

The resulting system is a mess. Cars show up at rental branches unannounced. Cars show up on sales lots, and the salespeople have to re-enter basic data such as odometer reading. The car buyers won't give the salespeople the original purchase price, so to calculate profit, the accountants have to take data from used cars and match it to data on car purchases. The owner/sponsor of the project has a new job washing cars. Due to the tight labor market, the analyst changes jobs at a higher salary.

You ask me to summarize the first analyst's work, which I do as follows:

Buyer's Predicates for cars are

- purchase price
- promised-by date
- electric option

Rental's Predicates for rental units are

- intracompany holding charge
- odometer at last reading
- anticipated date back on lot

Seller's Predicates for used vehicles are

- asking price
- manual windows
- price paid to manufacturer
- mileage

In reviewing my work, you find one error. What is it? (Due to our limited scope, assume for a minute that all the Predicates describe the car; for instance, forgive that date car is due back in is probably a Predicate of the rental agreement, not the car.)

The rental manager listed four Predicates. I combined the dates into a single field, perhaps planning to use the field for the date the car is to arrive from the manufacturer to hold the date the renter is to return the car since I can't rent a car that I have not received. Many analysts want to reuse fields in this way, but this approach causes so many problems. Recycle glass, aluminum, paper; but please, do not reuse Predicates. If you store the value for the date a car is to be returned to a rental lot in the same Predicate as the date the car was to have been delivered to that lot, then you have lost data. The Car Buying Department would be robbed of the opportunity to compare actual delivery dates and planned dates.

My analysis parallels that of the earlier project for the hospital. There is a missed opportunity, the same missed opportunity that led to the first bad system. If you don't already see what needs to be done, then take a minute to ask yourself, "Which of these Predicates are redundant?"

Asking whether a car has manual windows or whether it has the electric option is really the same question, and so one of these Predicates is redundant. That is, if I told you the car had the electric option, you would know (ipso facto) the car does not have manual windows. This data about the windows is captured by the buyer but needs to be available months later for the Used Car Department—even though electric windows are not of interest to the Rental Department, which holds the car between the time it is bought and sold. In the same way, you can safely assume that the purchase price entered by the buyer is the same data that is needed by the seller. Irrespective of security concerns or just bad blood between the two departments, the data model must reflect this fact about the nature of the data. Further, the promised-by date captured by the buyer is what the Rental Department needs to know to determine when a car is going to be available to rent. If the Rental Department does not take advantage of this data when the buyer enters it, then they probably will not get the data in a timely fashion. Finally, the Predicate mileage when car was last checked-in from a rental is probably close enough to the Predicate mileage that the used car salespeople need. A careful analyst, of course, would double-check.

Each department has its own perspective on cars and wants some different and some of the same data. Each department needs many Predicates. Some of the Predicates were needed by more than one department. Why don't you send me back to create a spreadsheet and eliminate the redundant Predicates you found in my first attempt?

Here's the spreadsheet you requested, but again I made a mistake. Can you find it?

Predicate	Buyer's Perspective	Rental's Perspective	Seller's Perspective
Purchase price	Required		Required
Promised-by date	Required	Required	
Electric option (y/n)	Required		
Intracompany holding charge		Required	
Car due-back-in date		Required	
Odometer at last reading		Required	Required
Asking price			Required
Window type (manual/electric)			Required

"Window type" is essentially the same thing as "Electric Option," irrespective of the different presentations chosen for the basic Domain of "true/false" involved in this case. The information system needs a consistent interpretation of the data, and so the name of the Predicate (the meaning) has to be unified. The corrected table is shown below:

Predicate	Buyer's Perspective	Rental's Perspective	Seller's Perspective
Purchase price	Required		Required
Promised-by date	Required	Required	
Intracompany holding charge		Required	
Car due-back-in date		Required	
Odometer at last reading		Required	Required
Asking price			Required
Window type (manual/electric)	Required		Required

Tip for System Analysts

It doesn't matter whether you choose to say "Window type" or "Electric Option"; irrespective of which you choose, those who design the user interface can put anything they wish in front of the owners.

Why I remain so optimistic about system construction is a real mystery. The interface designers won't do anything but use their screen generator, feed the owners some line about how they cannot change the defaults, and the owners will just live with it as usual.

Data that is relevant in one State is also relevant in another State. If the data carried over from one State to the next is not relevant, then either you are dealing with different Entities altogether or you are dealing with altogether different Predicates. In this case, the data is the same, proving that it is the same Entity being moved through States. For example, it is no coincidence that the odometer at check-in describes the same vehicle when it is being rented as it does when it is being sold.

Two Predicates that have the same meaning and that describe the same thing will have the same value and are in fact the same Predicate. If I have only one Predicate, I cannot have more than one Entity. The fact that the Entity has States does not change this fundamental rule. Let's say you and I are bickering about the mileage on a car. You might say, "This is dopey; let's go out and look at the odometer." The key to resolving our bickering is the actual car; my perspective and your perspective will then come together. I say, "Oh, THAT car. I thought you were talking about this car." Same car, same reading—different car, different reading; what does all this tell us? Odometer reading is a single Predicate of a single car; we use a Name such as "vehicle identification number" (VIN) to stand in for the actual car because I cannot park a Buick in a floppy drive. As a convenience, as a matter of practicality, we say that the argument is the VIN and the resolution is the odometer reading. Given a VIN, I can tell you what the odometer reading is.

Tip for System Analysts

Do not confuse this concept either with the Union or with union sets. The Entity with States is more similar to a join; unions come into play in the concept of Superclasses.

States Integrate Perspectives

In the example spreadsheets above, I have chosen to title the columns perspectives in order to emphasize the role that the system owners play in the formation of these States. Imagine that the project progresses in phases; the owners pay for the development of a buying system, then an audit system, and then a renting system. How would this change the previous analysis? At the end of the first project for the buying system, we might not even recognize that multiple States were possible. The original notes, repeated below, would be adequate.

Buyer's Predicates for cars are

- purchase price
- promised-by date
- electric option

The buyer gave us the set of Predicates needed to support the buyer's needs. We develop systems based on our scope and what the system owners can offer us. We cannot build the whole of the car table without the perspectives of the rental and sales departments. These Predicates represent the perspective of a single department, which was the scope of the project, and which then is a correct data model.

The second project is to satisfy the needs of the Used Car Department. Remember that they required the following Predicates:

- asking price
- manual windows

- price paid to manufacturer
- mileage

With the second project, we recognize for the first time that a car has States. As before, we create a table to document additional perspectives without replicating Predicates. Note the resolution of the different ways of expressing the Predicate <u>electric option</u>.

Predicate	Buyer's Perspective	Seller's Perspective
Purchase price	Required	Required
Promised-by date	Required	
Electric option (y/n)	Required	Required
Odometer at last reading		Required
Asking price		Required

What I hope you see from this illustration is the way the user requirements cannot conflict with each other and that the resolution is always synergistic. Of course, disagreement about the meaning of a column can arise. When this happens, one of two resolutions are possible; either is a win-win for the system owners. They can come to an understanding that they are really talking about the same thing, as in the case of the electric windows. The resolution then is to share the data and hence create a more integrated and thus smarter system. Or they can come to understand that they are talking about different things. Notice that the <u>purchase price</u> is not confused with the <u>asking price</u>. In this case, the Predicates are kept distinct; a clearer understanding of both Predicates is gained, and each owner can operate in a way that does not interfere with the other. This solution assumes that the analysts don't disintegrate when they should have integrated and vice versa. Either way that conflicts are resolved—by agreeing to integrate data or by agreeing to keep separate data—the owners win.

Whereas an Entity is the set of all Predicates irrespective of who might want them, the State is a subset of the Predicates required to accomplish some process or processes. At this point in our sample analysis, the Entity is comprised of all five Predicates that begin each row of the table. That the Entity is the aggregation of all Predicates is the essence of integration. When someone says that Data Modeling somehow separates the data from the processing, this is the meaning. Aggregating all Predicates that have a common argument, that describe the same thing, is a rote task. The set of all Predicates that comprise an Entity is a consequence of the analyst's specification of the Predicate's arguments; no business knowledge is added to the data model when the Predicates are drawn together into the Entity. On the other hand, the State is a subset based on the knowledge provided by the system owners. The Predicates included in any perspective are those deemed relevant by the owners; relevance is determined only by owners. The composition of a set of Predicates, a State, is new information about the business.

You might be familiar with Buddha's parable of the blind men who each feel different parts of an elephant in the hope of describing the entire elephant. The conclusion of the parable is painful because it is too true to life. The blind men end up in a fight because each felt only a part of the elephant. When different perspectives are sought, the natural outcome is frustration that the owners don't use terms consistently, that we can't get them to agree to a single definition, that they feel like they own the data.... The truth is that all the perspectives are valid, and a properly defined system allowing for multiple perspectives gives the owners the 3-D view they need.

What might you conclude if another perspective were added that had the same data requirements as an existing perspective? The third project is to prepare reports for the auditors. After speaking with them, you determine to extend the table as follows:

Predicate	Buyer's Perspective	Seller's Perspective	Auditor's Perspective
Purchase price	Required	Required	Required
Promised-by date	Required		Required
Electric option (y/n)	Required	Required	Required
Odometer at last reading		Required	
Asking price		Required	

The buyer's and the auditor's perspectives are probably the same. By definition, and only by definition, States have a unique set of data requirements. States may be called different things by different departments, but until those departments have different requirements for the Predicates there is no need to identify a new State.

Processes require a certain and unique set of Predicates, and the composition of a State is business knowledge. We can respect the need of departments for States while maintaining the system integration that the corporation demands. Integration results from recognizing when differing perspectives want the same questions answered, the same Predicates. Independence of operation results from recognizing when different departments have different intentions for some Predicates.

How States Relate to Each Other

I have talked about sets of Predicates. What would you call a set of States? When we have identified an Entity but have not recognized any more than a single State, then we are disinclined to speak of the State of that Entity at all. For example, when we discovered the Predicates required just to order a car, forgetting the subsequent rental and sale of that car, then we did not speak in terms of the ordered car State. Once alternatives were discovered—for instance, a car that had been received and made available to rent—then we recognized the two alternate States of ordered and rental.

As further evidence of the existence of sets of States, owners will tell you that there are rules about State transition. For instance, a vehicle cannot become a used car unless it was first a rental car. It is common to create State transition diagrams showing what transformations are allowed. A State transition diagram for the car rental case would look like Figure 5-3.

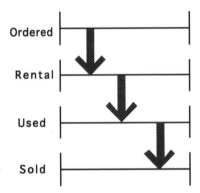

Figure 5-3

A diagram like this one is easily understood by the owners of the information system and proves that in their mind the States (ordered, rental, used, and sold) are related by the fact that a sensible map of possible transitions can be described.

Tip for System Analysts

These diagrams are often referred to as life-cycles or Entity life-cycle analysis. This is a good way to start thinking about State transition in that it is a metaphor to which we can all relate. True, all data within the information system comes from somewhere and has some ultimate State in which it becomes irrelevant. The difficulty comes when you consider that many State transitions are not linear, that things go back to earlier States, skip States, and sometimes even exist in multiple States. Some Entities seem to be completely lawless: hopping between any two States is allowed. If you cling too dearly to the metaphor of the life-cycle, the unpredictable nature of some Entities will be upsetting.

The rules governing the transition from State to State do not change the Predicates or how the Predicates are used within a State. For this reason, I consider the State transition rules to be outside the data model and will leave this long story alone.

Multiple Statehood

Keep in mind that States are more than merely Predicates; if all that is needed is a simple Predicate, such as "Licensed yes or no," then the following discussion does not apply. States change data requirements so that a "licensed" vehicle is one for which the license number, governing body, and expiration date are all required. It would not be reasonable to require this license information of an unlicensed vehicle.

Cars have other States besides rented or sold and licensed or unlicensed. They can be operable, under repair, or totaled; they can be owned, owned by the bank, or leased. A licensed vehicle is opposed by an unlicensed vehicle; that is, a car cannot be both licensed and unlicensed. However, whether something is licensed or not has nothing to do with whether it is mechanically operable. So while sets of States represent mutually exclusive alternatives, an entity may nonetheless be in more than one State when those States do not conflict.

For example, it is sensible to speak of a car that is at the same time part of the rental fleet, being owned, licensed, and operable. In this case, we are dealing with an Entity that at any one time can be placed on many State transition diagrams. The general assumption is that Entities are in at least one State of each set and that the States in each set do not interact. Imagine one of those cylindrical combination locks that has one tumbler for each set of States. Each tumbler is marked with the all the names of the States in that set. By spinning the individual tumblers, you can create any combination of States while maintaining the mutual exclusivity between the States of each set. To test your understanding consider this: In our example we have four sets. Set one describes the life of a vehicle from ordered through sold, four distinct States. A second set describes the licensing process in two States. A third set describes maintenance in three States. The fourth set describes the ways a car could be financed in three

States. So 4 x 2 x 3 x 3 = 72 possible combinations. Good thing we have a computer.

When more than one set of States is at work for an Entity, then I like to visualize it as existing on multiple planes. So rather than placing the Entity on a line, you can place it on two or more dimensions. Walk through the example as I add dimensions (States) to the car Entity. Note that the following set of tables is to help you visualize the concept; the tables are not suggested project deliverables.

Start by placing car #54 on the following axis:

State
Ordered
Rental   Car #54
Used
Sold

The table shows that Car #54 is a rental. You can take it to a second dimension by including the transition from unowned, owned, owned by bank, or leased, as follows:

State	Unowned	Owned	Owned by Bank	Leased
Ordered				
Rental			Car #54	
Used				
Sold				

The table shows that car #54 is a rental owned by the bank. You can add a third dimension, placing car #54 in the State axis of licensed or unlicensed (see Figure 5-4). (You have to use your imagination a bit since I cannot put three dimensions on a two-dimensional page.)

Figure 5-4 shows that car #54 is a rental, owned by the bank, and currently licensed. What's to keep me from adding a fourth, fifth, or any number of dimensions? For one, I imagine that your patience is growing thin. For another, I could no more draw a four-dimensional picture than I could walk onto the set of *Singing in the Rain* and dance a number with Gene Kelly. But I can imagine that I can imagine these higher dimensions, and

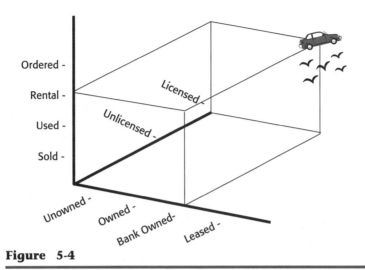

Figure   5-4

that is all I need to relax and realize that Entities with even large numbers of States do not have to be difficult to understand.

Don't like the visualization? Follow this dialogue between a film editor and a director:

Director: I saw the boom mike in one of the clips I reviewed yesterday.

Editor: I can't believe it. Where?

Director: It was in the foreground. (one dimension)

Editor: Work with me, baby. That isn't much help.

Director: It was stage right. (two dimensions)

Editor: It was a boom mike, so it was at the top of the frame (three dimensions), but we got about ten million stills here. Help me out a bit.

Director: It was about two minutes into Gene's number in the downpour. (four dimensions)

Editor: Good, good. WE DID THIRTY-FIVE TAKES OF THAT NUMBER!

Director: Relax. I only saw take five. (five dimensions)

Editor: I'll be Bonzo the monkey. There it is: top, right, foreground, two minutes in, on take five.

Director: Who's that dancing? Wait a minute. Is this studio 34?

Editor: No, this is 43!

Director: Sorry, wrong movie!

Whew, five dimensions! I was imagining a rim shot each time I tossed another one into the phrase. Placing an Entity into multiple perspectives is analogous to the director finding the right part of a film or finding a shaggy dog in New York City.

Tip for Project Managers

I suppose it would be natural for someone reading this to decide, "To hell with this. There has to be a simpler way!" This *is* the simpler way; in fact, the more States you identify and the more transitions you document, the easier the whole mess is to understand. It is precisely when the Predicates seem to whirl around in chaotic activity that things get really complex— so complex that the analysts usually shove it off on the designers who shove it off on the programmers who end up getting blamed for everything. Remember, chaos is the way things look before you discern the pattern. When you discern the pattern, the underlying chaos is unchanged; it just seems manageable.

Tip for System Analysts

Almost all Entities could be said to exist in a State of being either valid or invalid. You can consider this to be another dimension of your State transition analysis. It is not part of the conceptual or logical model but can simplify the database design tremendously. You avoid setting up separate "suspense files" that have necessarily all the same Predicates as the intended file with the valid data.

The Relation of States to Hidden Modifiers

You may find that this entire discussion is very similar to the previous discussion of hidden modifiers. (I spent a long time thinking about it, anyway.) Before, I said that a salesperson was a person who was employed selling and that a manager was a person who was employed managing salespersons. The confusion enters if we see a salesperson and a manager as States of an employee. It would appear that if you eliminate the hidden modifier type of employment, you would also eliminate the States. I agree that the two issues seem to occur together like opportunistic infections. However, there are fundamental differences. The hidden modifier is a Predicate that has buried itself within a noun so as to confuse the real nature of the Entity. The State is a Name given to a set of Predicates. When you eliminated the hidden modifier and stripped salespeople and managers down to just people without reference to any process as you should, you were unpacking a word into its simpler parts. Nonetheless, once you consider some processes, you might discover that there were distinct States of persons such that the terms Salesperson and Managers come back into the data model. A short example follows; the Entity in question is person.

Predicate	Human Resources Perspective	Sales Department Perspective
Quota		Required
Commission amount	Required	Required
Manages who	Required	
Sales region		Required
Charitable contribution	Required	

The Human Resources Department probably speaks of Managers and Salespeople, sometimes referring to the State and sometimes simply burying a modifier. This is why analysts get paid well—because the owners are so accustomed to very sophisticated uses of language that they make it difficult to simplify things for the dense computer.

Relevance of the Data From State to State

As always with Data Modeling, the key is relevance. The following example is intended as a counter-point to the previous examples. Imagine this same rental company. They now want to be able to keep track of their offices, of which they have two types: rental and used cars. An exuberant modeler, having read almost as much of an excellent text on the subject as you are about to, completes the following table:

Predicate	Rental Perspective	Used Car Perspective
Office hours		Required
Monthly Gross Revenue	Required	Required
Location	Required	Required
After hours drop off (yes/no)	Required	
Notary		Required

The analyst's conclusion is that there is a single Entity, office, with two States, used car or rental. Why is this wrong?

This is an example of two Entities whose Predicates are the same but whose data loses its relevance if you try to transform one into the other. *But*, you protest, *the two offices have the same office number.* You can easily fall into this trap. The office number is a made-up number; another analyst could easily have decided that rental offices are different from sales offices and given them different office numbers without affecting any other result. If you say that the value of the Predicates is determined by the key, but you make up the key, then you have let go of any principles that would otherwise guide your analysis. You are saying that you could do anything you want since you made up the key. The office number itself is a mere stand-in for characteristics that truly identify the office. You cannot turn around then and say that the values of the Predicates are dependent on the office number; that would be circular logic. Whenever you have a Name such as office number, you cannot rely on that argument.

Okay, what if we walked into a rental office #0101 in May and told everybody that starting tomorrow they no longer were to rent cars but rather to sell them? Even though these are the same people, at the same location, with the same cars, I assure you that rental office #0101 and sales office #0101 are not the same Entity. The problem is that the data from the Rental office is no longer relevant to the Sales office. You have defined it to be merely coincidental. Consider what happens to the Monthly Gross Revenue. Would the following report be useful?

Office #0101

Month	Monthly Gross Revenue
March	$100,000
April	$100,000
May	$150,000
June	$150,000

Did that office really increase in revenue, or did that location increase in revenue? Clearly, the gross revenue for that location has increased; whether the office has more revenue is not so clear. To say that the office, now a used car office, has more revenue than the old rental office is to compare apples to oranges. Wouldn't you expect that an office that sold cars for thousands of dollars would have a higher gross revenue than an office that rented those same cars for hundreds of dollars a week? It would be more informative to compare the new used car office to similar used car offices rather than any rental office.

Consider area code 222 defined to cover a region such that in 1980 it had 10,000,000 residents. In 1985, the area code is split into 222 and 333. Would the following news report make sense, "In the last ten years, area code 222 has lost almost half of its population"? Is it inaccurate? Area code 222 is the same only in name in the same way the office is still office 0101. It is more accurate to say that the region that was 222 has been redefined, and that statistics on old region 222 will no longer be gathered. It is more sensible to say that old rental office 0101 has been closed; a new sales office—unfortunately also called 0101—is now open for business.

State analysis is a very powerful concept that not only has a profound effect on the information systems we create to assist us with the processes we perform, but also may actually transform the processes themselves. Perhaps for this very reason, analysts can sometimes get State-happy. They see States in everything. True story: I know of one analyst who quit and moved to India to meditate. A different true story: imagine a sophomore guru speaking with a quavering, hushed voice that a caterpillar sheds its skin to become a butterfly. Okay, but what if the guru was really a systems analyst and the audience was made up of his peers and superiors? I was there; it was ugly. No one wanted to sit with him at dinner. Is it any coincidence that at about the time Codd worked on his seminal "Normalization" scheme, Nixon was in China and thousands of young people believed that they were star-dust in some non-trivial way? I don't think so. You have to use these concepts responsibly. State transition analysis will not change the world; but it can lead to some pretty heavy analysis, man.

"Becomes a" vs. "Is a Part of"

The critical thing to keep in mind is that one State has to share Predicates with at least one other State of the same Entity. The office example puts a fine point to the issue of relevance; what is apparently the same Predicate, gross revenue, means something different in the context of rental than sales. Another circumstance that causes confusion is the issue of components.

A simple way to think of States is to see them as something that "becomes" something else. The Purchase Order becomes a Receipt Voucher. The rental car becomes a used car. This next example deals with circumstances in which one thing becomes something else, and the data of the original thing is still relevant to the resulting thing, but, nonetheless, the State analysis as described above is not useful.

There is an entire class of examples that create this confusion; anytime one thing is made of other things, then the relationship between the parts can seem to be one of becoming. The crux of the problem is that the relationship is not one thing becoming one other thing; it is one thing becoming two or more things, or one thing becoming a part of another thing, or even one thing becoming a part of many things. The confusion can be eliminated if you take these examples out of the State context entirely and create another kind of Predicate, is part of.

Take, for example, a board that has been cut into two pieces. Much of the data about the original board is still relevant to the pieces, such as the source of the board and the type of wood. Now is a good time to stop trying to be super-modeler and look at the real circumstance with fresh eyes. Are there now two boards? True enough. Do each of the resulting boards have Predicates that can be evaluated independently of the original board? Yes, but they may have other Predicates that, not coincidentally, do have the same values.

My eyes tell me I have two existing Entities, the board pieces, and one historical Entity, the original piece. What I see is important; what the system owners direct me to keep data about is very important. What I have to do is to balance the rules of the real world and the principles of modeling with the directives from the owners.

Assume the owners tell me they want to know the following about all boards:

- Who sold the wood in the first place?
- What type of tree did the wood come from?
- What standard board was it (example: 2x4)?
- How long is the board?

If I know these facts (if I can evaluate these Predicates) for the original board, which of these facts do I also know about the board pieces? Everything except the board length. Therefore, I need to add just one more Predicate to answer all the questions from the owners—that is, I have to keep track of what long board the short boards came from. Call this new Predicate originating board. To help understand this concept, evaluate the Predicates for the circumstance given. Assuming that the original board is board A and the resulting pieces are boards B and C, then the following two tables satisfy the needs of the owners:

Board	Vendor	Tree	Dimensions	Length
A	Weyerhaeuser	Alder	2x4	8'

Board	Originating Board	Length
B	A	3'
C	A	4' 11.9"

These tables allow me to answer all the owners' questions. For instance, I can determine that Board B is Alder by referencing Board A.

Tip for System Analysts

Figure 5-5 shows a data model using a "becomes a" type Relationship.

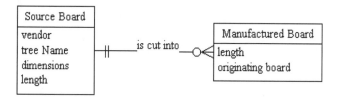

Figure   5-5

Under the given circumstances, it would be reasonable to expect that the type of tree and the manufacturer are not going to change except if some error had been made in the original entry of the data. Duplicating these Predicates to the MANUFACTURED BOARD Class would be a second normal form solution as effective as a third normal form solution. It is also possible that despite documents pledging away first-born children, the owners may someday want to plane a 2x4 down to a 2x2. Again, in this case it might be better to copy the Predicate to the MANUFACTURED BOARD Class to provide flexibility. Ultimately, the familiar involuted or recursive Relationship results.

I chose the example of a board being sawed in half as a simple way of introducing a number of real problems. What is a car made of except parts from vendors? The parts are still there; together they form new parts that may or may not have independent data. What is software made of but components copied into other programs? A bug in the component is a bug everywhere it has been copied, so the component still exists; the resulting software has its own existence as well. What happens to the hops when I make beer? In each of these cases, the analyst has to consider both the inherent facts, those things that owners cannot change, and the relevance that the owners see in those things.

These examples are more counter-points to the State analysis. The "is a part of" examples given here are not the same as the "becomes" relationship between two States. The practical divide between these examples is the fact that States become one other thing whereas parts can become components of more than one other thing. Perhaps if we thought of States as "becomes one of" another State, we could avoid this confusion.

Here's what you should have learned from studying about the concept of States:

- Entities integrate by pulling all the Predicates from many perspectives together and recognizing where those Predicates actually have the same meaning.
- States, on the other hand, keep the perspectives intact.
- The State itself has characteristics that may change either what owners call the Predicates or which Predicates are required.
- States may interact with each other to either disallow an Entity from existing in two or more States simultaneously or disallow certain State transitions.
- States may form independent sets, each set defining its own world of Predicates and rules but only interacting with other sets at the nexus of the Entity.

- State analysis is a way of making sense of complex data.
- State analysis can lead to business process improvement in demonstrable ways, even more so than other Data Modeling techniques.
- State analysis is very compatible with the aims of software developers in that the results of the analysis are easily transformed into database and software specifications that optimize development time and system performance.
- State analysis is distinct from "is part of" type Predicates.

Part THREE

Sets of Entities

We are concerned with three sets of Entities: Classes, Super-classes, and selections. I intentionally do not capitalize "selections" because I do not consider it a Data Modeling concept in that it is not data about data but involves values of data. All three sets are groups of things based on some criteria; the way the criteria differ is critical to your understanding of the sets and your ability to construct databases.

A Class is the set of all Entities having all the same Predicates and arguments regardless of what process needs the data. Compare this definition to that of an Entity, which is the complete set of Predicates for the same thing, regardless of what process needs the data. Over and over in this text we run into the distinction between a thing and the idea of a thing. That is the case again here: an Entity is a thing, or just one symbolic step away from the actual thing; a Class, on the other hand, is a further abstraction. In the sentence "Telly Savalas is a person," Telly is the Entity; PERSON-HOOD is the Class.

A State is a subset of the Predicates needed for some subset of all processes. In the sentence "Telly Savalas became an actor," actor is a State. But there is nothing stopping you from creating any subset of the Predicates of an Entity. If you ask me to write a check to Mr. Savalas, I don't need to know the details of his union membership. Any subset of the Predicates of an Entity is a projection.

A Superclass is the set of Entities having the same projection. The projection could be a State, but it could be any subset of Predicates. For instance, if we projected just those Predicates we needed in order to print checks, we could then group every Entity that had those Predicates. Regardless of where the projection comes from, the set of all Entities that have those Predicates is a kind of Class because it groups Entities. We call it a Superclass not because it has fewer Predicates than the Class but because its inclusion criteria consists of fewer Predicates and thus encompasses more Entities than the Class. When it comes time to pay for one of Mr. Savalas's films, the Accounting Department will write checks not only to actors but also to the companies that supplied the film. The Accounting Department is interested in the Entities included in the Superclass they may choose to call VENDOR. The short set of Predicates the Accounting Department cares about makes Mr. Savalas and Kodak indistinguishable.

Finally, you can create a set of all Entities based on the value of Predicates rather than on the existence of Predicates. These sets are called selections. When you ask somebody to give you an example of a set, they will say something like "All the blue things." I get the sense that a selection is the archetypal set, and for this reason, it confuses many analysts. It is of the utmost importance that analysts see the distinction between sets based on the existence of a Predicate, versus a set based on the value a Predicate might have assumed. Classes and Superclasses are the basis of database design; selections are used extensively in programming but never in the design of base tables. Since selections are based on data rather than on descriptions of data (meta-data), they are part of the software system itself rather than being a part of the data model. The term "selection" will appear in order to contrast with the other sets, Classes and Superclasses, but I will not discuss further in this text.

You do all the above setting and subsetting so naturally you might not even be aware you are doing it. You are such a set-master that you easily combine the above types of sets into even more complex criteria such that a set might be composed of all the Entities of a particular State that have a particular value. You might want all the "transactions posted to the ledger in March." A TRANSACTION is surely a Superclass including EXPENSE and ALLOCATION; those that are posted are in an advanced State having initially been unposted, and only those transactions that have a date of March are selected. As we said in the Introduction, you don't need to know how to build a stove to make soup; you do need to know how a stove works if someone is paying you to fix one. We still have more study ahead to understand how information works. Remember, the appliance guy makes good money, and so we will now return to the study of Data Modeling.   ■

Classes

Why Should I Study Classes?

As you study Classes, you may feel as though this course has come home, not only because we are finally getting to the discussion with which most other courses begin but also because it is very restrictive to have to think solely in terms of Entities, as we have up to this point. In our everyday speech, we use class words constantly. "I spilled my coffee. May I have another cup?" "My coffee" refers to an Entity. When I ask for "another cup," I am not asking for that of somebody else; I am speaking of a general Class. Generally when one discusses the data used in a procedure, one refers to that data in terms of the Classes to which it belongs. For example, a clerk may explain that "the red copy of the invoice goes to the shipping department." INVOICE is a Class. Imagine how impossible it would be for the clerk to make herself understood if she had to refer to each individual invoice Entity. You have been speaking in terms of Classes all along—you just haven't used this term. You should feel very at home with this concept.

Language had to develop a set of words that stood for a generalized set of things. Data Modeling borrows that idea; it is called a Class. In this section, you will come to understand this idea in detail and learn how to make it work for you. Don't try to make Classes a complicated topic. The underlying idea is Sesame Street simple. Basically, you need to be able to answer the question "Which of these things is not like the other?" This ability to generalize and distinguish is all you need to master Classes. As with every topic in this text, you are trying to understand something that you do intuitively; I am not trying to teach you a new skill but rather to appreciate the mastery you already possess.

Classes and Computer Systems

Classes are the most visible product of data analysis. Managers will use the number of Classes to estimate the cost of building information systems. Quality Assurance consultants will likely start with the Classes to check the validity of the model. The construction team's first request will be for the finalized list of Classes so that they can begin to build the database and generate prototypes.

The Classes that you use in carrying out your activities will become files in the computer system you develop. Classes translate into files during the prototyping phases of software development. In a perfect world, translation is one-to-one, that is one Class becomes one table. The basic principle is so straightforward that most CASE tools do it for you automatically.

A Class is the set of all Entities that have all the same Predicates. Once people have decided what the Predicates are, creating the set is a simple matter of matching up Entities—a stupid computer could do it. In this case, the task is even too inane to turn over to the computer. It is so trivial for we human analysts that we think in terms of Classes from the outset. We skip the step of generalizing in the same way we skip the steps of long division—for persons practiced at modeling, I do not think it even occurs to them what they are doing. Once analysts properly identify Predicates and classify Entities, then the computer can do the mindless work of repeatedly executing some action on all the members of a Class.

Classes do not translate into computer screens or reports or any other output! Watch for this mistake; you will see it from analysts who want to take existing output and call it a Class. You will also see this mistake committed by designers who complain bitterly that all these Classes are going to make system owners pass through several screens to do some simple task. The confusion here stems from the fact that screen painters will default to provide one screen per table. If you have the patience, then explain to them that there is no direct relationship between a Class and a screen or report. Any output device can show any part of one or many Classes.

Many analysts talk about the need to denormalize the database. Denormalizing is their way of saying, "If you guys are through cogitating on your navel, I'd now like to go build a database the way I always have." The only need being met here is to calm the nerves of old-line programmers by avoiding a relational model.

Denormalizing is justified in the case of exceptional performance or security requirements. Take, for example, a data warehouse: in the warehouse you have giant volumes of data, which implies a need to be very sensitive to access speeds. In the warehouse, the assumption is that the data is historical and will not change. When the data does not change, then the third normal form will not provide benefits. In any case, the denormalized design must be reviewed in light of all accesses to the data, not just the needs of the first programmer who wants access to the database. That is, if one set of programs requires very fast access and another involves a high volume of change, then you will have to weigh the one access against the other. Don't ignore the option to replicate data. You may use the "Create Read Update Delete" association matrix to be sure every access is being considered. Denormalize and replicate as necessary, but assume that the relational model is correct until a very compelling argument for denormalizing (debasing) the data model can be made.

Nowadays, the denormalizing argument is less often heard because our models and our databases are better, and more often we can translate the data model into the ideal database. The goal of the Data Modeling and the database manufacturers has always been that databases should be built to mirror the business information requirements. Practically speaking, this means a Class becomes a table. In the past, database administrators were comfortable because they could alter analysts' models. Today, a properly defined data model, when targeted to a feature-rich and very fast database, translates into a system that resembles the data model. To the frustration of modelers, some database administrators are standing up and saying that our modeling is too physical—that is, too similar to the database. They have a sense that the logical model isn't logical if it can be interpreted easily into tables. They want to go back to the days when data models had to be altered before workable databases could be generated.

You will be pummeled by designers and programmers screaming that they cannot work with this "overly-normalized" database.

Any change you make to the data model will affect more than just the individual who is complaining. If you denormalize (debase) the model to facilitate one person, you are almost certainly creating work for somebody else. That somebody else may be in the next room already working on that part of the model. More likely that person has not yet learned enough about the affected section to object. Quite possibly, the section affected by the change belongs to some future phase of development not yet specified or to the way the system is to integrate with some other department.

The normalized, relational data model is designed to optimize over the entire project scope; almost always, some individual programming problem would be better served by some other data structure. If you start to make exceptions, you will be visited by the ghosts of projects past, over-budget, and over-promised. Deviate from the normalized model very reluctantly.

What Is a Class?

Everyone classifies things all the time. Think of organizing the stack of papers on your desk. The idea is to file the paper into folders such that a folder can be treated as a whole for some purpose. Take, for example, those invoices that need to be paid. To get a basic handle on Classes, think of them as folders. But if you really want to understand Data Modeling, you have to play "Which of these things is not like the others?" Study these short lists and see if you can pick out the entry that doesn't quite fit.

PRODUCT
Shoes
Sweaters
Pants
Freight

Freight is very different from shoes and sweaters, even if all the items on the list do show up on invoices. Just for example, freight has no color or size. The rule is: items in the same Class can be described the same way.

BANK
1st Natl Bank
J&J Caterers
Banco Nationale
Banco Credito

You might want to have a Class such as COMPANY that would encompass this whole list. Banks, however, might need their own list; for instance, we can have multiple accounts with a bank. Banks could have their own Class, since they have different Predicates.

INDIVIDUAL
Olga Schmidt
Carl Husmann
Exxon Corporation
Abra Lyons-Warren

You should have chosen Exxon. Exxon could not be a passenger on a flight; Carl could. Members of the same Class can be treated the same way.

It is an amazing fact that children could make the same distinctions, selecting freight, the caterers, and Exxon as different. No single person in any group I have ever spoken with has argued this point. Nonetheless, getting those same people to agree on how they came to make the distinction is an impossibility. It is as simple as asking, "Why do we put some records in one file and others into other files?" Doggedly, over the course of this text, I will try to convince you of what has already been stated: we put all Entities that have the same Predicates into the same Class.

Groups of Similar Things

Sorting things is as natural as breathing. Children sit for hours and put all the smooth rocks in one pile and the rough ones in another. Likewise, we put all the drinking glasses in the cupboard and silverware in the drawer.

We organize filing cabinets by correspondence, policy bulletins, bills to be paid, and so forth. Piles, shelves, and files: all these groupings can be Classes. As we go about sorting things, we don't pay much attention to the criteria we use, much less the kinds of criteria we use.

There are two kinds of criteria: we may group things based on what we can know and what we do know. When we group things based on what we can know, the Predicates, then we are classifying in the strict sense called for by Data Modeling. For example, when I put all my financial records together, I am putting together things that have dates, amounts, and descriptions I can use, for instance, to calculate my taxes. Dates, amounts, descriptions are Predicates, that is, things I can know about these records. Next, I separate my records into my receipts and my disbursements. Whether the money came in or went out is a discrimination based on the value of the Predicate amount. Whether the record pertains to my current tax bill or next year depends on the value of a Predicate, date. I can set aside my receipts for the year 1998, that is, group things based on the value of these two Predicates. The first act, that of setting apart the financial records from the general debris of my desk, creates a Class, FINANCIAL TRANSACTION. Before I can select records, I have to have created the Class; I have to know what I can know of something before I try to ascertain anything. I always select from a Class; in this case I select from FINANCIAL TRANSACTION. First I classify; then I select.

Classes are groups of similar things, but similarity is defined in terms of the Predicates of an Entity, not the value a Predicate has taken on. For the purposes of Data Modeling, what makes one thing like another is not the color of the thing but the fact that it can have a color. The data model does not ask you to distinguish between rough and smooth but between things you care to feel and things you don't. If all that you are interested in is the way something feels, then you can put frogs, puppy dogs' tails, and rocks into a single Class because they have the same Predicate, feels like.

We put Entities into the same Class because they share the same Predicates. Remember, "If it smells like a duck, if it walks like a duck, and if it quacks like a duck, then it must be a duck." If I have a 1099 stating I was paid something, it is a financial transaction. I cannot pretend it is one of the thank-you notes I meant to write. The tangible piece of paper is evidence that a FINANCIAL TRANSACTION took place because the paper has the Predicates value paid, recipient, and date. I cannot have a Class called BALL, meaning the act of throwing a bowling ball down a lane, and then try to pretend that the ball I put in the gutter was not a BALL. Analysts will commit the error of taking two Entities that have the same Predicates and putting them into different Classes when they do not recognize that each are in different States. Remember, States are pieces of Entities. When defining your Class, ignore any States that the Entity exhibits. Don't cheat on your taxes, your game, or your modeling. Two Entities that have the same Predicates have to belong to the same Class.

The other side of the coin is the notion that if two things have different Predicates, then they must have different Classes. Remember, "A place for everything and everything in its place." I do not want to put people and businesses into the same Class, because people have first names and businesses do not. Businesses are chartered by some government and people are not. If you allow yourself to put dissimilar things into the same Class, eventually you have no organization at all. So let's exercise these ideas.

For example, say your company sold caskets. Is casket a likely Class? CASKET is a good candidate Class. (The term "candidate" is used to imply that the Class is under investigation.) Caskets are a central part of many processes: they are designed, invoiced, manufactured, and so forth. Caskets have Predicates, such as manufactured date and sold to. A good, strong candidate Class such as CASKET helps nail down a corner of the total data model and helps to focus further discussion. Although Classes are not always as tangible as a casket, Classes that are easily visualized by the project team are good places to start your investigation.

Now, to carry the example further, assume your company sells a wide variety of final resting homes (caskets). You have economy model #100. On the other hand, an all-metal luxury CASKET model #123 for $2,500 is the top of the line. Would model #123 be a good candidate Class?

The #123 should have been a dead giveaway that in this instance we are talking about an individual CASKET. Yes, there are a lot of caskets of model #123 but there are also a lot of other models of CASKET, too. Perhaps there is a model #124 and model #125. For instance, all these models have the Predicate material type. The Predicates of the models are different from the Predicates of the individual caskets, so they belong to different Classes. Think of a dialogue with the undertaker.

> **You:** What makes one casket model different from another?
> **Undertaker:** Some have locks. Some are painted. Some are wood. Some have gaskets....
> **You:** What can you tell me about Model #123?
> **Undertaker:** That baby is water-proof, tight as a drum. Comes in Titanium and Platinum; special orders don't upset us. I can fit you this week at 10% off.

When you ask the undertaker about a Class such as MODEL, he tends to give you definitional answers. If you ask about an instance of the Class, such as Model #123, then he can respond with specific descriptions of that individual thing. His different responses are cues that give us our intuition about Classes.

An Entity Is What It Is

Remember the duck. Two Entities that have all the same Predicates must belong to the same Class. This fact highlights an important difference between the file folders you typically set up to organize your taxes and the Classes you would set up to computerize them. For your taxes, you would likely have created a different set of file folders for each tax year. In Data Modeling terms, you would have created file folders by the value of the Predicate tax year. However, you should not have a separate Class for each tax year. Classes are distinguished by the existence of the Predicate itself, regardless of the value the Predicate may have taken on. All the expenditures share the Predicate tax year, which, therefore, cannot be used as a rationale for separating expenditures into different Classes.

In the above example, even though the value of the Predicate tax year would typically cause us to have different folders in a manual system, the data model would have a single Class. Although we need to develop a system of processing data that is intelligible to the way we humans organize data, simply replicating the way we organize data, especially tax data, would be a mistake. Consider another example that demonstrates the same idea from another perspective.

Allow me to role play. What if my project were to create a data model of the petty cash function?

Me:	Let's walk through some typical transactions.
Clerk:	On 1/1/97, I gave $2 to Jaime. On 1/1/97, I gave $3 to Bill. On 1/1/97, I gave $4 to Mark.

Some time later...

Me:	Okay, show me just one more.
Clerk:	On 12/2/99, Jaime gave me the $2 back.

I return to my desk to write the following:

Transaction of 1/1/97

Predicates:
date
amount disbursed
recipient

```
┌─────────────────────────────────────────────┐
│                                              │
│    Transaction of 12/2/99                    │
│                                              │
│                                              │
│    Predicates:                               │
│    date                                      │
│    amount received                           │
│    donor                                     │
│                                              │
│                                              │
└─────────────────────────────────────────────┘
```

I deduce that <u>donor</u> = <u>recipient</u>. Further, I realize that the difference between a disbursement and a receipt is simply the sign on the transaction. I write, "Note to the files: rename Predicates; use <u>amount</u>." I retire to the coffee machine. Upon returning to my desk, I make the big leap: "All these doggone transactions have the same Predicates! There's only one Class, TRANSACTION!"

This story is so compelling, I think that I will finish it later. For now, I hope I am making headway with my steady repetition that <u>Entities with all the same Predicates belong to the same Class.</u>

CLASS = TABLE

Do Classes Have Predicates?

A Class is a list of Entities. Entities with all the same Predicates belong to the same Class. You will almost certainly hear someone say that Classes have Predicates. I too say that Classes have Predicates when I am not speaking precisely. When I am careful about my words, I say a Class is a set of Entities that are described by a particular set of Predicates. What does the book you are holding smell like? Go on, get in there and smell it. Am I back in focus? Okay, let me ask you, "Does your book have an odor?" Then the Entity, this book, has a Predicate, <u>smells like</u>. Now, let me ask you, do books have an odor? Are you thinking something like *Some books more and some books less*? That is not my question. If you are thinking in terms of some books, then you are thinking of the odor that individual books may or may not have. I am asking does the abstraction BOOK have odor? You might want to answer that *Whatever you printed on is potentially going to have an odor; whether you could actually smell it, I don't know."* This response is what I would characterize as a definition of the set BOOK in terms of its Predicates. From your response, I learned that a book is something that <u>has printing</u>, <u>is made of something</u>, and <u>may have an odor</u>. You can evaluate the Predicate of an Entity; you can define a Class in terms of the Predicates any member of that set must have; but it is a fallacy to say that the Class has a Predicate, at least not in the sense that an Entity has a Predicate. I keep data about Entities, not Classes. By definition, anything I keep data about is an Entity. Entities have Predicates so that I can keep data. Classes use the Predicates of an Entity to include or exclude that Entity.

A Place for Everything

As an analyst, you must recognize and document a Class for any Entity that has a unique set of Predicates. This rule is a corollary of the rule stating that Entities with the same Predicates must belong to the same Class. Returning to my project to create a data model of the petty cash function, I pick up the story after I, playing the role of persnickety analyst, have spent a restless night worrying that I hadn't covered all the bases.

Me:	Show me just one more transaction.
Clerk:	Well, on 12/3/99, I received check #213 from Pat for $5.
Me (stunned):	Check #! You record that?!
Clerk:	Of course, check number is what is missing from our current application. Recording check number was the A-numero-uno raisin-eter of this new system.

I return to my desk to write the following:

Transaction of 12/3/99

Predicates:
date
amount
party
check #

I slip my flowchart template out of its protective sleeve and carefully highlight <u>check #</u>. This new document is filed accordingly, and the file drawer is slid shut. "Tonight," I think. "Tonight I rest easy."

That night I confide to my significant other, "I knew it was all too easy, all those transactions with the same Predicates. Now I know; they have cash transactions and check transactions. Tomorrow, I'm gonna go in there and create a new Class so that all the transactions can have their own place in the data model."

So one lousy Predicate is different. This one Predicate is just the beginning. Once I dig in, I am going to find lots of different Predicates. Besides, it is just an example. Imagine how many different Predicates exist among wire transfers, credit card transactions, and all the other kinds of money in the world. As we analyze any Class, it will become more differentiated, not less.

What Really Happens on a Project

In practice, you will recognize Classes without being fully cognizant of having identified Entities. You find out you are working for a car rental agency and immediately you think about a Class, CAR. You will find that you have an intuitive feel for Classes and Superclasses. Your intuition is probably good; you should go with it. Describing a Class and the Predicates that the Class uses to discriminate Entities is sufficient for analysis.

Despite the extensive discussion of Entities in this text, you will be not be entering the Entities into your CASE tool. Instead you will enter the Classes to which those Entities belong. The Classes are meta-data (data about data). The ones and zeros we use to represent Entities are simply data and are entered into the finished system. Keeping on file an example or two of the Entities you find during interviewing is a good idea. For instance, if you were to document a Class such as EMPLOYEE, then a copy of an employee record would be very helpful.

So how should you think about the Entities during analysis? If you find an Entity during an interview that has a unique set of Predicates, you cannot simply forget to include it in your analysis. You must create a Class for this new Entity. If, on the other hand, you find a Class in your data model that can have no Entities, then you should delete that Class. Ultimately, <u>Entities lead and Classes follow.</u>

Tip for Project Managers

Be ready to make mistakes and to correct them later when under closer scrutiny you discover that your data model has not considered all the different kinds of Entities. You have probably heard the facile phrase "analysis paralysis," meaning that everybody is so caught up in thinking about what they should do that they don't ever do it. An analyst might be showing a little paralysis if he or she is always hedging: "We are not completely sure that this is a comprehensive list of all the types yet. We haven't gotten complete agreement from everybody yet. We are still reviewing the existing system for anything we may have missed." Analysis paralysis is real, but project members can become prematurely analysis-weary. Here are a few telltale comments you might hear: "Oh, that transaction is just like the other transactions; I hear what you are saying, but I just can't bear the thought of changing that diagram again; I was sorta avoiding talking to her." A good manager will step in and encourage the weary and push the paralyzed.

Here's what you should have learned from studying about the concept of Classes:

- A Class is a set of Entities that is described by the same Predicates.
- An Entity having all the Predicates that a Class requires belongs to that Class.
- If two Entities have different Predicates, then each must have its own Class.
- Stages an Entity may exhibit are not considered when determining whether an Entity participates in a Class.
- A Class is said to have the Predicates that constitute the membership criteria for any Entity.
- A Class is not formed based on a selection of data.
- A Class is generally implemented as a table in the database.

Superclasses

Concept 7

Why Do I Need to Bother With Superclasses?

An organized person is someone who knows where things go and puts them there. A disorganized person is someone who sees that just about anything could go just about anywhere and gives up.

An Entity is recognized to be a company because it has the Predicates of COMPANY. An Entity can belong to only one Class. In Figure 7-1, you can note that any Entity belonging to the Class COMPANY, for example Exxon, also has the Predicates required to be a member of the Superclass EXTERNAL AGENT. In other words, Exxon is an EXTERNAL AGENT. Although not shown here, in other contexts, Exxon is a PROPERTY that can be bought and sold; Exxon is a LITIGANT; Exxon is an EMPLOYER. Entities such as Exxon can belong to any number of Superclasses such as PROPERTY, LITIGANT, and EMPLOYER.

131

Note that creating the new Superclass, EXTERNAL ENTITY, does not create any new data and has minimal impact on storage. The Superclass can be implemented with a SQL union statement.

The concept of the Superclass both satisfies the compulsively organized and saves the hopelessly divergent. The computer is like a magical cupboard: a single thing can be in more than one place at the same time.

Consider how allowing an Entity to be in more than one place at a time can be useful. Have you been confronted with situations in which a single thing could belong in more than one file? What if you kept your medical expenses so that you could see when you had met your deductible or exceeded your limits? What if you reported those same expenses along with other deductions on your income taxes? Would you put the expense receipt in a folder labeled MEDICAL EXPENSE or in a bigger folder labeled TAX DEDUCTION? What about putting the MEDICAL EXPENSE folder within the TAX DEDUCTION folder?

The computer can make the single Entity appear to be in any number of places at the same time. Even when circumstances are too complicated to allow simply placing one folder within another, the data model can show you how the pieces can be organized to suit everyone. You do not need to worry how the computer does this organization; as a data modeler, you need to know only that a single Entity can belong to any number of Superclasses.

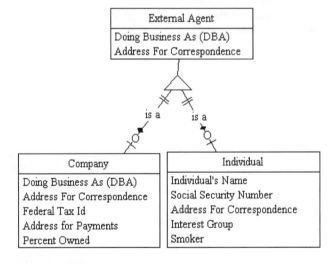

Figure   7-1

Superclasses and Computer Systems

Superclasses, like Classes, are a set of Entities. From outside the database looking in, Superclasses appear to be the same as a Class, whether you are accessing data via an application, or whether on the other extreme you are a programmer building a new application. A Superclass presents to the owners a set of Entities that all have the same Predicates.

Superclasses are implemented within the database very differently than Classes. The database sees the Superclass as a set of Classes, or what is called a union set. A union set is a set that includes all members of the constituent sets. If I union the set of apples and the set of oranges, I get a set of fruit. If I had four apples and five oranges, my union set has nine pieces of fruit.

Superclasses are extremely helpful, but they are optional. You cannot build an information system without Classes; Superclasses are used when a process calls for them. In fact, support for union sets varies by database manufacturer.

What Is a Superclass?

A Superclass is the set of Entities having the same projection. The projection could be a State, or it could be any subset of Predicates. This definition has a ring of erudition to it, ironic in that so many Superclasses are actually the result of ignorance of the business system being analyzed. Let's talk products.

Let's say you ran a little hardware store. You needed an inventory system, so you bought some package off the shelf and started entering data:

Part No.	Description	Qty-on-hand
1	24 inch Lawn Mower	4
2	18" Mini-mower	5
3	36 inch Lawn Mwr	3
4	Weed eater - electric, 2 amp	20
5	Weed eater - gas 1.5 hp	5
6	Weed whacker - 1 amp electric	2
7	Weed eater - gas 2.0 hp	10
8	1 gal Walnut wood stain	30

When you get comfortable with your inventory records, you start to get ideas such as "What size mower is best for my customers? Do I sell more electric weed eaters or more gas? Do people prefer the more powerful whacker? What is my most popular stain?" The data is "in there," but it is locked in this non-Predicate called description. Computers cannot effectively ferret it out. When you started your project, you were ignorant of all the detail you might later realize that you needed.

You decide to create a spreadsheet of your weed whackers to do a special study:

Part No.	Power Supply	HP Delivered	Description	Qty-on-hand
4	electric	1.0	2 amp	20
5	gas	1.5		5
6	electric	.5	1 amp	2
7	gas	2.0		10

The part numbers are the same because you have not recognized or created any new Entities; these are the same Entities from the inventory records. The useless description has been parsed into the relevant Predicates <u>power supply</u> and <u>horsepower</u>. AMPERES were converted to HORSEPOWER so that <u>horsepower</u> would draw values from a single Domain. The description field is left for notes that teeter on the brink of irrelevance. The quantity-on-hand values are associated with this more detailed Class so that there is only one master record of all data about a weed whacker. The old inventory record is a transcription of data rather than an original source.

In this scheme, the old inventory record is now the Superclass; the new weed whacker file is now the subclass or simply the Class. The original Class of inventory looked the way it did because we didn't have the benefit of the new requirements—the inventory Class was the result of our original ignorance of the owner's needs. Over time, as we learn more about our business, we add Predicates. As we add Predicates, we create new Classes, which has the effect of elevating the old view to the status of Superclass.

The idea of elevating a Superclass while moving the real interest down to the Class is not unlike modern management techniques of giving people really rotten jobs and sugar coating such jobs with fancy titles. Speaking of rotten jobs, we haven't checked in on the VP of Petty Cash recently. (Editor's note: The author assures me that this installment is absolutely the last of the case of the petty cash clerk.)

I was a bit nervous that Monday because I knew I had to face the VP of Petty Cash. I had to cool my heels while he made a short call. After a little while, he offered a demitasse and some small talk. I sipped the coffee. I had glanced at an abstract on interpersonal relationships while on a commuter flight. In short, it said, "Remember the small things." So I kept up my end of the "chit chat." But finally, it was time to speak plainly. While maintaining perfect eye contact, I breezily straddled a chair and let my large frame glide down in front of his desk. I banged my knees hard.

VP o' PC:	When we started this affair, you promised me that I would be driving the process.
Me:	That's how I operate.
VP o' PC:	So why when I look at your logical model do I see two (2) Classes?
Me:	CASH and CHECK. You admitted on 12/7/99 that checks had check numbers.
VP o' PC:	Maybe so, Joe, but now you are telling me I gotta look in two places to find all the items that affect my cash balance!
Me:	Easy, big fella. You have three (3) Classes, counting the Superclass. If you want to balance cash, the Superclass has every transaction, either CASH or CHECK. You don't even need to worry about the Classes. Just take a gander at Figure 7-2 and tell me I can't accommodate your every little desire.
VP o' PC:	I am so impressed.

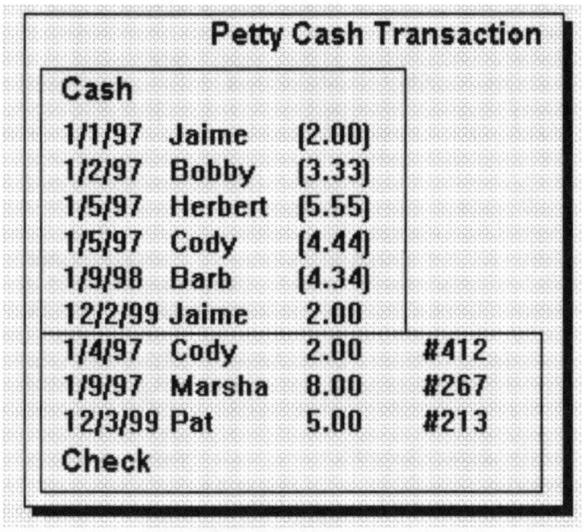

Petty Cash Transaction

Cash

Date	Name	Amount	
1/1/97	Jaime	(2.00)	
1/2/97	Bobby	(3.33)	
1/5/97	Herbert	(5.55)	
1/5/97	Cody	(4.44)	
1/9/98	Barb	(4.34)	
12/2/99	Jaime	2.00	
1/4/97	Cody	2.00	#412
1/9/97	Marsha	8.00	#267
12/3/99	Pat	5.00	#213

Check

Figure 7-2

The identification of Classes is a very intuitive and natural skill. It is an exercise in discriminating and generalizing. Bigots have given these basic logical methods a bad name, but telling one thing from another and making assumptions about a group is much older than hatred. Or maybe not—but as in the case of atomic energy, there are peaceful purposes for these skills. Perhaps the atom bomb is not such a good example. Try to see it this way: when a bank robber flees, only to find that he has locked his keys in his car, he pushes a kid off his bike and rides away. The robber had one Entity in mind but generalized his need to MODE OF TRANSPORTATION. (Editor's note: to the best of my knowledge, the author does not go around pushing kids off bikes or building bombs.)

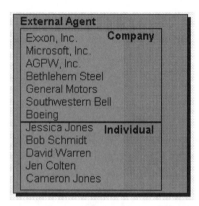

Figure 7-3

Take a look at Figure 7-3, a Venn diagram using boxes instead of circles to list a number of companies and a number of individuals. The companies belong to the set COMPANY, the individuals to the set INDIVIDUAL. These sets are specialized; we distinguish one from the other. The companies and the individuals together belong to the set EXTERNAL AGENT, which indicates that somebody somewhere has a reason to see individuals and companies as the same—perhaps because companies and individuals can bring lawsuits. The EXTERNAL AGENT set is a generalization about the Entities. After studying Figure 7-3, would you say a Class is a table in a computer, a set of Entities, or a selection of Entities?

I hope you didn't choose "a table in a computer." I said that tables correspond to Classes; that is not to say that they are the same thing. Remember, this course is not about computer systems! It is about how you and I organize and process information in our heads.

The names all represent Entities. From there, you can see that the Classes—COMPANY, INDIVIDUAL, and EXTERNAL AGENT—are sets of Entities. Is saying that a Class is "a selection of Entities," the same as saying "select all the external agents in Texas"? That query would yield a set of Entities; however, when we are defining Classes, we never include Entities based on the value of some Predicate but only on the existence of the Predicate. When we select all the external agents in Texas, "Texas" is the value of a Predicate. On the other hand, if you say, "Put all the Entities for which we can know what state they are in over here," then you are classifying.

i) CLASSES = ENTITIES with the SAME PREDICATES.

2) Superclass = Entities that have SAME Predicate Value.

What state they are in is a Predicate; a Superclass is a set of all Entities that have the same Predicates.

You may have thought that you had found all the kinds of EXTERNAL AGENT. But if your projects go like mine tend to, then something unexpected will occur before they are finished. For example, what do you do when you find out that governmental bodies are treated like EXTERNAL AGENT for purposes of paying tax bills? Should you allow them to be included in the EXTERNAL AGENT Superclass without requiring them to be either a company or an individual? The answer is no. (You should know that some CASE tools allow this practice, and some writers promote it.)

A simpler rule is to have a place for everything—that is, a separate Class—anytime you have Entities with a different set of Predicates, even if that set of Predicates is a subset of some other Class. In this case, that rule calls for a Class TAX AUTHORITY. Maybe there is already such a file on the system. Integrating an existing file (or adding another) in the manner shown for COMPANY and for INDIVIDUAL is no more difficult than it was to set up INDIVIDUAL in the first place. On the other hand, creating something that is not purely a Superclass nor wholly a Class creates a new topic to cover, and both you and I would rather not.

If tax authorities don't have Predicates found in other members of the Superclass, for example credit ratings, that lack is okay because those other Entities are set off in their own Classes, as shown in Figure 7-4.

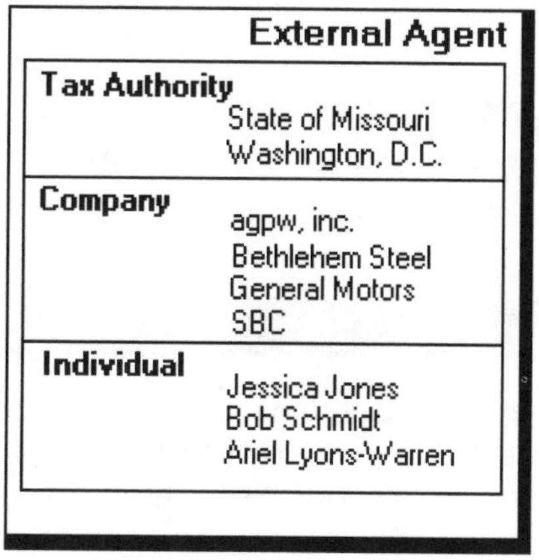

External Agent	
Tax Authority	State of Missouri Washington, D.C.
Company	agpw, inc. Bethlehem Steel General Motors SBC
Individual	Jessica Jones Bob Schmidt Ariel Lyons-Warren

Figure   7-4

If tax authorities have Predicates not found in the Superclass, such as sales tax rate, or if new Predicates are added at a later date, there is no problem since the Superclass EXTERNAL AGENT can ignore any Predicate it does not need.

Consider how an infinite number of places to put things can be useful. How many times have you been about to file something and thought, "I really should set up a separate folder for this thing, but I already have so many folders—and, anyway, what a hassle." You might have stuck the document into some folder containing the least dissimilar Entities. For instance, a moment ago I put information about my homeowner's policy in with my auto policy for this very reason. I may as well have thrown it away. A computer allows you to create an infinite number of Classes such that you never need to compromise your organizational scheme by putting dissimilar items in the same place.

Too often analysts treat the computer as if it were getting too many files. (It will not get too many files.) They think it is a hassle to recognize new Classes. The real hassle, however, is trying to work with a system in which dissimilar things have been placed into the same Class. This just turns the computer into an electric replica of the manual system you spent all this money to improve. Create as many Superclasses as you find useful, and associate an Entity with as many Superclasses as is warranted.

Tip for Project Managers

If a file of all the agencies to which we pay taxes is already in the system, then integrating that file would be great. Because if you do, it does not need to be kept current by more than one department. You may save time on your current project because you will not have to load your own file.

Some other departments will scream, "That's my file!" If they do, they are literally acting like children. It is the corporate file, and if they don't let you read it, go tell mommy and daddy.

Tip for System Analysts

The great thing about finding a new requirement such as these governmental agencies late in development is that you can blame it on other analysts or on the owners. Then you can get your deadlines pushed out or time added to your budget. (Do not accept more bodies as the solution. If you don't know why you shouldn't, then go ahead and accept more bodies—everybody has to make that mistake in his or her career.)

Then since you cleverly used a simple SQL union statement to pull COMPANY and INDIVIDUAL together, all you do is loop TAX AUTHORITY in as well, and you are through. Take all the time you saved and fix something that was your own error.

SuperClasses can be SQL union statements.

Generalizing

Sometimes you want very specialized information about something. For instance, you might need to know the smoking preference of an individual. You might want to know the state of incorporation for a company. Data Modeling requires you to set up a separate Class for any Entity that has a distinct set of Predicates. These specialized Predicates, smoking preference and state of incorporation, distinguish the Classes INDIVIDUAL from COMPANY.

The Superclass allows you to recognize a generalized Class for all Entities that have the same Predicates so far as is needed for some purpose. When you want to write checks, you want very generalized information about EXTERNAL AGENT. For example, you will want to know where to send the check. Both individuals and companies have addresses. You will also want to know to whom to make it out. Both individuals and companies have names. These Predicates, address and name, belong to both INDIVIDUAL and COMPANY.

Remember, a Class is the set of all Entities with all the same Predicates. If you forget those Predicates of companies and individuals not involved in check writing, then the remaining Predicates are the same. That is, both Exxon and Bob Schmidt have an address to send check and a name used as external agent. Therefore, these Entities naturally fall into the Superclass EXTERNAL AGENT, since they have all the needed Predicates to be external agents.

The Predicates held in common must have the same Domains. They may have different names, but they must have the same meaning—that is, the same function. For example, you can combine Social Security Numbers for individuals and Federal Tax Identifiers for companies into a single Domain for our purposes, since they both have the same underlying use, to uniquely identify taxpayers.

Specializing

Imagine you have been asked to develop a simple computer application that writes checks. You might need only one Class for EXTERNAL AGENT. But if you end up doing a good job, the system owners might well ask you to extend their application. For example, they might have been writing checks to employees but now want to keep track of the evaluations that these employees have received. Average evaluation is a Predicate not applicable to all external agents, nor is it important to the original check-writing program.

To extend the application, you add the new Predicates to the data model. Do not stuff the new Predicate <u>average evaluation</u> into the EXTERNAL AGENT Class. To do so would violate a crucial principle: Entities with different Predicates belong in different Classes. Instead, you split the EXTERNAL AGENT Class into Classes to reflect the different Predicates each has. Recognizing the differences between Entities and creating new Classes is called specializing (see Figure 7-5).

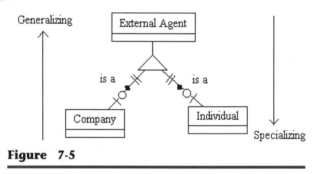

Figure   7-5

Tip for Project Managers

Analysts waste weeks arguing over the proper way to analyze a system. Frankly, if they haven't found some common approach before the project has begun, they risk losing client confidence, ungluing team cohesion, and suffering setbacks.

One popular and spectacularly unprofitable argument is whether 'tis better to begin with an inclusive idea, such as EXTERNAL AGENT, and then work down, say to COMPANY and INDIVIDUAL; or whether 'tis more noble to start small and aggregate.

The broad Classes such as EXTERNAL AGENT are called Superclasses. Many people prefer to recognize the Superclasses before they recognize specialized Classes. Rather than building Superclasses up from Classes, they will break Superclasses down into specialized Classes. This approach is called specialization.

Many people prefer to start with the most highly specialized Classes and group them into Superclasses. This technique is called generalization.

This issue is not the kind of thing that should divide people. The truth is you have to follow the analysis where it takes you. You will often find false bottoms—thinking you have found all the Predicates of a thing only to realize that you have missed some and be forced to specialize your Classes further. You will also find many cases in which a system owner thinks in general terms about a number of Classes, so you should generalize and recognize a Superclass. Your team should master both the skills of generalizing and specializing.

It would also help if they were less stubborn.

Tip for System Analysts

This book does not use the term subclass, although when talking about models, it is a very useful term. You might say that COMPANY is a Subclass of EXTERNAL AGENT—that is, COMPANY is relatively more specialized than EXTERNAL AGENT. As you can see, subclasses are the product of specializing; Superclasses are the product of generalizing.

A Class is the set of all Entities that have all the same Predicates. Since the Entities in the Class account for all the Predicates, then the Class is by definition the ultimate subclass. Consider the term Class to mean the most specialized Class and the term Superclass to mean any generalization.

Building hierarchies of Superclasses is rational; you can say that a Superclass is made up of other Superclasses. As a general rule, I do not recommend this as a Data Modeling practice, because you introduce an unnecessary complication. Changes made at intermediate levels have implicit effects at higher levels in the hierarchy, which may or may not have been intended. You can create all the Superclasses you need in terms of the individual Classes in one step rather than an entire staircase.

One other point: when Entities of two or more Classes are combined to form a union, a Superclass, the Entities must still be uniquely identified. This often requires advance planning.

Avoid layers of Superclasses.

Entities of Many Classes

You may conceive of Superclasses made up of other Superclasses nested like Russian dolls. This conception is not necessary; no matter how general a Superclass may become, you can still define it in terms of the Classes without reference to any other Superclass. You may also find Classes that belong to more than one otherwise unrelated Superclass.

Figure 7-6 shows two Classes of transactions that affect the balance due on a reservation: (1) RESERVATION RECEIPT and (2) RESERVATION RECEIPT, LESS COMMISSION. Two Classes of transactions that affect our accounts with sales agents are also shown: (1) RESERVATION RECEIPT, LESS COMMISSION and (2) COMMISSION PAYMENT. These payments

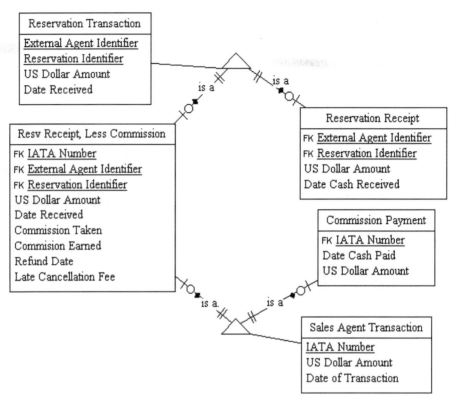

Figure   7-6

include commissions for side-trips that may have been paid for by the tourist without notification of the sales agent but for which the sales agent is given incentive.

A reservation receipt for which the sales agent has withheld his or her commission is a RESERVATION TRANSACTION, and it is a SALES AGENT TRANSACTION. It is a member of both sets, both Superclasses. A reservation receipt for which no commission is due is not a SALES AGENT TRANSACTION. The Commission Payment is based on a recap of many different transactions and does not itself affect the balance due on a reservation, so it is not a RESERVATION TRANSACTION.

Note the general sense of Figure 7-6. The statements about the model should seem sensible to the owners. The diagram meets the modeling principles of different Predicates, different Classes; and the same subset of Predicates, the same Superclass. Also note the usefulness of the Superclasses from the perspective of the processes that are implied. Insofar as Accounts Receivable is concerned, all transactions that affect the balance due on a trip are unified in the Superclass. From the perspective of the Sales Agent Accounting Department, all transactions affecting the balance due an agent are likewise unified. A change to a reservation receipt for which the sales agent has withheld commission is reflected accurately in both Departments. And finally, note how much Superclasses simplify maintenance. The owners invent new transactions yearly—credit cards, wire transfers, promotional coupons. As each new Entity is introduced, new Classes can be set up to accommodate the new Predicates. These Classes are easily incorporated into the Superclasses without affecting the processing of either Receivable or Payables.

Tip for System Analysts

The Superclasses are important because they are simple for the system owners to understand, and because they improve integrity and reduce maintenance costs.

For example, the RESERVATION TRANSACTION Class creates a simplified view of all the accounting for a reservation. The system owners readily understand the idea of "anything that changes in the customer's balance." For the programmer, the balance due on a reservation is the sum of all reservation transactions. This makes programming simpler, since only one file is referenced in documentation and ultimately only one view of the database is read. Finally, maintenance is simplified because adding new Classes for new types of transactions does not affect the programs that use the RESERVATION TRANSACTION view. The same benefits are true of the transactions that affect our balance with our sales agents, that is, SALES AGENT TRANSACTION.

Superclasses Serve Some Purpose

One could classify things endlessly. For example, cans of paint in the hardware store could be a part of a Class INVENTORY-FINISH. They might be lumped with other materials in a Class HAZARDOUS MATERIAL. Another possibility is a Class GOODS, LIQUID.

Classes must have a reason to exist. In the above example, INVENTORY-FINISH is important for stocking and accounting. The Class HAZARDOUS MATERIAL may be needed for a local fire ordinance. However, try to imagine the need for a Class that is the set of all liquids. Would anyone want to know how many gallons of liquid were in the store? Although liquid goods might meet all our criteria for a Class, it is simply unnecessary.

Do Not Simply Put All Instances Into the Same Class

One way to solve the conundrum of Entities that belong to many Classes is to shove all the Predicates into the same Class. Let's call this the one Entity fits all approach. Refer back to Figure 7-6. This approach would eliminate two Classes, Reservation Receipt and Commission Payment. The Super-classes, Reservation Transaction and Sales Agent Transaction, are no longer unions of their constituent Classes but instead are simple projections of Predicates found in the one remaining Class. On the surface it would seem that the situation is thereby simplified; but what has really happened? The diagram would be simpler. However, the business would be unchanged; only the system owners can simplify their business. The diagram would be simpler because it reflects less of the business, and therefore it would be less capable of informing the system designers. In particular, the diagram does not show the business rule that when the Entity is a receipt for a reservation that was not made by a sales agent, then those Predicates dealing with sales agent transactions must be blank. That is, if Joe got the reservation directly from Dynamite Tours, then the sales agent's IATA number must be blank and the commission fields must be zero. The hidden rules about when one Predicate is required become very intricate and you find yourself in a much deeper conundrum than had you created separate Classes.

Tip for System Analysts

The logic that is missing from the one Entity fits all approach takes the following form:

```
If Entity is type "Resv Receipt Less Commission" or
"Reservation Receipt" then
  Require user to enter reservation number
Else
  reservation number must be blank.
End if
```

This kind of validation requires that there be a Predicate <u>type</u> added to the Class. Ultimately, no matter how you might squirm, you end up with type values "hard coded" in the programs. As a result of this, to add new types you have to reprogram. Of course, you always have to specify what type of Entities you are working with whether you use a Predicate, about which I warned you, or a table name, which I suggest you do use. The general rule is do not put data about data into your database. The Predicate type is data about data. The practical upshot of this rule is that application logic does not have to have logic to account for Entities having different Predicates. A design that in fact has many tables corresponding to many Classes, each Class being a set of Entities sharing the same Predicates, is simple relative to managing application logic to do the same thing.

The one Entity fits all approach is contrary to the idea of a place for everything and everything in its place. Either idea has the quality of allowing a team to apply the approach consistently to arrive at a single, coherent, correct answer for a given set of owner's requirements. When a team always recognizes a Class as any set of Entities that have the same Predicates, then the analysis will result in a large number of highly specific Classes with Predicates being either optional or required depending only on the State of the Entity. When a team takes the one Entity fits all approach they have no objective rule to prevent the collapse of the entire model into a single Class. In the one Entity fits all approach Predicates are optional or required depending on the State and some type indicator. Although I never expect to see a one Class data model, the only thing that prevents models that mix Entities with different Predicates into the same Class from collapsing into a single Class is the intuition of the analysts.

Every Entity sets itself apart from other Entities that do not have the same Predicates. An Entity's place is with all other Entities that have the same Predicates.

Do Not Create Superclasses Just to Hold Common Predicates

Some analysts take exception to the diagram of Figure 7-6 because Predicates are repeated; for example, US Dollar Amount. Those analysts would want to move any Predicate that repeats to its own Class and "inherit" the Predicate to all Classes that need it. Figure 7-7 demonstrates this "inheritance" approach.

I do not recommend inheritance of Predicates because the approach will not work in all circumstances: it forces unnecessary revisions during analysis, it is not a good basis for database design, it is confusing to system owners, and it has no basis in the way humans are accustomed to organizing data. There is controversy about this approach. The paragraphs that follow expand on each of the reasons not to inherit Predicates.

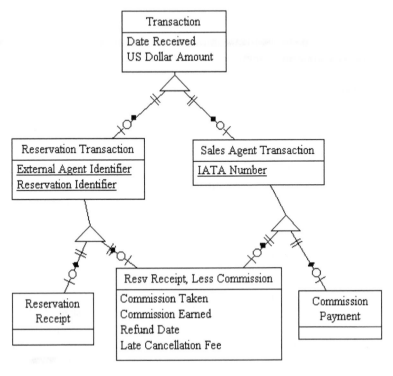

Figure   7-7

It is usually possible to create hierarchies of Classes such that the Predicates need only be noted one time; however, as with the Predicate US Dollar Amount there is no objective way to determine whether the Predicate is inherited from the Reservation Transaction Class or the Sales Agent Transaction Class or both. In a larger model, Predicates such as US Dollar Amount become especially challenging since such a Predicate is so pervasive. In this case as in many others, the inheritance approach does not provide objective guidance. Remember that a Predicate is bound to the thing that determines the value of the Predicate. These made-up abstract Classes such as RESERVATION TRANSACTION have no correspondence to things in the system owner's world and so cannot be the source of Predicates.

If the database administrators use the common rule that one Class is implemented as one table, then the inheritance approach is misleading. I can think of no reason why a single Entity corresponding to some one thing in the system owner's world should have the values for its Predicates spread across multiple tables. If creating a single consistent record for everything the system owners want to know about some thing is integration, then creating multiple tables would have to be called disintegration. The current disintegration of systems is the understandable result of rapid growth without a guiding data model; this would be more like a self-inflicted wound.

Irrespective of the prior problems, the inheritance approach makes more work for analysis teams whenever they discover a new Class or a new Predicate. If a new Class shares some Predicates but not all the Predicates of a Superclass, then the shared Predicates have to be moved between Superclasses to maintain the idea of not repeating Predicates. If a new Predicate is found that is shared but not in exactly the same way as other common Predicates, then again new Classes must be inserted into the Superclass scheme. All the moving of Predicates is meaningless but nonetheless must be incorporated into each team's models to maintain the consistency of approach.

The inheritance scheme does not serve analysts or database administrators; perhaps it is a better way to talk to the system owners. Plainly, the non-technical person would rather not have to follow lines from one Class to the next to figure out whether their data is represented in the model. Further, the Predicate that is shared cannot be called one thing in one Class and something else in another. So, for instance, the analyst may be very comfortable with something called <u>date received</u> as a generic name for the date the transaction is to be posted. The system owners may want the Predicate for COMMISSION PAYMENT to be called <u>date paid</u> but the same Predicate to be called <u>date cash received</u> when referring to RESERVATION RECEIPT. There just is no way to explain this to system owners without leaving them with the idea that you are not listening.

The reason the inheritance scheme fails so miserably is that it has no basis in the way we humans organize data. The confusion seeps in when we let ourselves think that Classes have Predicates in the same way that Entities do. How can a Class have a Predicate if you cannot evaluate it? What is the length of the Class of things called pens? What is the length of an Entity such as your pen? Your pen has a length, the Class of pens does not. If you cannot evaluate a Predicate, how can you say that it is functionally dependent on any argument? The Predicates associated with an Entity define what we can know about that thing. The Predicates associated with a Class constitute the criteria by which an Entity is included into the set. That is, a Class is the set of all Entities that are described by the same Predicates. The Class is not the source of Predicates, the Entity is.

Create one unique Class to be the set of all Entities that have all the same arguments and Predicates. Omit no Predicates; combine all Predicates from all States. Do not be concerned that a Predicate may be found in more than one Class. Create all the Superclasses you need to simplify communication with the system owners and to signal the designers that some kind of union set is needed. As with Classes, the Predicates you associate to the Superclass form the membership criteria of the Superclass; that is, every Entity that has those Predicates belongs to that Superclass. Each Superclass necessarily repeats Predicates already documented in Classes; no new Predicates are identified as Superclasses are formed.

Too Many Classes?

Dear Doctor Data,

I followed your instructions carefully. Each time an object had different Predicates from another object, we set up a new Class. We are swimming in Classes.

Signed,
Going Down for the Third Time

Dear Going Down for the Third Time,

Once you start allowing variances between the definitions of instances of Classes, what have you got?

Everyone is afraid of having too many Classes, but no one can tell you how many is too many or what evil will befall you for having lots of Classes.

I can tell you that the project that sticks a bunch of dissimilar Entities into the same Class will pay a big price. Here are some tips to help you mange complex data models.

1) Be sure you don't have a bunch of Domains in your model acting like Classes.

2) Be sure you are not showing States as separate Classes.

3) Presentation can help. Contract neighborhoods of Classes into Entity Groups.
4) Be sure you are recognizing Superclasses when the business justifies them. Superclasses can clean up diagrams dramatically.
5) Use your judgment. Be sure you understand how Classes are used in design and construction. Sometimes, leaving some detail undone is better than confusing everyone with a model that is complete but as big as West Texas.

Signed,
Doctor Data

Having more Classes will not create more work. There will be a perception of more work because your estimating guidelines probably use number of Classes as a parameter. Going around and eliminating Classes will not make the project get done more quickly, but a good model will.

Here's what you should have learned from studying about the concept of Superclasses:

- All Entities must belong to a single Class but may belong to any number of Superclasses.
- A Superclass is the set of all Entities that have the same subset of Predicates.
- Superclasses are more general than Classes.
- Every Superclass must serve some purpose.
- As long as every Class and Superclass serve some purpose, then you cannot have too many.

Part FOUR

Back to Predicates

I n one sense, you've seen it all. Let's review. Data Modeling gives us a way of making sense of the data with which we work. Just as chemistry makes use of models to help scientists work with invisible elements, Data Modeling helps us to work with abstract structures of data. Our minds work unconsciously with Domains, Predicates, Entities, States, Classes, Superclasses, and even more complex elements of language. The kind of close attention we have given these elements of information may strike you as confusing, or academic, but you should remember that the computer has no native intelligence. You must provide 100% of this structure for the information you intend to store there.

When you studied Domains, you became aware of the many ways we can gauge any experience. We may evaluate NUMBER OF CARS, NUMBER OF DOLLARS, or WEIGHT IN KILOS.

When you studied Predicates, you realized how we describe Entities—how the evaluation of an experience is applied to the object, how the Domain meets the Entity. When we sell a box of white rice, the white goes with the rice; it doesn't stay on the shelf. Color is a Predicate of rice. You saw how you can also describe an Entity in terms of another Entity, as in the company's assets.

When you studied Entities, you became aware of the way we carve out distinct objects from our experience. Somehow, we believe that a tree is dif-

ferent from the ground it grows out of. We separate a customer from his money. We can take a product apart. States are not difficult if you see that they are formed by the same rules as are Entities—the difference being that you consider only those Predicates known to a certain part of the business.

When you studied Classes, you realized how Entities that have the same Predicates can be grouped. Thus, all the boxes of rice must belong to the same Class, there being no distinguishing Predicate. The shelf must be its own class because its Predicates are different from those of GROCERY. Superclasses are formed the same way as Classes, except that you ignore some distinguishing Predicates—you generalize.

A computer can record Entities, facts about those Entities, and then group those Entities six ways from Sunday; that is about all computers can do. You may know a lot more about your business than just that, but these elements are enough to structure information for the purposes of study and systemization.

So what's left?

If you understand all of the concepts I have so far discussed, then you have a grasp of all the basics. However, there is a lot more to learn, especially about Predicates. Predicates put the information into an information system. Through the proper analysis of Predicates, the real power of an information system is exploited. Remember that there are two kinds of Predicates, Relationships and Attributes. For those of you who work with CASE tools day in and day out, you may be more comfortable with these terms than with Predicates. In any case, you must always make the Relationship versus Attribute distinction before you sit down at a CASE tool.

So, what brand of hieroglyphics are you going to show me now?

By dissecting each element of information and by providing numerous examples from real-life situations, this text tries to instill a natural understanding of the elements that make up an information system. Rather than advocating rote learning, such as learning to recite definitions, my goal has been to promote real learning, for example being able to express the ideas using your own terms. In actual practice, particular terminology and particular ways of documenting a data model become important. No project of any real size is completed by a single analyst; generally, a data model is reviewed by many people. Standard language and standard documentation are needed to allow everyone involved to work together smoothly.

In order to present real-life examples in this book, I had to choose some particular presentation style. (Learning the type of presentation used on your immediate project is easy once you understand the elements I teach here.) This text has been developed over a seven-year period during which I have received support from the Sybase PowerDesigner team in Boston and Paris, the IBM DataAtlas team in San Jose, California, and Baden-Württemberg, Germany, and the SILVERRUN Technologies team in Woodcliff Lake, New Jersey, and Quebec. I was presented with a devil's bargain—in the end I chose the tool my employer chose, SILVERRUN. Not incidentally, SILVERRUN is very easily customized to a wide variety of presentation styles. The repository, when loaded to their application, can be customized to resemble the style you prefer.

But isn't a data modeling language like IDEF1X better than Information Engineering?

The question is a little like asking, "Is Greek better than English?" Try this: approximate with your fingers something 3" long. Now approximate something 100mm long. While I have assumed that the reader does not speak Greek, I will assume that you are somewhat bilingual when it comes to measurement. (Who could forget that famous jingle about the cigarette being one silly millimeter longer?) But you might remember a time when you didn't have any understanding regarding the length of 100mm; at that time, 100mm might as well have been Greek. Once you are familiar with different ways of measurement, or language for that matter, which one you use becomes insignificant to you.

Languages, like standards of measurement, have become wildly different. Witness the way the Systems Programmer cannot seem to speak with the Marketing Manager. Even within the language of Data Modeling, a number of different dialects have evolved such that there are a number of different ways of representing a data model. To name only a few, there are IDEF1X, Merise, and the Universal Modeling Language.

As with the difference between Greek and English, the differences between Data Modeling languages are greater than the differences of opinion about the meta-model. That the language seems so different misleads people into thinking that there is a difference of thinking. But we find that a diagram in Merise is easily converted to IDEF1X, and from this fact we infer that the two Data Modeling languages have a common meta-model.

An understanding of the differences between Data Modeling languages will help you see that it is not meaningful to argue about whether an X or a crow's foot should mean "many" (any more than it makes sense to say that English is better than Greek).

Why are there so many CASE tools if the meta-models are so similar?

It is easy to see how the tools of language have evolved into thousands of dialects, but it is hard to understand why a modern society would have created so many word processors. Hard for a Marxist. If you have an ounce of entrepreneurial blood, you understand that everybody thinks he can write the better word processor and get famously wealthy, perhaps owning a vacation home in Greece. The same unstoppable force has people writing new accounting packages, new computer-aided design software, and new CASE tools.

Do not confuse the presentation style with the CASE tool. Your CASE tool may even support various styles of presentation. A CASE tool such as SILVERRUN supports many Data Modeling languages, but each tool must support at least one. A Data Modeling language may be supported by none or many CASE tools. Be sure to keep the tool and the language separate in your thinking.

I did not say that CASE was unimportant, only that the tool is subservient to the Data Modeling principles in the same way a general ledger application has to follow accounting principles. While the first concern is how well the CASE tool supports your understanding of modeling, your second concern is how the features of your CASE tool make modeling easier. CASE is the tool of the professional analyst. A CASE tool is not optional equipment. Without a CASE tool, it would be impossible to work in teams with the complexity that comes with even modest projects.

Tip for Project Managers

The CASE tool does not support a lot of different formats because each of your analysts should be allowed to express themselves. It supports a lot of formats because the CASE tool vendor sells to many different companies.

Here's what you do. Find the guy whom nobody likes and upon whom you plan on blaming a lot of stuff. Tell him he has a very important job to do—to choose the background and foreground colors, and to create standards for use of shadowing, font size, and color. Then in front of a mirror practice sadly shaking your head and mouthing his name.   ■

Relationships

I now return to the idea of Predicates to look at a specific type, the Relationship. A Relationship is a Predicate in that its purpose is to describe something. In common with all Predicates, a Relationship must answer a relevant question about some Entity, and it may evaluate none or many answers to that question. A Relationship is different only in that rather than requiring the answer to be drawn from a Domain, the answer to the question must be the unique identifier of some Class.

It is a little misleading to minimize this difference because this is all the difference in the world. What this means is that the Relationship in and of itself does not describe anything any more than the unique identifier of any Class tells us anything. To know that my name is Robert tells you nothing about me. You can use my name to find out a lot about me. A Relationship gives you the name and points you towards other Predicates—Attributes, as you will learn—that are informative.

Because Relationships connect Classes together, they are the transportation network of the database. I once had a client derisively refer to the Entity-Relationship diagram (ERD) as those "damn railroad tracks." I have thought of them in that way ever since. You ride the Relationship railroad, getting on the rails with any unique identifier you know. If you know my name, you could get on at the AUTHOR Class. From there you could ride the railroad to the PUBLICATIONS Class to get a list of all my publications and to learn their publication dates. From any publication, you could ride the rail to the PUBLISHER Class to learn its mailing address or the name of the CEO. (Editor's note: Feel free to write the CEO of Prentice Hall; the author took his advance and rode the train to Mexico.)

What Is a Relationship?

One sentence does not constitute an information system. However, we can look at a sentence and speculate about what kind of data model would be built from it. The following sentence contains an example of a Relationship: "Stock car 54 may be driven by many drivers."

What part of it would be the Relationship? "Stock" qualifies "car." It sets this car apart from a custom or street car. Probably this is indicative of a Predicate, type of car. (You might prefer to see it as part of a specific Class, STOCK CAR.) "54" is an identifier, not really a Predicate in that it doesn't describe anything, but it is your cue that we are talking about a specific Entity. "May be driven by many" describes the car by referring to another Entity or Class, DRIVER—"may be driven by many" is what we are talking about, the Relationship.

Pairings versus Relationships

Contrast these two sentences: "Stock car 54 may be driven by many drivers"; "Stock car 54 may be driven by Mario Andretti." You could say the first sentence sets up the possibility of the second, or that given the latter sentence you could generalize to create the former. I can know who may drive cars; I know that Mario drives car 54. This distinction between that which I can know and that which I know was made earlier in the text when the concept of Predicates was introduced. Again, a Predicate—and by extension, a Relationship such as "Car may be driven by"—is what you can know. Some authors have used the term "pairing" to refer to a fact that is the evaluation of a Relationship, such as "Car 54 is driven by Mario."

Throughout this text, you must realize that individual facts or instances are distinct concepts from generalizations such as Predicates. A Relationship is not an individual fact; it is an abstraction, a Predicate.

Relationships Are More Than You Link

The following sentence does not contain a Relationship: "Stock car 54 has a relationship with many drivers. Your reaction should be, *What's that supposed to mean?* Precisely my point! The sentence doesn't provide enough meaning to be a Relationship. A Relationship has to provide some relevant information. The sentences

- Stock car 54 has many drivers
- Stock car 54 is for many drivers

have the same problems. You might be assuming these sentences mean something that they do not say. This creates a real problem when others look at your data model and make assumptions that seem reasonable to them but are actually contrary to your intent.

The stock car may have many Relationships with the same Class. Some drivers may not be allowed to drive the car. Some drivers may have ownership in the car, may have wrecked the car…. Each of these Relationships, in contrast to the earlier examples, seems to have enough meaning. You cannot know if it is truly enough meaning until you understand the process that the Predicate is intended to support. The essence of the Relationship is not the link; the value of the Relationship is what it tells you about the Entity being described.

Relationship Names

The meaning of the Relationship is abbreviated into its name. Without a name, a Relationship is largely meaningless. In Figure 8-1, there are two Relationships between currency futures contract #124 and CURRENCY. The Relationships are named "commits to sell" and "commits to buy." Obviously, the names are needed to distinguish one Relationship from another, but if that were the only reason to name them, then you could just call them Rel1 and Rel2. What is more important is that Relationship names tell you what the Relationship means.

By convention, the Relationship name always contains a verb; this convention allows the entire structure to be read as a sentence. (There may be

Described Entity

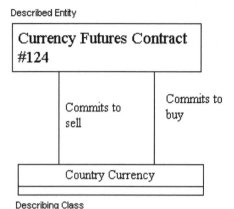

Figure 8-1

Describing Class

reason to establish more exacting standards. David Hay in *Data Model Patterns: Conventions of Thought*[1] has established some excellent guidelines.) The subject of the sentence is always a single Entity; in Figure 8-1 the Entity is "Currency Futures Contract #124." The subject of the sentence is described by the object of the sentence. The object of the sentence is always some Class; in Figure 8-1 the Class is COUNTRY CURRENCY.

Okay, so putting everything together, the two Relationships in Figure 8-1 tell us that

- Currency futures contract #124 commits to sell currency.
- Currency futures contract #124 commits to buy currency.

Currency futures contract #124 is described by both the currency it will buy and the currency it will sell:

"Tell me about contract #124."

"Contract #124 is to buy French Francs with German Marks."

Tip for Project Managers

Listening to all the bickering about Relationship naming standards is sometimes dizzying.

Some people are adamant that words such as "has," "is for," "is described by," and so forth must not be used. It is hard to argue with their point: "If you can't describe it, you don't understand it." But how long can

1. *Dorsett House, 1996, ISBN 0-932633-29-3.*

you stand to see a roomful of people looking like an amateur poetry society struggling over tiny changes in wording?

The truth is that all Relationships are different and require a different degree of exactitude in naming. Ask an experienced analyst to review the data model and verify that the Relationships are adequately specified.

Tip for System Analysts

These names are adequately specific. They say enough that a reasonable person would be expected to use the information responsibly. Sounds like legalese, but I'm making an important point here. You will never describe the Relationship so well that some bozo isn't going to stumble along and try to misuse the data—hence the reasonable person caveat.

The name of the Relationship must convey an understanding of how the data is to be used. A vague name encourages analysts to scavenge Relationships to use for their purposes, ignoring the original intent. A Predicate must have one meaning, adding a second analyst's meaning atop the original meaning leads to analysts working at cross-purposes. For example, needing to identify the country in which the currency exchange is to take place, an imprudent analyst might decide he or she could just use the "commits to sell" Relationship. Such a decision would lead to problems because you can exchange Francs for Pounds in New York City. In such a case, you need a new Relationship CURRENCY FUTURES CONTRACT is transacted in COUNTRY.

A clear Relationship name encourages people to make informed choices about how a Relationship should be used.

Pairing for Life

Sometimes a Relationship, once established, cannot be changed. Figure 8-1 demonstrates a contract that specifies the purchase and sale of specific currencies. When a Relationship is non-modifiable it is commonly said to be "non-transferable." Should the Relationships in Figure 8-1 be transferable?

    a. The type of currency involved is a part of the unique identifier and should therefore not be transferable.

b. The nature of the contract would be fundamentally changed if the type of currency were changed and should therefore not be transferable.

Well, the type of currency might be a part of the unique identifier for currency contracts. And, if that were so, then it would be reasonable to make the Relationship lines non-transferable (option a). However, Predicates such as these Relationships are non-modifiable first and then may become a part of a unique identifier second. (The rule is not that you cannot change the identifiers to a Class but that if you change identifiers, you are referring to a different Entity.)

Once the contract is established as trading British Pounds for Canadian Dollars, the result just wouldn't be the same if we switched to Pounds for Francs (option b). You probably understand this intuitively, and, if so, then you should leave it at that. However, if you need more convincing, then consider the effect on other Predicates. If you changed the deal from Canadian Dollars to French Francs, would you expect that the exchange rate would be different? The rate might be coincidentally the same, but only coincidentally. Think of what you would say if your trading partner wanted to make such a change. Wouldn't you say something like, "That is a different deal altogether"? In common language, you see that the non-transferability is assumed by the trading partners rather than imposed by the information system. Option b is the correct answer.

All graphical notations use a line to relate the instances of one Class to another. Beyond that a variety of markings are used to describe the nature of the Relationship. Focus your study on the kinds of things the markings represent rather than the shapes of the markings themselves.

How Many Answers Do You Expect?

Any Predicate can have more than one value for a single Entity. An example of a Predicate that can have more than one response is "What credit cards do you accept?" The number of answers a Relationship can have is called the cardinality of the Relationship. The example "Macy's accepts many credit cards" is what is called a "many" or "more-than-one" Relationship. If a Relationship can have only one response, it is said to have a cardinality of "only-one."

The cardinality of a Relationship is an answer to the question "How many Entities of the describing Class may be associated with the single described Entity?" Figure 8-2 drops one Relationship and adds the short stroke at the bottom of the remaining Relationship to highlight the manner in which cardinality is expressed graphically. A Relationship that is limited in this way has an only-one cardinality.

Described Entity

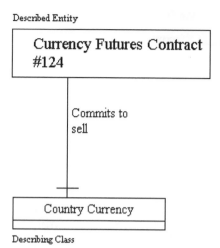

Figure 8-2

A Relationship that allows many pairings between the Entity being described and Entities of the describing Class has a cardinality of many or more-than-one. For example, in Figure 8-3, U.S. Dollars <u>may be committed for sale</u> by any number of CURRENCY FUTURES CONTRACT.

A more-than-one or many cardinality is shown as a crow's foot. (Editor's note: If the practice is going to be to draw on avian imagery, then the preferred term should be "cardinal's foot," for the sake of consistency.)

You can be more specific if your situation calls for it; for example, cardinality could be any whole, positive number. Some examples:

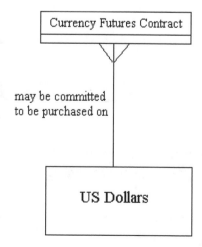

Figure 8-3

- A currency contract promises to sell one type of CURRENCY.
- A marriage contract weds two INDIVIDUAL.
- A fiscal year has thirteen PERIOD.

However, the Relationships having cardinality of only-one and more-than-one are far and away the most common.

Cardinality has implications to your database design far out of proportion to this short explanation. For instance, if you know what Entity you are interested in and want to use an only-one Relationship to learn more about the Entity, then you can get a single answer. For instance, the fact that every copyrighted book has only one current publisher exemplifies only one cardinality. If you know the name of a book and you want to know the name of the publisher, then you can count on getting a single answer. If you wanted to use a more-than-one Relationship to go get information about a describing Class, then you have to expect to get a number of answers back. So, for example, if you wanted to know the authors of a book, you might get more than one answer. This situation is more complex: to whom do you write to complain? If you wanted to talk computers for a moment, how would you display it on a screen or report? With more-than-one Relationships, you have to be able to list all answers.

You might want to cover the right-most column with your hand to test your skill at identifying cardinality.

Described Entity	Relationship Name	Describing Class	Cardinality
The Pope	employs	CARDINAL (s)	many
The St. Louis Cardinals	play	BASEBALL GAME (s)	many
A cardinal	is born of	MOTHER (s)	one
A flock	consists of	CARDINAL (s)	many
A compass	indicates	CARDINAL DIRECTION (s)	four

Optionality or Minimum Cardinality

Conventionally, whether or not the Relationship is required is considered an issue separate from the issue of cardinality. Whether a pairing is required or not is called optionality. It is becoming much more common to

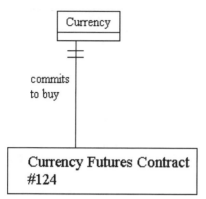

Figure 8-4

think in terms of a maximum and minimum cardinality. Up until now, I have talked about the maximum cardinality, how many pairings there might be. Now consider how many pairings there must be.

Optionality is indicated by marking the Relationship line with either a short perpendicular stroke just inside the cardinality mark, meaning required, or a zero, meaning optional.

For example, a futures contract is not a futures contract without Relationships to a buying and a selling currency, as shown in Figure 8-4. Therefore, these Relationships are required. An example of an optional Relationship, on the other hand, would be U.S. Dollars <u>may be committed to be purchased</u> on zero or more CURRENCY FUTURES CONTRACT, as shown in Figure 8-5.

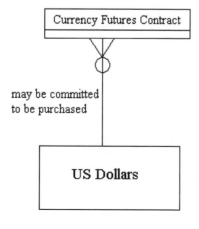

Figure 8-5

Often this question is asked: "What about the nanosecond between the time the futures contract record is written and the U.S. Dollars record is written? Isn't the contract out there without a currency record? Doesn't that condition make it optional? Or what if the person keying the record gets up to go to the bathroom after entering the futures contract but before the U.S. currency is entered? What about that?"

When I get a question like that, I call for a break, take the questioner into the hall, and explain to him that Data Modeling is not about computers. Insofar as the logical model is concerned, a Relationship is required if the database is incomplete without it. If a futures contract is invalid without the references to currency, then the Relationships are required. You gotta save something for software construction.

One way to figure out optionality is to ask the question "Can the first Entity exist without the second related Entity?" If the answer is yes, then the Relationship may be optional. If the answer is no, then the Relationship is required. In Figure 8-4, for example, a futures contract cannot exist without reference to some currency.

You might want to cover the right-most column with your hand to test your skill at identifying optionality:

Described Entity	Relationship Name	Describing Class	Optionality
Currency futures contract #124	commits to sell	CURRENCY	at least one
U.S. Dollars	are committed to be sold on	CURRENCY FUTURES CONTRACT	none
U.S. Filter Stock	is issued by	CORPORATION	one
Macy's	sells	PRODUCTS	none

To say that Macy's sells no products would seem absurd. But if Macy's went bankrupt, then it could happen. The general practice is to leave the minimum cardinality as none unless there is a compelling reason to do otherwise.

You don't want a data model that is predominantly optional Relationships. Such a situation indicates that the Entity Classes are not clearly defined.

Generally speaking, however, optionality is not a high-risk area of the data model. Optional Relationships will almost certainly get cleaned up in the design phase without causing any real problems.

Eliminating Optional Relationships

Sometimes, an optional Relationship is a sign that the described Classes are too general. The introduction of a less inclusive Class makes the Relationship required rather than optional. In Figure 8-6, you may specialize COMPANY by introducing FINANCIAL SERVICE PROVIDER to eliminate the optional Relationship to BANK ACCOUNT.

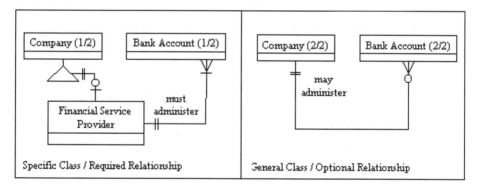

Figure 8-6

The real problem is not the optional Relationship; it is the weak Class, COMPANY. Trying to force dissimilar Entities into the same Class often results in optional Predicates, which are weak because they don't tell us how the business works. An unequivocal data model is much more useful.

Tip for System Analysts

Optional Relationships result in vague specifications, which result in weak code—code that either does not do all it can or contains unsightly exception logic.

For example:

> If the agent is a bank, then
> > Add bank account record.
>
> Else send msg to user: "Sorry, only banks may have accounts."

Screen design also becomes more effective. For example, with specializing, the owner selects a menu option to "Add a bank"; the resulting screen has only data applicable to banks, such as account numbers and bank processing codes. If the owner selects an option to "Add other external agent," the resulting screen contains no useless fields such as "ABA code" that the owner must tab past.

Relationships Always Go Both Ways

At the risk of sounding trite, I note that Relationships are always a two-way street. An Entity cannot be described by another Class without saying something about the describing Entity. Figure 8-7 demonstrates this principle. Currency futures contract #124 <u>commits to sell</u> some COUNTRY CURRENCY. Therefore, we can say that some country currency (such as U.S. Dollars) <u>may be committed to be purchased on</u> some CURRENCY FUTURES CONTRACT.

In Figure 8-8, the two Relationships have been merged into a single line. Note that after the merge, neither side is explicitly an Entity; both sides are

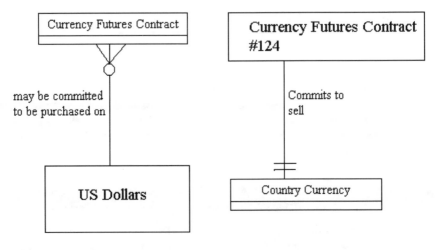

Figure 8-7

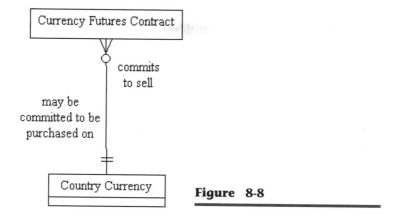

Figure 8-8

Classes, and the Classes describe each other. There is in fact no standard notation for an Entity. Nonetheless, you must understand the diagram as if it were two separate Relationships; that is, a single Entity may be described by its Relationship to some Class.

My terminology should be amended here. When analysts refer to Relationships, they are speaking of the two Predicates merged. Nonetheless, you will find occasion to work with one half of the Relationship or the other. I should have been using the terms "relationship membership" or "direction" when speaking of one half of the Relationship.

Analysts refer to the cardinality of the merged directions, or Relationship, by combining the individual cardinalities. So two directions, each with a cardinality of many, become a many-to-many cardinality. They speak of Relationships as if the various combinations of cardinality constitute types of Relationships, hence a many-to-many Relationship. If one direction has a cardinality of one and the other a cardinality of many, then we refer to the Relationship as a one-to-many Relationship. Analysts don't say many-to-one: it just isn't cool. If both directions have a cardinality of one, then we refer to that Relationship as a one-to-one Relationship.

Degree

When an Entity can be described in terms of some other Entity, it is said that the Entities have a Relationship. The basic Relationship consists of the described and the describing Classes—two Classes. The number of Entities involved in a Relationship determines its degree. The Relationship shown in Figure 8-8 is the most typical; it has two degrees and is said to be binary.

When both the describing and described Entities are the same, then the Relationship is often called unary. Figure 8-9 expresses the idea "An individual is recommended by one and only one INDIVIDUAL."

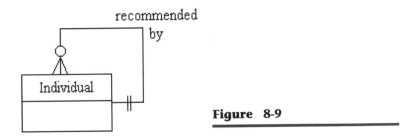

recommended
by

Individual

Figure 8-9

The unary Relationship is much loved by the modeling cognoscenti since it confuses novices in an amusing way. In order that the concept be maximally confusing, they have given several different names to this kind of Relationship. You may hear the terms "recursive," "involuted," "reflexive," or "unary." It might help you to understand how this type of Relationship works if I show you the same diagram with only one half of the Relationship, that is, just one direction (Figure 8-10).

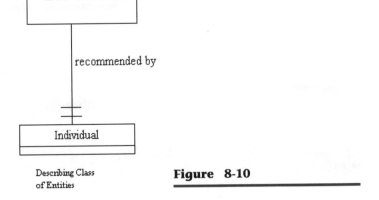

(Expanded for clarity)
Described Entity

Bob Schmidt

recommended by

Individual

Describing Class
of Entities

Figure 8-10

My advice is to always correct the terminology of the know-it-alls. When they, like Jack Horner, pull out what they might call a "recursive" Relationship, you say, "You mean an involuted Relationship." Or if they use the term "involuted," you correct them to "reflexive." (Editor's note: This kind of one-upping is covered in a separate pamphlet, "How to Get to Do Every-thing by Yourself.")

When more than two Entities must be involved to express a single idea, then we call that Relationship "n-ary." The "n" is like the "x" you remem-ber from algebra—the n stands for some number greater than two.

Imagine that your boss hollers out, "Each country has to know which of our employees is working for which of our companies in their borders!" What Classes and Relationships would you need to keep track of who works where for whom? Two alternative data models are given (Figure 8-11 and Figure 8-12); the one with the n-ary Relationship is the only model that expresses your boss's data requirements.

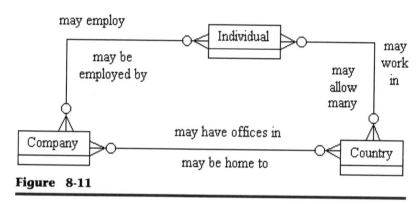

Figure   8-11

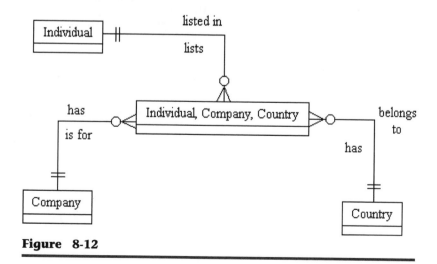

Figure   8-12

It is not so obvious which diagram contains an n-ary Relationship. N-ary Relationships are usually disguised as a series of binary Relationships. The n-ary Relationship is, however, not separable into parts; all the parts must be working together to have the intended effect.

The Relationships in Figure 8-11 cannot answer the question "Who works where for whom?" To demonstrate that you cannot answer the question, transform the Classes specified in Figure 8-11—COMPANY, COUNTRY, INDIVIDUAL—into tables. (Make up the names of the Entities.)

COMPANY
Zapata
Zaragoza
Zblx

COUNTRY
Honduras
Guatemala
Costa Rica
Jamaica

INDIVIDUAL
O'Hanahan
Morales
Mamhood
Forest

Next, transform the many-to-many Relationships into tables and fill the tables with sample data. The two columns link Entities in the Classes.

COMPANY operates in COUNTRY	
COMPANY	**COUNTRY**
Zapata	Honduras
Zaragoza	Honduras
Zblx	Guatemala
Zblx	Honduras

INDIVIDUAL works in COUNTRY	
INDIVIDUAL	**COUNTRY**
O'Hanahan	Honduras
Morales	Guatemala
Mamhood	Honduras
Mamhood	Guatemala

INDIVIDUAL works for COMPANY	
COMPANY	**INDIVIDUAL**
Zapata	Mamhood
Zaragoza	O'Hanahan
Zblx	Mamhood
Zblx	Morales

Does Mamhood work for Zblx in Honduras? The tables indicate that Mamhood works for Zblx, that Zblx has operations in Honduras, and that Mamhood does work in Honduras; so Mamhood might work for Zblx in Honduras. But what you cannot tell from the tables is that when Mamhood is in Honduras, he actually works for Zapata, which also has operations in Honduras. In any case, you shouldn't have to go chasing around a model like this to answer a simple question.

There is no other way to express the idea that a company employs many persons in many countries, except by creating an n-ary Relationship. As shown in Figure 8-12, COMPANY/COUNTRY/INDIVIDUAL is the n-ary Relationship. It looks like a Class, and it is, sort of. The COMPANY, COUNTRY, and INDIVIDUAL tables that you conceived of before are unchanged. However, instead of the three binary tables, create and populate a table such as would be implied by the n-ary Relationship.

COMPANY	COUNTRY	INDIVIDUAL
Zblx	Honduras	O'Hanahan
Zblx	Honduras	Mamhood
Zblx	Guatemala	Morales
Zblx	Guatemala	Mamhood
Zaragoza	Honduras	O'Hanahan
Zapata	Honduras	Mamhood

Each Entity, each row, clearly states that a company employs certain individuals in a country. The second line tells me that I lied; I guess Mamhood does work for Zblx in Honduras. Really, if you just sat down with a pad of paper and tried to satisfy a barking boss, you would probably have come up with something like this table. Only when we get drunk with the flexibility of computers do we envision wild maps of tables that in this case cannot do the job of a single, intuitive table.

Since I have slid into the nasty world of actually developing a system, I should note a few items. The micro-case assumes that the only thing the system had to do was to answer the question "For each country, who works for what company?" If this were an actual system, individual, country, and company codes would stand for the actual names, and only these codes would be seen in the n-ary table. In an actual information system, you would likely see other Predicates of each of the three Classes and in the n-ary Relationship itself; for example, you might have a Predicate expressing when person began working for COMPANY in COUNTRY. If you also needed to know who worked for what COMPANY regardless of COUNTRY, you might just infer that data from the n-ary Relationship; however, this approach would be poor form since there would then be more than one record that described Mamhood as working for Zblx. A more sophisticated approach would be to institute the many-to-many Relationship between INDIVIDUAL and COMPANY as shown in Figure 8-13.

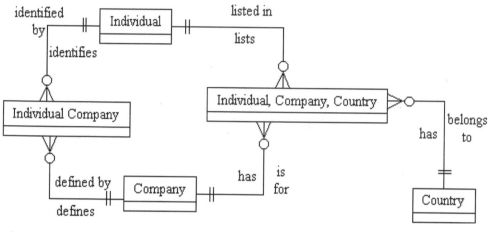

Figure   8-13

Ten Possible Relationships

I have discussed four important characteristics of a Relationship: its name, degree, cardinality, and optionality. Additionally, there are only three combinations of cardinality: many-to-many (M to M), one-to-many (1 to M), and one-to-one (1 to 1). In all, there are only ten possible combinations of cardinality and optionality. Relationships are not all that intimidating when you see that there are only ten of them!

	Direction X *Cardinality*			
Direction Y *Cardinality*	maximum = many minimum = one	maximum = many minimum = none	maximum = one minimum = one	maximum = one minimum = none
maximum = many minimum = one	1) Fully dependent M to M. e.g., An employee <u>must work in at least one</u> COUNTRY /A country <u>must have at least one</u> EMPLOYEE	2) Partially dependent M to M. e.g., An individual <u>may be the target of none or many</u> MAIL DROP /A mail drop may <u>target one or many</u> INDIVIDUALS	4) Mutually dependent 1 to M. e.g., A rooming party <u>consists of one or many</u> RESERVATION / A reservation <u>belongs to one and only one</u> ROOMING PARTY	5) Dependent group. e.g., A travel group <u>is made up of one or many</u> RESERVATION / A reservation <u>may be a part of none or only one</u> TRAVEL GROUP
maximum = many minimum = none	Same as 2)	3) Fully independent M to M: e.g., An external agent <u>may pay for many</u> DEPARTURE /A departure <u>may be paid for by many</u> EXTERNAL AGENT	6) Parental or descriptive. e.g., A departure <u>is for one and only one</u> TOUR /A tour <u>has none or many</u> DEPARTURE	7) Independent group or optional descriptor. e.g., A sales agent <u>may sell none or many</u> RESERVATION / A reservation <u>may be sold by none or only one</u> SALES AGENT

	Direction X *Cardinality*			
Direction Y *Cardinality*	maximum = many minimum = one	maximum = many minimum = none	maximum = one minimum = one	maximum = one minimum = none
maximum = one minimum = one	Same as 4)	Same as 6)	8) Mutually dependent 1 to 1. e.g., A place is followed by one and only one PLACE /A place follows one and only one PLACE (Think of Monopoly.)	9) Partially dependent 1 to 1. e.g., An individual may have been named via none or only one BOUNTY / A bounty must name one and only one INDIVIDUAL
maximum = one minimum = none	Same as 5)	Same as 7)	Same as 8)	10) Fully independent 1 to 1. e.g., A travel coupon may discount none or only one RESERVATION / A reservation is discounted by none or only one TRAVEL COUPON

Numbers 1–3 are the M to M Relationships, which have a cardinality of more-than-one on both ends of the Relationship. For example, a person may own many cars; a car may be owned by many persons. Jaime loves cars; he owns an Olds, a Chevy, and a Lincoln. That old Ford has had many owners, including Nelson Rockefeller and now Henry Ford III.

Numbers 4–7 are the 1 to M Relationships. The idea is that Entity A may be described by many Entity Bs; however, Entity B may be described by just one Entity A. This arrangement would be typical of a bank: a President employs many Vice Presidents, but a Vice President is employed by just one President.

Numbers 8–10 are the 1 to 1 Relationships. They are called 1 to 1 because the cardinality of both halves of the Relationship is only one. For example, at any one time, I am allowed to be married to one person, who at that point must be married to just me.

1 to M Relationships

The 1 to M Relationship has many uses. The familiar organization chart depicted in Figure 8-14 is represented in a data model as a 1 to M Relationship. For this reason, you might think of these Relationships as indicating groupings or subdivisions. For example, a Vice President is responsible for a number of MANAGER; or a finished product is made up of many COMPONENT. This kind of 1 to M Relationship might be described as fatherly.

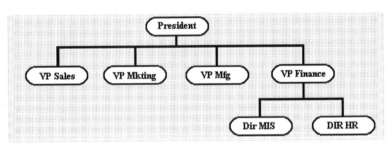

Figure 8-14

Many other circumstances are also depicted as 1 to M. The Descriptive 1 to M is the simplest case. For example, a sale is denominated in one CURRENCY; a currency may denominate many SALE. This Relationship is shown in Figure 8-15.

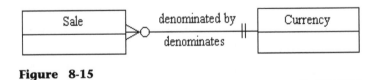

Figure 8-15

Lastly, you will see large numbers of 1 to M Relationships that are the remnants of M to M Relationships cut in two. For this reason, you might think of these Relationships as being one-half of an M to M association, rather than a true 1 to M Relationship. (Do not confuse this severed Relationship with the concept of direction introduced earlier. Note that both resulting Relationships have two directions.) This text provides examples of this type of Relationship in the discussion of M to M.

Examples of 1 to M Relationships

The most common type of Relationship is the 1 to M. There are only four combinations of optionality and cardinality that make up 1 to M Relationships:

There are, however, six business circumstances that call for a 1 to M Relationship:

- Father
- Required Descriptor
- Independent Group
- Optional Descriptor
- Dependent Group
- Mutually Dependent Group

Father Relationship

The most common 1 to M Relationship describes the circumstances in which a thing might or might not be related to many things of a Class; and every thing of this Class must be related to only one thing of the Class represented by the first thing. No wonder we never understand our father. This 1 to M, partly optional, Relationship may be used for two different business circumstances, a required group or a required descriptor. The first situation, as shown in Figure 8-16, is like a fatherly Relationship: a single Entity may describe many children. In this first situation, we see things from the perspective of Dad. The Dad seems to be controlling.

Here is one way of looking at the fatherly Relationship: Dad exists independently of the children; but if there are children, they have only one Dad. The example in Figure 8-16 describes the way planners develop a European tour. First, the planners decide on an overall tour theme, for

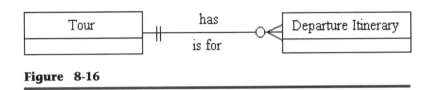

Figure 8-16

example, "The Winter Light of Paris." Later, the planners decide on departure dates, for example, 1/1, 2/1, 2/13, and 3/3. The tour is like a template that is used to create departures for different dates; it is in fact more analogous to a clone than a parent. The Relationship describes the tour in this way: a tour <u>may have none or many</u> DEPARTURE. This same Relationship describes the departure as <u>for one and only one</u> TOUR.

Each departure is its own Entity and is a clone of its related tour. Each departure has the same itinerary as the associated tour; you might say it inherits those characteristics from its parent. (But don't, because the literature uses the term inheritance in the context of Classes and Superclasses.) The departure must have a tour; even if there were just one departure, the diagram says the departure is for a TOUR.

On the other hand, the father in this Relationship, the tour, may have no departures if the tour seems uneconomical. In that case, the planners may scrub the tour. The father exists as a partial plan or something to be reviewed later. In any case, the tour exists independently of the child.

Required Descriptor

In the second situation, as shown in Figure 8-17, the describing Class plays a subservient role to the Entity that is described, and we tend to view the Relationship from the perspective of the described Entity.

The descriptive Relationship is a very common one. Read the Relationship in Figure 8-17 as a currency futures contract <u>commits to purchase one and only one</u> CURRENCY and a currency <u>may be committed to be purchased on none or many</u> CURRENCY FUTURES CONTRACT. The contract

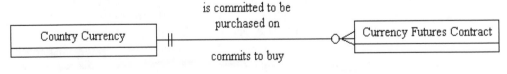

Figure 8-17

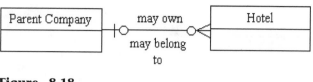

Figure 8-18

is described by the Relationship that answers the question "What currency are we committed to buy as a result of this contract?" The Relationship also answers the question "What contracts do we have on this currency?"—but we tend to see this second direction as subordinate.

Independent Group

The second most common 1 to M makes both ends of the Relationship optional and therefore changes the character of the Relationship. In this case, neither Entity requires the other. Such a Relationship occurs when there is an independent group or an optional descriptor.

The Relationship in Figure 8-18 indicates a situation in which some group, a parent company in this case, can exist without any members. Furthermore, the potential members, hotels, can exist regardless of whether they belong to a group. The Relationship recognizes that a number of hotels may be grouped under one parent: a parent company <u>may have none or many</u> HOTEL. For example, Dynamite Tours established an agreement with Hilton's parent company in 1988 for reduced rates and simplified arrangements at all Hilton Hotels worldwide. This Relationship makes it possible for Dynamite Tours to store the contract one time with the parent company, Hilton, and to pass it down to the individual Hilton Hotels. It also allows Dynamite Tours to summarize total expenditures for all Hilton Hotels. On the other hand, not all destinations of Dynamite Tours have Hilton Hotels. Many use independent operators with no parent company. Therefore, a hotel <u>may have none or one</u> PARENT COMPANY.

Tip for Project Managers

This relationship assumes that if a hotel is sold by Hilton, the business we gave that hotel is no longer associated with Hilton. A report of "Total Hilton Business" before the sale will show different totals for the same time period, an event sure to bring howls from the accounting department. The same kind of thing will happen if Hilton buys a hotel.

This example highlights a common dilemma. Does an information system record things as they were when the report was printed, as they are now, or as they should have been? We can model for any and all of these Predicates. A good manager will be sure everyone knows the limitations of each approach and the costliness of trying to do everything.

Optional Descriptor

Figure 8-19 illustrates the following Relationship: a sales agent <u>may sell none or many</u> RESERVATION; a reservation <u>may be sold by</u> SALES AGENT. For example, sales agent 99 sells a trip to Bora-Bora. In this case, a pairing of the Relationship would exist to describe the reservation to Bora-Bora as having been sold by a sales agent, 99. In a different situation, a customer uses the Internet to make her own reservation. In this second case, there is no sales agent, and the Relationship is not used.

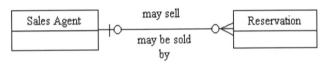

Figure 8-19

Tip for System Analysts

The example in Figure 8-19 demonstrates the essence of optionality. In any specific instance, a reservation may or may not involve a sales agent. You might want to distinguish between a Class of reservations made in-house and a Class made by sales agents, thus making the Relationship mandatory for the latter type of reservation and impossible for the former. Generally, this is a good direction for your analysis to take; however, when the only distinguishing characteristic between two Classes is a single Predicate, then there is little to be gained relative to just having the optional Relationship.

Some would make the Relationship mandatory by insisting on setting up a dummy sales agent for in-house sales or setting up some fictitious in-house sales department. This argument is completely crazy. To the computer, sales agent 9999 is no different from sales agent (blank). I feel myself being sucked into the black hole of a discussion over null values and so will simply turn away. The great fear is not that programmers are going to write commission checks to a dummy sales agent but rather that they

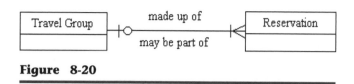

Figure 8-20

would just code around it all the time: "If sales agent is 9999, then skip to...." This kind of inventiveness is the antithesis of Data Modeling.

Dependent Group

The next most common 1 to M Relationship functions as a group defined by its members; it could be called a dependent group. If the group has no members, then the group ceases to exist.

Figure 8-20 indicates that

- Reservations may be grouped.

- A travel group cannot exist without reservations.

- A reservation belongs to only one travel group.

- A reservation may be associated with no group at all.

This kind of Relationship is fairly unusual. Use it when you want to treat a number of Entities in the same way for some process, but the group has no meaning beyond binding the individual Entities together. In this case, Mom and Dad are taking the kids to Antarctica. Each individual has his or her own reservation, but when Mom calls up to make a change, you make the same change for all the members of the family. If all the members of the family cancel, the group is dissolved.

So far as this example of the airline reservation goes, many analysts would set this up as a unary (or involuted) Relationship rather than having a new Class for the group. The Class, TRAVEL GROUP, more accurately reflects the business because it is independent of any particular member. Any member can drop out of the group without forcing the Relationship pairings to change. In a unary (or reflexive) Relationship, one member of the group would have to be head honcho. If that person were to drop out, the group would disband.

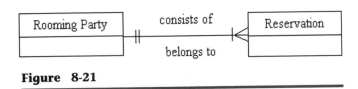

Figure 8-21

Mutually Dependent Group

The least common 1 to M Relationship makes both Entities required. In familial terms, now parent and child are co-dependent. This type of Relationship is unusual, is probably indicative of an error, and should be questioned when you find it in a data model. The Relationship illustrated in Figure 8-21 is plausible.

The Rooming Party/Reservation Relationship means two things: each member must belong to only one group, and a group cannot exist without members. For example, assume that the owner of the information system is a tour operator specializing in shuttling wealthy persons around the world. Because of a history of gigolos and gold diggers making trouble on tours, the tour company has instituted a couples-only policy. That is, you may take one of the tours only if you are accompanied by a friend or spouse.

You won't see many circumstances when this Relationship is needed. It is used when a number of Entities are treated the same way for some process, but the group has no meaning beyond binding the individual Entities together. That explains why there must be at least one Reservation. What makes it rare is that at the same time there is some reason why a member must belong to a group.

M to M Relationships

The M to M Relationship is an idea that is a bit awkward to define but easy to see by example. Teenagers are masters of M to M Relationships: "She went out with who!?" You work with M to M all the time; it's nothing new to you, just a new term to describe something very familiar. An M to M Relationship is one in which the Entity being described is free to associate with any number of Entities of the describing Class and vice versa. I could spend 1,000 words trying to clarify that, or you could just look at a spreadsheet. A spreadsheet or a table (columns and rows) is a common way to present information that is structured as an M to M Relationship. You may read a spreadsheet across a row, studying the values for each of the columns. A row can have a value for any column. You may read a spreadsheet down a column, studying the values for each of the rows. A column may have a value for many rows. A spreadsheet is a natural representation for a binary, M to M Relationship. The following is an example of a spreadsheet showing the kind of data that typifies the M to M Relationship:

Person	Data Whse	Accts Rec	Year 10,000 Project
William	25%	25%	50%
Patricia	10%		90%
Mamhood			100%

Could this spreadsheet be rotated 90 degrees, that is, make the rows column headings and the column headings rows? Would it still seem natural?

Project	William	Patricia	Mamhood
Data Whse	25%	10%	
Accts Rec	25%		
Year 10,000 Project	50%	90%	100%

The difference between the two spreadsheets is purely one of personal preference or perhaps perspective. The information is exactly the same. When the spreadsheet is representing an M to M Relationship, then the name of each row is some Entity and the title of each column is another Entity. It doesn't matter which Entity is which.

What do the values in the cells represent? You cannot tell just by looking at the individual cell; when we put together spreadsheets like this one, we assume that the name of the Predicate that is the cell is the same for every cell. The name of that Predicate would be placed at the top of the spreadsheet, in this case "Percent of actual hours billed—by project and by consultant."

Hacking an M to M in Two

An M to M Relationship can be shown as two 1 to M Relationships with a new Class tying everything together. This is common practice, but I assure you that it is not good practice. Way back in the dawn of CASE tools somebody reduced the programming budget by forcing analysts to enter M to M Relationships as two 1 to M Relationships. The CASE software could already put Predicates on Classes, but it was not programmed to put Predicates on another Predicate such as in an M to M Relationship. This work-around practice of showing binary and n-ary Relationships as Classes has become so standard that most analysts think it is supposed to be this way.

This hacked-up diagram only becomes necessary when there are Predicates that belong to the Relationship itself rather than either one of the Classes (and when your CASE tool has no way of putting Predicates on a Relationship). In this circumstance, the Predicates are associated with the new Class.

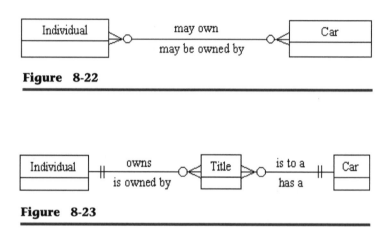

Figure 8-22

Figure 8-23

The original M to M Relationship between cars and individuals shown in Figure 8-22 defines an interaction between things in the real world and so makes sense to us. Notice that when the M to M Relationship is hacked into two 1 to M Relationships, as shown in Figure 8-23, the sense of the original Relationship is lost. The new Class and the two new Relationships are difficult to name. That there are now two Relationships is deceptive because they are not independent of each other; if you delete one without deleting both, the resulting diagram is probably no longer accurate.

Tip for System Analysts

An M to M Relationship is very much like an Attribute that is not in its first normal form. For example, if the project determined that INDIVIDUAL would not be considered a Class, then the Class CAR would have an Attribute <u>owner</u>. The Attribute would repeat since there could be more than one owner.

The same situation works from the perspective of the individual. If the project determined not to have a Class CAR but instead to have an Attribute <u>cars owned</u> for the Class INDIVIDUAL, then <u>cars owned</u> would repeat.

The solution for getting an Entity to first normal form and the solution for resolving M to M Relationships are essentially the same: create a new Entity. When you normalize a repeating Attribute, you get a new Entity whose unique identifier is the same as the original Entity. The repeating Attribute is plucked out of the original Entity and plopped into the new Entity. The original and new Entities are related as a 1 to M; what was a repeating Attribute is now a single Relationship with a many cardinality. In the same way, when you resolve an M to M Relationship, you get a new Entity whose key is made up of the key of the described Entity repeated as necessary and a Predicate that happens to be the key of the describing Entity.

Tip for Project Managers

Some analysts insist that all the M to M Relationships be resolved into two 1 to M Relationships with a new Entity in the middle tying everything together. I suggest that the M to M stay until the analyst can add to the new Entity some new Predicates. Most of these new Entities will find Predicates of their own and be broken into separate Classes. In the meantime, you can enjoy a simpler data model that is easier for everybody to read.

Examples of M to M Relationships

There are three types of M to M Relationships. Far and away, the most common is the M to M in which the Entities are independent of each other. The other two types of M to M are much less common. The partially dependent M to M, in which one Entity is independent of the second Entity but the second can only exist if it is related to the independent Entity, is rare. The mutually dependent M to M, in which both ends are required, is almost non-existent. Whenever either of these types is seen in a data model, question it.

Examples of common M to M Relationships follow.

Fully Independent

In this Relationship, both ends of the Relationship are optional; either Entity may exist without the other. Three scenarios in which this M to M Relationship apply include

- Bills of Materials
- Records of Events, especially Contracts or Agreements
- Assignments or Allocations

Bills of Materials

An M to M Relationship can describe a structure such as the various steps taken to make a part or what parts make up a kit. Common examples of descriptive M to M Relationships include a distributor is authorized to sell many PARTS; a part may be acquired from many VENDOR; a customer has interest in many PRODUCT; a product has many PROSPECT; a part requires many ROUTING STEP; a routing step may be used by many PART; and a part is made up of other PART and vice versa. (Editor's note: Can we stop now?)

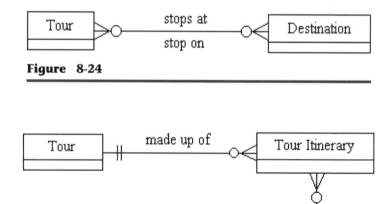

Figure 8-24

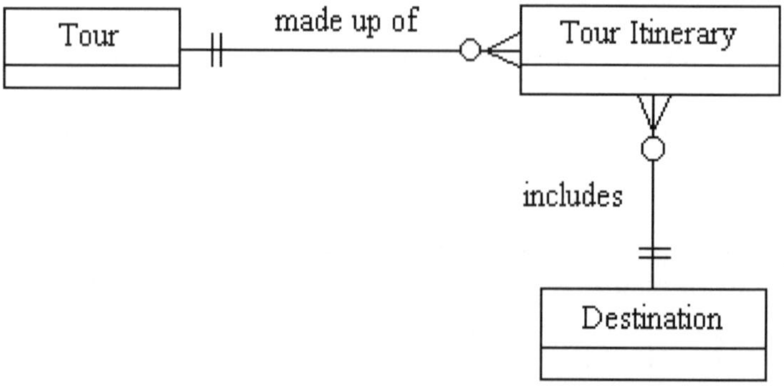

Figure 8-25

Figure 8-24 reflects the circumstance in which a tour is made up of destinations in the same way an assembly is made up of subassemblies. We can hack apart the M to M Relationship into two 1 to M Relationships, as shown in Figure 8-25. In this case, the new Class and the new Relationships make sense to the business persons. The new Class is their tour itinerary, a document central to their operations.

Records of Events

When we think of data, we think first of static things such as inventory or customers. (Editor's note: What a bizarre idea. He should get out of systems work. Who thinks of data but an analyst? If he were a ditch-digger, at least he could explain to his friends what he did all day and tell funny stories about silly things that happened. If he were a people analyst, then he would have these great secrets that everyone would try to pry out of him.) Okay, imagine some data. What jumps to mind? A product catalog? A name and address file? These concrete things are evidence of Classes, but the critical data is more often the things that happen, such as sales. Events such as "Analyst buys self-help book" are represented as M to M Relationships, because when the analyst picks up a copy of *Secrets of Intimacy,* he probably can't resist *Secrets of the 68000 Processor* and *An Intimate Guide to OS/2.* It is a safe bet that many such analysts picked up copies of *Secrets of the 68000 Processor.* However, some analysts will not seek help at all. (Editor's note: If you ask me, no one would read *Secrets of the 68000 Processor.*) The analyst <u>may buy zero to many</u> BOOK; a book <u>may be bought by zero or many</u> ANALYST.

For transaction-processing or real-time systems, these Relationships are the linchpins that connect everything else in the data model. I sometimes visualize the events as the spark between two conductors. Capturing data in these Relationships is the reason all the other Entities exist. There would be no reason to track customers if they never bought anything. There would be no reason to track inventory if none of it ever sold. Sales and the other side of the coin, purchases, are the most common examples of these kinds of M to M Relationships.

Tip for Project Managers

Further examples of events that drive Relationships include "salesperson calls prospect" and "customer buys item." Even remotely possible events such as "analyst reads book" would be an M to M Relationship. For every Relationship of this type, you should have identified at least one external

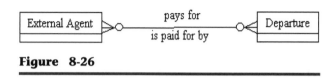

Figure 8-26

event. Every external event will be recorded with at least one Relationship of this type. Use this as a check of the process model.

The example given in Figure 8-26 represents the sale of some DEPAR-TURE (a tour) to somebody. As is typical of sales events, a lot of Predicates are hiding inside that M to M Relationship. I think rather than my crude language of hacking Relationships apart, it would be more meaningful in this case to talk about revealing the hidden Class. When modeling agreements with other parties, the hidden Class is a contract, in this case a Reservation, as shown in Figure 8-27. The Reservation is a promise by Dynamite Tours to provide passage on a departure to some EXTERNAL AGENT.

A couple of tangents relative to Figure 8-26 and Figure 8-27 are worthy of mention. First, why is there is no Class representing Dynamite Tours? And what is the unique identifier of a reservation? You would have a Class something to the effect of PARTY OF THE FIRST PART if you were modeling a circumstance in which it was not implied that all contracts were with the party owning the software. It is a simplification to not indicate a Class for the single Entity that represents the sponsor of the modeling effort. However, this simplification confuses the question regarding the unique identifier of a reservation. Since the reservation is an agreement between Dynamite Tours and some EXTERNAL AGENT entered into on some date, then it is sensible that the unique identifier would be a combination of Dynamite Tours, the Name of some EXTERNAL AGENT (e.g., Don Adams) and something, such as date, to distinguish the many agreements between the parties that might exist over time. The model would lead you to believe that the Name of the departure would be a part of the key, but the Relationship to some DEPARTURE answers the question, "You bought what?!" If I decide to go to Bora-Bora instead of Antarctica, and Dynamite Tours says it is okay; then we transfer the Relationship but we still have the same agreement. If on the other hand, you say that your wife was going to pay instead of yourself, I would respond either, "My agreement is with you; I

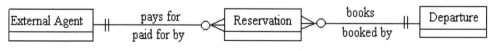

Figure   8-27

will bill you and you recover from your wife," or "I will have to get some-thing agreed to by your wife; until then I will not let you out of your obligations to our contract." The essence of a negotiation such as Reservation is the contract between some EXTERNAL AGENT and the system owner who is not shown.

Irrespective of whether the original idea of splitting an M to M Relationship was a programming work-around, when you put Predicates on a Relationship, the resulting data model object starts acting just like a Class. RESERVATION even has States, such as confirmed and completed.

Assignments or Allocations

Frequently the situation arises in which a resource is divided among a number of uses. For example, a sailor is assigned to a ship. In this case, the sailor may be assigned to only one ship at a time, but over time, that sailor may serve on many ships. Important Predicates of this Relationship would be <u>start date</u> and <u>end date</u>. Another example: an employee is assigned to several projects simultaneously. An important Predicate of this Relationship might be <u>percent of time dedicated</u>. Or another example: a traveler is assigned to a hotel room. In this case there may be no Attributes of the Relationship; only the assignment itself is important.

Consider the common event illustrated by Figure 8-28: "a receipt of money is allocated to payment for some goods or services rendered." This example is notable because the Class that would result from breaking apart the M to M is difficult to name inasmuch as it is not a common business document. The new 1 to M Relationships, as shown in Figure 8-29, are also awkward. As I mentioned before, this awkwardness is typical when M to M Relationships are divided this way.

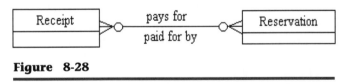

Figure   8-28

Figure   8-29

Figure 8-30

Partially Dependent

Sometimes an Entity must be described by at least one other Entity, but the describing Entity is independent of the described Entity.

The example in Figure 8-30 is taken from an experience with direct mail advertising. Individual prospects may receive no mail if they do not fit the characteristics of the target market. On the other hand, they may get buried by this mail if they ever once actually bought something. But a mail drop must have at least one letter, or it just isn't a mail drop.

Fully Dependent

This Relationship implies that if there is an Entity being described, there must be a describing Entity; moreover, the describing Entity can exist only so long as it describes something.

Here's the psychological profile of this Relationship: Pat joins a commune looking for meaning in his life. With someone from the commune, he feels good, although it doesn't seem to matter with whom. Curiously, the commune seems to need Pat too, or at least someone like Pat—why else would they have clonked him on the head and dragged him away from his six-figure job as a consultant? It is as though everyone feels like Pat, needing to be with somebody, anybody, to exist.

This Relationship is so demanding on the Entities that it becomes virtually non-existent. The example in Figure 8-31 is at least plausible. Consider a multi-national firm that moves its employees among various countries. The executives tell the analyst, "Each employee must be a citizen of some country; we also want to know if employees have dual citizenship and with which countries." Further, the executives inform the analysts, "We

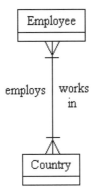

Figure 8-31

keep data only on countries in which we have employee citizens." In this case, any single employee justifies the existence of a country Entity. Once the country Entity exists, it can be related to many employees.

1 to 1 Relationships

1 to 1 Relationships are maligned, abused, forgotten; they are the underclass of the Data Modeling world. If they were a color, they would be hot pink. If they were a note, they would be discordant. If they were a piece of hardware, they would be the odd-shaped gadget that is just what you need but has to be ordered from Iceland.

A 1 to 1 Relationship is like a simple list. A wedding guest list is an example. The invitee is allowed one date; we could say, "A guest may bring one and only one date; a date must be accompanied by his or her one invited guest." Because 1 to 1 Relationships are restrictive, they tend to be more rare than other Relationships. They are essential and very powerful because they are specific.

Invitee	Date
Bob Thompson	Chris Short
Jaime Suarez	Ben Burreen
Justin Schmidt	Melissa Long
Kim Turkinian	George Kim

Tip for System Analysts

1 to 1 Relationships are maligned because some analysts are of the mistaken opinion that the Entities should be merged and the Relationship eliminated. However, something like the invitee list cannot be properly diagrammed without a 1 to 1 Relationship.

1 to 1 Relationships are abused when they are used to show a Class structure, such as "A car is a vehicle; a vehicle may be a car." This observation is necessary, but it is not a Relationship in the strict sense.

Examples of 1 to 1 Relationships

There are three kinds of 1 to 1 Relationships. None of these Relationships are very common; however, the mutually independent 1 to 1 is not so unusual. The familiar sign "Only one coupon per purchase" is an example. Whenever you see either of the other two types in a data model, question it.

Fully Independent

The promotion that Dynamite Tours runs to attract past travelers is a variation on the one-coupon-per-purchase theme. These past travelers can get certificates worth $300 if used within one year of their last date of travel. To avoid counterfeiting, Dynamite Tours numbers the certificates. As shown in Figure 8-32, passengers may use only one certificate per departure and must use the whole travel certificate on one trip. So we can say, "A travel certificate _may discount none_ (it's still in your drawer) _and only one_ RESERVATION; a reservation _may be discounted by none or one_ TRAVEL CERTIFICATE."

Only Child

The only child Relationship seldom occurs. You may, however, want to use it to improve the description of some situations. The example in

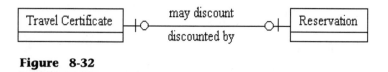

Figure 8-32

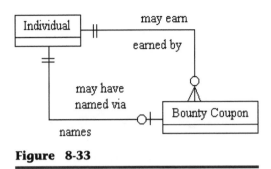

Figure 8-33

Figure 8-33 comes from a business practice designed to get the names of prospective customers.

Existing customers were offered a bounty for recommending their friends if those friends were not already active prospects. A customer could recommend any number of friends. For each recommendation, the customer received a certificate for a substantial discount if any recommended friend were ever to travel with Dynamite Tours. The diagram expresses the Relationships between an individual and the collected bounty coupons, and between the bounty coupons and the recommended individuals.

Mutually Dependent

Another rare example is the mutually dependent 1 to 1 Relationship. Think about a board game, such as the game of Monopoly. As the game is played, you move your token (the boot or the battleship or whatever) from place to place (Park Place, Broadway) around the perimeter of the board. The Relationship between places is a mutually dependent 1 to 1. Since the movement around the board is circular, every place must be followed by one other place, as shown in Figure 8-34; for example, New York Avenue is followed by Free Parking. (Is Kentucky Avenue next?) Anyway, I wouldn't waste your time with such a trivial example except to point out that anytime you have a sequence of Entities this approach is very useful. It is arguably better than the common practice of assigning a sequence number.

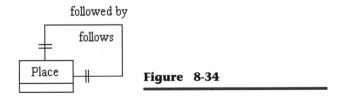

Figure 8-34

Before you begin to think that the example is not business-like, remember the travel itinerary in which one stop always follows another and always leads back to where you began.

Some may object to this Relationship being used, because in actual implementation the computer would not be able to validate any record until after all the records have been entered. This consideration is not legitimate when modeling data. The data model must show what Relationships are required for the data to be in a consistent state; later the computer wizards will have to choose a way to implement it.

A Phony Relationship

Sometimes a 1 to 1 Relationship is used to represent a Superclass. You will see this representation because historically CASE tools have not done a good job of documenting when a Class is a subset of another Class. When an analyst identifies a Class of Entities, for example EXTERNAL AGENT, and another Class, for example BANK, the analyst has no way of expressing the idea "A bank is an external agent." He or she may use a Relationship line to get this idea documented. The problem is that the use of a Relationship line introduces inconsistencies in the method because it does not describe as a standard Relationship describes; instead, it makes the statement "Entities of this Class are also Entities of this other Class." This statement is about set inclusion, not description. In Relationships, an Entity that is a member of one Class has a descriptive association with another Entity; in this case, Relationships should have nothing to do with generalization. There is only one Entity involved. The experienced analyst knows that these Relationships and/or Classes do not meet modeling principles. However, even experienced analysts can brainwash themselves looking at a Relationship style that evolved out of weaknesses of early CASE tools and deceive themselves about the nature of the Superclass.

Here's what you should have learned from studying about the concept of Relationships:

- A Relationship is a type of Predicate.
- A Relationship exists when there is reason to describe an Entity in terms of another Entity.
- Relationships imply something about all the Entities involved. That is, from the perspective of Entity A, Entity B is descriptive. From the perspective of b, a is descriptive. Each perspective is called a direction.
- A pairing or a Relationship membership is an instance of a Relationship, an individual fact as opposed to a kind of fact.
- Despite the term "pairing," a Relationship may involve only itself or any number of other Entities. The term "degree" describes the number of Entities involved in a Relationship.
- Like all Predicates, a Relationship must convey meaning rather than simply link Classes.
- Like all Predicates, the meaning of a Relationship is implied in its name.
- Like all Predicates, a Relationship may be such that pairings may not be altered once entered; when this is the case with a Relationship, we say that the Relationship is non-transferable.
- Like any Predicate, when an Entity is such that its Relationship may have no pairing, then that Relationship is said to be optional. Alternatively, if an Entity requires at least one pairing, it is said to be required. This is also called minimum cardinality.
- Like any Predicate, Relationships may evaluate to more than one pairing, in which case we say that the Relationship has a cardinality of many.
- Given the finite combinations of minimum and maximum cardinality, there are only ten possible types of Relationships.
- A Superclass is not a Relationship.

Attributes

Predicates describe things. Attributes are a special kind of Predicate that describes things according to some Domain. Common examples of Attributes are the <u>weight of a package</u>, the <u>distance to some destination</u>, and the <u>acidity of a solution</u>. How would you describe somebody? By her race? By her hair color? Height? Weight? <u>Race</u>, <u>hair color</u>, <u>height</u>, and <u>weight</u> are a few of the Attributes of a person. How would you describe a purchase order? By the ship date? Cost of materials? <u>Ship date</u> and <u>line item cost</u> would be Attributes of invoices.

You have probably done a research paper. You dig around libraries looking for references and write on index cards stuff that seems to fit. Late the last night, you finish the report. You re-read the professor's instructions and realize you need a "bibliography in good form." Scrambling, you also realize that when you were at the library, you didn't copy down the name of the publisher or the date of publication. At the time, you didn't know you needed that information. For each reference in your bibliography, you need a set of Attributes, such as <u>name of publisher</u> and <u>date of publication</u>. Knowing what you need to know is the key to designing an information system. Students are expected to make this mistake, but we can see how easy it would have been to create the bibliography if you had gone to the

library with a form indicating all the data you needed about each reference. The problems of trying to complete the bibliography are very similar
to the last-minute problems we encounter with information systems when
we haven't accounted for all the Attributes we need.

What Is an Attribute?

Words that stand for Attributes can be used to complete the sentence
"What is its...?" So, for instance, the question "What is its altitude?" indicates that whatever it is, it gets off the earth—it can be described in terms
of its position above the ground.

Take a look at the following table:

Which of the words in this column could be used to complete the sentence "What is its...?"	Does this word indicate an Attribute?
Temperature	Attribute
Hot	
Altitude	Attribute
Fly	
Status	Attribute
Closed	
Velocity	Attribute
Car	
July	
Date	Attribute
Color	Attribute
Blue	

Based on what you know about Predicates and what you can observe
from the table, which statement is most true of Attributes?

a.   An Attribute is a fact we know about something.
b.   An Attribute is an adjective.
c.   An Attribute is something knowable about something.

An Attribute is not a fact we know about something. Recording individual facts (or values) about something is the job of the data entry clerk. Figuring out what type of facts are to be recorded is your job.

Someone once pointed out that the difference between computers and humans is that humans know what they don't know. Ask a computer what is the altitude of an invoice, and the computer will look to see if it has that information. If some joker has indicated the altitude of an invoice, then the computer would swear to it in court. The human will answer with something sarcastic like, "Your bills are sky-high; get out of my office." Humans know that the literal altitude of an invoice is irrelevant, so irrelevant that it becomes ridiculous. Moral: Be careful what you tell a computer.

An Attribute is not an adjective; it is a noun. The values that are attributed to something are often adjectives. That is, Domains—not Attributes— can be a collection of adjectives. In the preceding table, <u>temperature</u> is a noun and an Attribute. Hot is an adjective but is a member of a Domain. Note also that not all the values attributed to something are adjectives. For instance, replace the word hot with 100° Celsius; 100° Celsius is not an adjective.

An Attribute is something knowable about something. People know facts about things; a person who knows a lot of facts is great to have on your team in a parlor game. The thing that distinguishes a person from a book is that the person also knows what they can know about something. That is, we can identify the characteristics of something. When you complete the question "What is its...?" you complete it with a word standing for some characteristic of something that can be known. For instance, temperature is a characteristic of a patient, or of an engine, or of a vat of chemicals. <u>Temperature</u> is an Attribute of patients, engines, and chemical reactions.

An Attribute is any property, quality, or characteristic ascribed to a person or thing.

People innately know not only what Attributes a thing has but also which of those Attributes are relevant to the current situation. I once used the weight of a coupon as an example of an irrelevant Attribute. The analyst from Kellogg's told me, "You obviously don't mail millions of them each year." If I had to sum the weight of all the components of a direct mail piece to be sure it didn't cost too much to mail, then I would care about the weight, and <u>weight</u> would then be an Attribute of a coupon. We know <u>altitude</u> is relevant to the jet, not the engine, and that <u>temperature</u> is relevant to the engine or separately to the cabin. We know that <u>temperature</u> of the patient is different from <u>temperature</u> of the engine.

Attributes and Entities

We understand things through their Attributes. A question such as "What is the eye's?" begs the response "What is the eye's what?" We learn about things by asking about their Attributes. An Entity without any Attributes is unknowable and, so far as information systems go, is not an Entity. And on the other hand, as with any Predicate, an Attribute is just not an Attribute unless it describes some thing.

Getting system owners to volunteer any number of things that they want the computer to record is no problem. Attributes jump out at analysts like locusts. Pressed for time and confronted with hundreds, sometimes thousands, of Attributes, analysts can be overwhelmed. It is common to mistake the Entity that is being described by an Attribute; consider price. On first glance, a product has a price. If the analyst asked, "Do we always charge the same price for a product?" then the analyst might have been surprised to find that price may be a function of customer, or customer type, or day of the week. Discovering the Attribute is never enough; you must know what that Attribute describes.

Attributes by themselves are meaningless. Try dropping the Entity from a phrase, for example, "What is the color?" The question begs the response "What is what's color?" It's like the old gag:

> **Curly:** I've the answers to all your questions.
>
> **Moe:** Oh yeah? Give them to me.
>
> **Curly:** Yes, no, and maybe.

In this scene Curly exploits the fact that the answers to all of Moe's questions are of the Domain "Yes, No, Maybe." Curly's response to Moe is a non-answer answer. Divorced from the context of an Entity, Curly's response is useless. Moral: Attributes are understood only in the context of the associated Entity.

Tip for Project Managers

Moe's understandable response is to try to gouge out Curly's eyes with his index and middle fingers. Curly responds with a kind of salute turned on edge, further frustrating Moe, who is clearly at some intellectual disadvantage in this conflict. Certainly, both Moe and Curly need to take a few days away from the project.

Attributes and Domains

Attributes are associated with a Domain; Relationships get their values from Classes; but whichever Predicate you are working with, you have to establish what kind of answer is expected. This is because computers are stupid as sticks. Computers can handle a multiple-choice question, but ask an essay question and they'd need an athletic waiver. If we were dealing with some real intelligence, a wide range of responses would be possible to any question. My <u>bowling average</u> is a miserable 65; "65" is the value of the Attribute. Let's compare a computer to a bowling buddy.

Computer:	Enter bowling average.
Me:	Miserable.
Computer:	Enter bowling average.

If I don't enter a number in the Domain of BOWLING SCORES, the computer just doesn't get it.

Bowling Buddy:	What's your average these days?
Me:	65.
Bowling Buddy:	Wanna go get a donut?

An Attribute poses a question in the form "What is its ___?" When dealing with computers, the value provided an Attribute has to be selected from a single Domain. The Attribute plus some value from the Domain is a fact about some Entity. The Attribute <u>current temperature</u> could be evaluated by the Domain DEGREES CELSIUS. A fact might be that the jet's <u>current temperature</u> is 100° Celsius.

Who decided that <u>engine temperature</u> is associated with the Domain DEGREES CELSIUS? The people who will use the information decided it. They could have chosen any sensible Domain, for example DEGREES FAHRENHEIT. But once decided, <u>engine temperature</u> is always measured in the same Domain; otherwise, the data would be a mess.

Although an Attribute relies on a single Domain, a single Domain can be associated with many Attributes. The Domain TEMPERATURE is associated with the Attributes <u>high temperature</u> and <u>last temperature</u>. The fact that Domains stretch across many Attributes is useful because we know that the Attributes of the same Domain are logically comparable or arithmetically compatible. For instance, a software program knows that it is logical to subtract the <u>last temperature</u> from the <u>high temperature</u> to calculate a <u>temperature change</u>.

Every Attribute has to be framed as some kind of multiple-choice question; that is, the set of possible answers has to be established. For each Attribute, identify the Domain you mean to use.

Description Is Not an Attribute

Take a complex question such as "Is the customer credit worthy?" Whereas a loan committee looks at the individual circumstances, the computer needs a hard-and-fast Domain such as "yes or no." Even sophisticated decision support systems are simply algorithms built on top of a number of Attributes, each with its own fixed Domain. Even if a loan committee were to type a lengthy rationale into the computer, the computer could do little with it besides type it back out.

Analysts will almost immediately imagine a Predicate called "Description." Supposed Predicates such as "notes, comments, description" are the antithesis of a thought-out data requirement. An Attribute like description is what we do when we can't think of what else to do. Figure 9-1 shows how free text is typically used in an information system. Note how this free text is largely useless.

Figure   9-1

The complete text reads: "Ms. Smith has asked for a single room and a cabin with an attached bath. If it is available, she would like a cabin on the lower deck amidships (she tends toward seasickness), port (for a view of the glaciers, you know), and no paislies on the bedding!" The data found in the comments can be reworked to make it more usable. Once reworked, as shown in Figure 9-2, the information makes it practical to list everyone

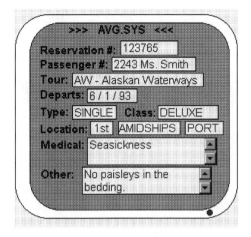

Figure   9-2

requesting DELUXE accommodations or wanting a room on the starboard side of the vessel.

The type of response to a question can be more or less fixed. The ship's physician may state that it would not be practical to classify all the kinds of medical alerts he or she would like to see. In that case, it may not be possible to set up a fixed list of values; instead, the Domain would be MEDICAL INFORMATION. Although it is not fixed, this information may be more easily directed to the ship's physician than were it still buried inside comments. Is MEDICAL INFORMATION a Domain? Just because a computer cannot validate it against a table or by reference to some range of values, it is still a Domain. Think of this: if you put "no paislies" in the medical record, then the doctor would complain that the data was corrupt; "no paislies" does not fit into the doctor's conception of the kind of values that answer the question "What is the passenger's medical condition?" Why would you assume that if the computer cannot validate it, that it is not a Domain? The computer does not define the structure of language. The question is whether our minds discriminate valid responses to the question, as we can with MEDICAL INFORMATION.

We can make only the barest discrimination with comments. Free text is a necessary evil; whether it is or is not a Domain gets to be an academic question. The fact that I know gibberish from a comment may be enough to convince you that there is a Domain for comments. Free text is its own information system with Entities and Domains imbedded in it! The mother of all description fields is the World Wide Web. A search for education in Data Modeling is more likely to yield model train enthusiasts than data modellers [sic] in London. Clearly, the more predictable the set of responses, the more suited the data is for automated processing. You must peel out the Attributes that are buried in comment fields. Reserve the use of free text for forms of data that could not be anticipated and will not be used to control processing.

Tip for Project Managers

Avoid fields with names such as comments, description, or notes. These do nothing but eat up time during analysis. These so-called Attributes are the refuge of slackers and pretenders who believe that once an Attribute named comment has been associated to a Class, then they have become embarrassment-proof. No Predicate suggested by an owner could ever be missing from these analysts' data model. If a system owner were to say, "Can I enter data about the passenger's luggage?" they can answer, "No problem, we'll put it in the Comments." "Can I enter information about the customer's dining preferences?" "No problemo, just put it in the notes." Eventually, your project will produce an information system with varying degrees of uselessness.

Consider a standard that omits such fields until Design. During the process of designing a database, a standard way of working with free text can be hammered out in one meeting and applied to the entire model at once.

Consistent Precision

Attributes have a consistent precision. Consider the example table below. Is it correct? Is it misleading? Can it be correct and misleading?

Sales Figures to the Nearest Thousand (except where noted)
15,000
23,000
45,000
24,124 ***
12,000
98,000
$217,124 total

It is correct plus or minus a thousand, but the final figure implies that it is correct to the nearest whole number. It might seem more correct if you get as much precision as you can into each number, but like the weak link in a chain, the result will be only as precise as the least of your measurements. Generally, circumstances will dictate how precise you can or want to be. Perhaps it is a limitation of the device, or it is custom. For example, automatic teller machines do not dispense coins, and many stock markets measure in 1/8 dollar increments.

Tip for System Analysts

I have engaged in a number of discussions as to whether precision is a characteristic of Domains rather than Attributes. I believe there are layers of abstraction in the meta-model not discussed in this text so that the answer may lie somewhere in between. I choose to keep precision out of the concept of Domains in order to focus on the meaning conveyed by Domains and to avoid comparison to picture or format statements used in programming.

Multiple Choices

Every Attribute, in fact any Predicate, is like a multiple-choice question. When the computer system requires something such as <u>weight</u>, it is looking for an answer from a list of choices, a Domain. The question is answered when you provide a value such as "170 lbs."

I would love to launch into another tirade about the profound ignorance of the computer, but this part of my discussion is about something the computer can do. The computer is limited to multiple choice, but it can compute a pick-all-that-apply type of response—provided you tell the computer ahead of time that more than one answer is allowed.

When might this situation arise? Consider a customer survey:

Which of your destination cities would you like to return to?

(Mark all that apply.)

—	London
<u>X</u>	Dresden
—	Paris
<u>X</u>	Barcelona

The usual technique used to document the fact that an Attribute may have more than one value is to use the CASE tool to draw a separate Class just for those Attributes. This new object is related to the Class they actually describe in a highly dependent way; that is, the values of the Attributes in this new Class are meaningful only when understood in the context of the original Class. This new Class is called an attributive Class. A data model with all the repeating Attributes separated from the Class to which they are functionally dependent is said to be in First Normal Form.

Figure 9-3 demonstrates the technique: CHOICE, SELECT ALL is the attributive Class. Each allowed destination city—London, Dresden, Paris, Barcelona—would be its own Entity in the attributive Class.

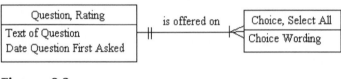

Figure   9-3

The first example (Figure 9-3) is a simple case of an Attribute that has more than one value. There is no other data about each of the choices to complicate matters. But what if the question had been a different one? For example:

Rank your destination cities.

(Mark each on a scale of 1–5.)

1	London
3	Dresden
4	Paris
2	Barcelona

Figure 9-4 demonstrates this more complicated case. The Attribute choice wording may still have four values, but additionally each value is complicated by a sequence. For example, London is first on the list; careful statisticians will tell you that position on the list is significant when weighing responses. These Attributes must be kept in their proper pairs to retain their meaning. The attributive Class can be used to document the way the

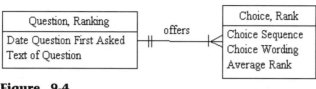

Figure   9-4

Predicates are dependent one on the other for meaning. This is another case of a Predicate having a Predicate.

Tip for Project Managers

You may be pressed to set up a standard that your data model be in First Normal Form. There are three universally accepted normal forms named First, Second, and Third. There are others—Fourth and so on—but they are not widely understood or even necessarily accepted as correct. The first three are considered fundamental; the remainder are almost derided. Despite the implication of the numeric names, an Attribute can be in Second and Third Normal Form and still have parts that are not in First Normal Form.

First Normal Form means that any multi-valued Attributes, such as those discussed here, have been set aside in their own Class. If you can wait to create these new Classes until after Analysis, you will certainly make the data model easier to read.

Three Types of Attributes

There are three types of Attributes: Elemental, Composite, and Derived.

Tip for System Analysts

Some texts would include a fourth type, Designed or Contrived Attributes. They are designed or invented to be simple handles for managing Entities. A Designed Attribute is a label intended to distinguish an Entity from all other Entities of a given Class. Despite being called an Attribute, a Designed Attribute is not a Predicate at all. This distinction is more than academic since, Designed Attributes may not act like Attributes, either: for instance, a designed Attribute cannot be the only Attribute of an Entity. An example would be a UPC code or a customer number. Designed Attributes are stand-ins for other Attributes. They do not describe anything; they can lead us to a description, but the code itself is not descriptive. Knowing that

I live in zip code 63112 tells you nothing about the area in which I live. You could find out a lot about the area by looking up 63112 in a reference.

Predicates are functionally dependent on an identifier. These Designed Attributes are not dependent on an identifier; it would be circular to suggest that they were. The key is a different part of an information system from the information it helps you to find.

Elemental Attributes

The most important Attributes are the Elemental Attributes. Most of the examples you have seen in this text so far have been of this type. In fact, in studying an information system, you need only to identify Elemental Attributes; the other types can come later. You cannot have an information system without Elemental Attributes.

One of the things that computers simply cannot do is to determine how to describe something. People have to determine what Attributes are appropriate. Attributes cannot be spontaneously generated within the system.

The values that Attributes take on come from somewhere. Often, system owners want systems to have data that you just cannot get. A bomb threat log requests <u>weight of the caller</u>. Great data, but how are you going to get it? The values ascribed to Elemental Attributes must be directly sensed from the world outside the information system. The sensors may be people, or they may be devices, such as temperature gauges.

Composite and Derived Attributes are made up of other, ultimately Elemental, Attributes. Composite Attributes string other Attributes together like beads. Derived Attributes combine other Attributes in mathematical or logical formulas. These types of Attributes can save time and improve the presentation of your information model. An example of a Composite Attribute is <u>customer address</u>. An example of a Derived Attribute is <u>total customer receivables</u>. Caution: these Attributes will cause problems if their component Elemental Attributes are not defined. Because Elemental Attributes are so important, I will resume further discussion about as well as practice with Elemental Attributes later in this section.

Composite Attributes

Composite Attributes are made up of other Attributes. The values of Composite Attributes are combinations of the values of other Attributes. Composite Attributes describe Entities in the same way as Elemental Attributes.

Indeed, Composite Attributes carry little more information about the data than do the Elemental Attributes that make them up.

Composite Attributes are conveniences intended to reduce the effort of tracking and referring to individual Attributes, and to simplify presentations. For example, it is simpler to refer to a <u>customer's location</u> instead of listing all of the Elemental Attributes that make up a location, such as <u>street address</u>, <u>city</u>, <u>state</u>, and <u>postal code</u>.

Somewhere in the analysis you should break down a Composite Attribute into its components. Combining elements to create a Composite Attribute is easier than counting on splitting them up later. For (an extreme) example, consider a hotel management system and hotel room number. The first digit signifies the floor the room is on. You should consider having two Attributes, <u>floor number</u> and <u>room number</u>. It sounds silly until you need to program a report of all rooms underneath room 2222. Recomposing an Attribute is much easier than decomposing one.

Derived Attributes

The value of a Derived Attribute is given based on logical or arithmetic operations using data from within the information system. Derived Attributes are a convenience to avoid having to show the entire formula for every calculated Attribute referenced in the system. An example of a Derived Attribute is <u>total sales for the quarter</u>, which is defined as the sum of all <u>sales amounts</u> excluding <u>sales taxes</u> for the quarter in which the current month falls. Since a Derived Attribute involves combining Elemental Attributes in a particular order with logical and arithmetical operands, the Derived Attribute has more information about data than is contained in the Elemental Attributes by themselves.

Tip for System Analysts

Composite and Derived Attributes do not necessarily become fields in files. In fact, the rule should be not to have a field for such Attributes. You should calculate the value of the Attribute only as needed.

The best reason to calculate just-in-time is that it is easier to program and less likely to be wrong. The value of each composite and derived field has to be changed every time the value of one of the component Elemental Attributes changes.

The decision to calculate in advance cannot be made until you can make a case based on all the ways the Attribute will be used by programs. Since during Analysis you cannot know all the ways an Attribute will be used, then this is the job of designers, and the decision should not be made until after the analysis phase is complete.

The convenience of Derived Attributes can be seen when you consider another example, <u>difference between actual and projected sales</u>. If you were never to use Derived Attributes, then some of your equations would be quite long and difficult to follow, for example, sum of all <u>sales amounts</u> excluding <u>sales taxes</u> for the quarter in which the current month falls less <u>projected sales</u> for the same quarter. Using Derived Attributes, your formula can build on earlier formulas: <u>total sales</u> for the quarter minus <u>projected sales</u> for the same quarter. Not only do the Derived Attributes make your formula shorter, but also consider what happens if the formula for <u>total sales</u> changed. If you did not use Derived Attributes, you would then have to browse your entire data model to correct the <u>total sales</u> formula everywhere it had been replicated.

Attributes may also be derived from rules as well as from simple mathematics. For example, a Frequent Flyer Program might have a rule such as "If the customer has more than 50,000 miles accumulated, then the Customer is a VIP." The Class CUSTOMER could have a Derived Attribute <u>VIP</u>, the derivation of which is based on this rule.

Derived Attributes can save considerable effort and can also lead to more consistent use of information. In the examples above, the question of including sales tax in sales figures has been resolved at the level of <u>total sales</u>. This encourages others to do the same when totaling sales. The second example, the VIP rule, is kept in just one place. Now when the big boss decides "What the heck. We'll make it 50,000 miles if earned during our fiscal year," you can make the change in one place and effect the change everywhere.

You must document the formula or rule for any Derived Attribute. If your formula refers to another Derived Attribute, be sure that formula is also documented. Ultimately, you must be able to expand a formula such that only Elemental Attributes are referenced.

Tip for Project Managers

Because people break this rule every time, someone is bound to suggest, "We should have a standard so that nobody can set up Derived Attributes!" This is simply not going to stick. Do make it a point to verify that all Derived Attributes are supported with a formula and that ultimately all Derived Attributes are based on Elemental Attributes.

Others will spend hours talking about the pros and cons of Derived Attributes as they relate to programming efficiency and response time, because these issues are easier to discuss than real models are to build. Do not worry about whether or not Derived Attributes are fields in files or whether they will be in-line code, function calls, or objects until the design phase. You know that if you blow your budget here, there won't be any design phase.

More on Elemental Attributes

An Elemental Attribute is an indivisible Attribute whose value relates to something in the world outside of the computer system. One way of defining an Elemental Attribute is in terms of what it is not. An Elemental Attribute cannot be a Composite Attribute because a Composite Attribute can be divided into simpler Elemental Attributes. For the same reason, an Elemental Attribute cannot be a Derived Attribute because a Derived Attribute is the result of combining Elemental Attributes in a rule or formula.

So an Attribute that is not composed of other Attributes and is evaluated outside the information system is an Elemental Attribute. An example of an Elemental Attribute would be your <u>height</u> or your <u>weight</u>. I cannot take apart your weight to find discrete Attributes. I cannot determine your weight except to ask you to weigh yourself.

Elemental Attributes are the building blocks of the information system. They are sometimes called atomic because they are the smallest pieces of data about an Entity and because all other information is made up of Elemental Attributes. Keep splitting Attributes until you discover the atomic level. For instance, an address can be subdivided into a <u>street address</u>, <u>city</u>, <u>state</u>, <u>country</u>, and <u>postal code</u>. Be ruthless with this rule; it really can't hurt. It can get ridiculous, but ridiculous depends on the application. Most people would not split address into <u>street number</u>, <u>street name</u>, <u>apartment number</u>, and so on; however, if you intended to verify street addresses, it would not seem so ridiculous.

There are a number of reasons for such hair-splitting. The first is discovery. For instance, if you look at an address as a lump all the time, it might slip by you that foreign addresses use a different postal code. The second reason is to maintain flexibility in the data model. Elemental Attributes can always be recombined without losing any detail or specificity. Composite or Derived Attributes, on the other hand, are convenient in many cases but cannot be used in every case. For example, the Composite Attribute <u>customer's address</u> makes the statement "Print the customer's address on mailing labels" very succinct; however, <u>customer's address</u> is no help if you need to express the idea "Print all customers who live in apartments." To get a list of all customers who live in apartments, you need to refer to the Elemental Attribute <u>apartment number</u>.

Practice: Finding Elemental Attributes in the Mail

When I was a yard man, I couldn't go by a lawn without making mental note about whether it needed a trim. Now that I am an analyst, I can't look at anything without trying to figure out what the Predicates are—yet another occupational hazard. Take, for example, this coupon I got in the mail (see Figure 9-5).

This **COUPON** entitles
The Bearer to
15% off
Everything in our store!

Coupon type A — expires 12/31/98

Figure   9-5

Is discount percent an Elemental Attribute of the coupon?

Yes, the <u>amount of the discount</u> given for use of the coupon is an important Elemental Attribute. It tells the sales clerk how much to discount the purchase. The amount cannot be calculated; presumably the inscrutable sales department divines the percentage; the information system cannot spontaneously generate it.

Would the coupon information system require a "yes/no" expired flag?

The idea of a coupon being expired is based on the business rule "If today's date is later than the coupon's expiration date, then the coupon is no good." So the flag expired with a "yes/no" Domain is actually a Derived Attribute based on the rule given above. The Elemental Attribute that you need to capture is <u>expiration date</u>. In fact, an expired flag by itself would be trouble. Attributing the coupon with a simple "yes/no" makes the computer stupider than it already is. First of all, the computer has to wait around for someone to tell it that the coupon has now expired. Second, the computer doesn't have any way of informing anyone of when the coupon expired or when it might expire in the future.

Is weight an Elemental Attribute of the coupon?

Initially I offered weight as a possibility to help you distinguish between Attributes that are true of a thing but not important to the business. For example, the weight of the coupon would not be an Attribute if you were considering an Accounts Payable system. However, someone pointed out to me that if you are planning a direct mail campaign, then the weight of each component of a letter is important. Relevance is a function of context; the Predicates of a thing are determined by what is important to the process.

Finally, is quantity distributed an Attribute?

To have correctly identified that <u>quantity distributed</u> is an Attribute, you must have understood that the Entity was not the individual piece of paper. Did you notice that there was no serial number or other identification on the coupon? No doubt you reasoned that each coupon was identical and, therefore, could not be an Entity. The Entity is probably coupon type A. (It is always difficult to be sure without an entire business case.) Assuming that this is true, the salespersons would be interested in how many of an individual coupon were distributed. That number would be important in determining the effectiveness of their promotional campaign.

More Practice: Finding Elemental Attributes Between the Pages of Books

Study the following from *The Telemarketer's Handbook*:

> People are creatures of habit—only, everyone has different habits. Some people are easy to reach early in the morning, others at dinner time. Remember the telemarketer's credo: "Discover a person's habits and exploit them."
>
> Go down your list of prospects, phoning each in turn. When you get to the bottom of your list, start over at the top. Many calls will be unsuccessful (rude response, no answer...). Try to call each number 5 times during each "Calling Period" (e.g., morning, afternoon, dinner, evening). Cross a prospect off the list only after you have had 5 unsuccessful calls in each calling period.

Based on the above business scenario, which of the following are Elemental Attributes?

a. Prospect Status, e.g., "contacted, not contacted, unable to contact"

b. Result of Call, e.g., "successful, no contact, rude response"

c. Date & Time of Call, e.g., "while you are trying to enjoy a meal"

d. Next Time to Call a Prospect, e.g., "morning, afternoon, dinner, evening"

Prospect status (a) is a Derived Attribute. In part, its derivation rule is "If one of the calls made to a prospect is successful, then the prospect has been contacted." When a Derived Attribute such as this one is confused for an Elemental Attribute, then there are real problems. Some analyst identifies it; some database designer adds it to a database; and some programmer writes volumes to keep it updated. Then, somebody in Telemarketing redefines what constitutes a "successful" call. When that redefinition happens, more than just changing software, you have data that is no longer factual in the database. Only you can put an end to this waste of money. By capturing all of the Elemental Attributes of the Entity sales call, the Telemarketing owners of the system can combine Elemental Attributes into any formula they wish.

Result of call (b) is an important Elemental Attribute of the Entity phone call. For each call made, we know that we want to know "What happened?" Is there any way that this could have been derived? What if the automatic dialer detected busy signals and automatically updated the prospect record? That is still data coming from outside the system; it is not based on data from within the system. Either someone must select the value from a list of possible outcomes, or the outcome must be detected by some other input device.

Date & time of call (c) is also an important Elemental Attribute. Some analysts would rather record calling period. However, for much the same reason you wouldn't want to record whether the call were successful, you don't want calling period. The date & time of call cannot be reinterpreted; it is objective. On the other hand, what the telemarketers consider calling period is subject to change. They may think they can ruin your favorite TV program if they call between six and eight, but they may want to extend into nine o'clock during the holiday season. If you know the date & time of call, you can always figure out the calling period, so why record it?

Next time to call a prospect (d) pushes the idea of a Derived Attribute. Next time to call a prospect is an example of confusing an action with data. The next call time depends on the result of the last call and the current time of day. You cannot calculate the next call time in advance. The telemarketing professional will call when he or she gets to the name on the list. Often, it is beneficial to calculate the value of a Derived Attribute and to store that calculated value in the database. In two previous examples, calling period and prospect status, it would likely be perfectly acceptable practice so long as all the constituent Elemental Attributes were also stored. In the case of next call time, however, it cannot be done because part of the derivation is time of day. Next time to call a prospect partly depends upon the length of the list.

Even More Practice: Finding Elemental Attributes in Policy Manuals

Study the following paragraph from *The Customer Service Manual*:

> Customers who have been told that their reservation is confirmed are entitled to double their money back if later denied a reservation. If there is an overbooking situation, customers will be bumped based on their "Priority Rating" as established by the inscrutable divination of the Sales Department. For customers with the same Priority Rating, the last reservation received will be the first one bumped.

From the evidence above, which of the following are Elemental Attributes?

a. Seats Remaining to Be Sold, e.g., "original seats available less total reservations"

b. Customer Has (Has Not) Been Told He Is Confirmed, e.g., "T/F"

c. Customer Priority Rating, e.g., "1-5; 1 is highest priority"

d. Time Reservation Taken, e.g., "date and time to the nearest second"

Seats remaining to be sold (a) is not an Elemental Attribute because it should be derived; seats remaining is calculated based on the number of seats originally available and the number of seats already sold. The rule may be more complex; note the ambiguity of the term sold. Is a seat sold if the customer has not been told that he or she is confirmed?

<u>Customer has been told he is confirmed</u> (b) is an Elemental Attribute. In order to execute the business rule "If a reservationist tells a customer he or she is confirmed and the company later bumps the customer, then the customer is compensated," the system needs to know whether or not the reservationist spoke the magic words. Do not struggle against these Attributes that seem to be made up by a single person or department; they are a necessary evil.

Given scant information, you should assume that <u>customer priority rating</u> (c) is an Elemental Attribute. It is significant that the Sales Department has no rigid procedure for establishing <u>customer priority</u>. If, for instance, customers were ranked based on total purchases, then <u>customer priority</u> could be derived and would therefore no longer be Elemental.

The <u>time reservation taken</u> (d) is a pretty safe bet as an Elemental Attribute. The time something happens is just about always something somebody wants to know. In this case, <u>time reservation taken</u> happens to be critical because the information is needed when a reservation gets bumped.

And a Little More Practice: Finding Attributes in a Hotel Room

The following might be found in a brochure for a hotel:

> Our hotels have double-occupancy first-class rooms (type a), single-occupancy first-class rooms (type b), double-occupancy economy rooms (type c), and triple-occupancy economy rooms (type d). Recently, we have divided the rooms into smoking and non-smoking rooms.

From the evidence above, which of the following are Elemental Attributes?

    a. Smoking Allowed, e.g., "yes/no"
    b. Type of Room, e.g., "A through D"
    c. Maximum Occupancy
    d. Room Value Rating, e.g., "Economy/First-Class"

Smoking allowed (a) is an Elemental Attribute of a hotel room; it is indivisible, and it must be established by someone setting up records for a room. Type of room (b), on the other hand, is a problem. The ambiguity of the name, type, is a clue that this is a lousy Attribute. The name has to be ambiguous because it mixes two disparate ideas, occupancy and value. The values that make up Elemental Attributes, however, cannot be compounds of simpler values. Type of room makes a single Attribute out of two basic ideas, how nice the room is and how many people can sleep there. Thus, maximum occupancy (c) and room value rating (d) are both Elemental Attributes. When they are combined in this way, as in (b), it makes access to the data much more complicated: for instance, to get a list of double occupancy rooms you would have to select those records that have a type of room of A or C. If later there were a third type of double-occupancy room, E, then the method for getting double-occupancy rooms would also have to change. Splitting the Composite Attribute type of room into its component Elemental Attributes not only makes the example query simpler but also makes the system easier to maintain and less prone to error.

Here's what you should have learned from studying about the concept of Attributes:

- An Attribute is a type of Predicate that is the association of a Domain to an Entity.
- An Attribute is a question in the form of "What is its…?"
- Any property, quality, or characteristic ascribed to an Entity may be an Attribute.
- Elemental Attributes are most important. Composite and Derived Attributes are made up of Elemental Attributes.
- Attributes should have a consistent precision.
- Like any Predicate, an Attribute might allow more than one value—in which case, we say that the Attribute is not in First Normal Form.

Part FIVE

Conclusion

I have had the good fortune to have started my career with Arthur Andersen & Co. It cost me my youth, but from the first day I wrote a line of code, I worked under a project plan and according to what was then the first methodology, Method/1. By the time I moved to Arthur Young, their Information Engineering Methodology was being released. So I was never allowed just to hack out systems; I always had to struggle with a set of guidelines. Despite the structure, I confess to having learned more from living through errors than by breathtaking inspiration.

Since I left the security of the Big *n*, I have seen a lot. My first education was working on a project that had no methodology—just some pretty smart people working their way through some very tough requirements. I came to realize that for all the heartaches I had building systems with a method, developing systems without one is bush league.

Despite the obvious advantages of structure, I have also seen the struggle people experience adopting structured methodology. Catholicism in Haiti spawned Santeria, a merger of European and African theology. That people would not abandon their practices entirely but would rather try to paint their old faiths with new colors is natural, something we all do unconsciously. That natural fact of seeing new things through the lens of old ways is an important evolutionary mechanism. On the other hand, sometimes entrenched interests intentionally frustrate the introduction of new things.

That new ideas are so difficult to effect may be best expressed by the true story of one Ruth P who worked for a company in a small town in the Old South that made handles and ornaments for caskets. I was sensing that the friendly introductions to our project were enough and that I could begin to ask some questions about her job. She had a rubber stamp which made the mark "BLUE COPY." It looked like a good entrée into a substantive discussion. "Oh, we stamp all the pink copies 'BLUE COPY.' We had some consultants in here a few years ago and they changed the receipt vouchers from blue to pink. Since then we have stamped the pink receipt vouchers 'BLUE COPY' so that nobody would get confused."

When you have a good sense of how difficult small changes are—and you have seen that the problem seems to scale up from there until even the Pope seems to be at wit's end—you wonder, "What should a person whose job is to change things do?" Suicide brings on many changes, but... People who want to make things better are just too optimistic to become jumpers. I have personally tried the work-every-available-hour and throw-lots-of-fits approach without much success. Resignation is something I have seen others try; they always remind me of the novel *1984*, in which Winston Smith in the end gets it in the back of the head. This is just not my way.

I hope you can excuse me for reflecting a little as we enter the last part of this book. You and I have come a long way at this point, and I feel a little license to speak about the really difficult parts of our jobs. We have somehow to crack the riddle "Make things better, but don't change anything." The secret I can now reveal, now that you have largely read this book, is that Data Modeling is only about 5% of your job.

I took something like 75,000 words to cover 5% of your day. You don't want me to start writing about the other 95%. This last part is meant to help you keep from having Data Modeling grow into something more than the simple skill it is meant to be. On my projects, I do not worry so much about the large number of people who admit to having difficulty with Data Modeling. In the first place, the most intelligent thing I can hear from somebody is "I don't understand." To have a sense of the difference between understanding and not understanding is like the gift of sight or touch. Until you appreciate the difference, you are blind; like a sailor that cannot feel the breeze, you cannot find your way to shore. In the second place, you can rattle around trying a jillion different ways to structure data, but eventually you will, like thousands of others, find a way to model data that works and will then roughly conform to the basic principles first established by E. F. Codd.

I do worry about analysts who have become so enthusiastic about the idea of Data Modeling that they have waged religious wars in their companies, taking it to extremes and into places it does not belong. You don't want ideas to be dead; they need to evolve and grow. To be sure, every software project everywhere is an opportunity for new ideas to be tried out and for our understanding of systems development to grow. Of course, this view is very optimistic about what is really going on out there. It is Pollyanish to suggest that every analyst is somehow making a positive contribution. Some analysts are dangerous because they convince their managers that they represent Data Modeling and therefore their failures are the failures of the model. When I heard Michael Stonebraker of Informix declare, "You are not doing a good job," he was speaking to a group of Data Administrators, not a bunch of beginners.

You should avoid a few recognizable extremes. First, do not try to do everything absolutely correctly. You cannot always be right, and in any case, not every detail matters. Second, do not go too far with the notion of modeling the real world. The real world is so complex that if you try to model every circumstance, you will go bananas. Third, the current modeling techniques cannot express every rule you might encounter. There are limitations to the meta-model and to the notation. If you tried to write a technical manual in iambic pentameter, you would find yourself sometimes taking a very long route to solve a simple problem. You might be able to write poetry using debits and credits, but it would find a pretty small audience—maybe your mother. Likewise, the language of Data Modeling cannot easily express certain things. This final part will help you avoid some common pitfalls. ∎

You Could Do Everything Right... but Still Make a Mess

Don't Pick a Fight With Your Friends

Take it from me. I have been monomaniacal towards Data Modeling for fifteen years. That attitude is not worth it. Once upon a time, clergy argued about how many angels could dance on the head of a pin. (Early in this century, certain denominations resolved the issue by outlawing dance.) How similar are so many of our arguments? Let me try to explain my perspective this way. It's June: the Houston Astros are meeting the Cincinnati Reds for the first time this season. The commentators are relaxed, the Astrodome is practically empty, the play is sloppy, and the'stros lose. Flash forward to August: the Astros meet Cincinnati again. All of a sudden, the one-game difference is a big deal, "Dis is da game of da season...blah blah blah." Well, guys, if we had whooped 'em back in June, we wouldn't be one game back now. The popular perception that the last games of the season are somehow more important is yet another example of media hypnosis.

Let me try again. It's June: the project team is meeting for the first time. The project stretches out in front of us, and I imagine myself Napoleon on the edge of the Russian steppes. The general's staff has just spent the last hour discussing whether Attributes always have Domains or just usually have Domains. Flash forward to August: the general's staff is crying for more troops, later deadlines, and earlier bedtimes. Nobody has time to eat, file paperwork, or test; they would let blood for an extra half-hour.

You can easily begin to see time as the enemy. When you first start working projects, you think, if only I had more time. You dread Fridays because

221

you have to account for your week. A mania can grip the whole project team evidenced by everyone trying to squeeze time out of everything. You might get hyper-efficient counting the steps to the coffee machine. You have no time for family, let alone exercise. The daily dicker replaces the usual chit chat and wastes away the goodwill you had invested in each other. You might begin to see yourself as Napoleon pushing onward despite all. Hello, Mr. Napoleon, the army has missed every deadline by 150%. Did I just hear you tell management that we were going to "make that up"? Freezing to death on the endless steppes is the hard way to solidify friendships. Trivial issues are the poisonous dope of divisiveness. Divisiveness is the spy. Time is in fact your ally: when the team is delirious with dopey discussion, just stick your hand in your shirt and say "We're out of time."

The examples that follow are intended to exercise the most important skill of a good analyst, judgment. Not all issues are as trivial as whether Attributes always have Domains or just usually have Domains. And sometimes you have to choose between maintaining relations with the owners and holding on hard to your modeling principles.

This first example describes a contentious issue being played out between management, the accountants, and the systems analysts. In your opinion, is this a time when the analysts should stand up and push for their solution, or is this a case in which the analysts are being dogmatic, sticking by principle beyond practicality?

Dear (your name):

You have helped us with our computers in the past, so I hope you don't mind helping to settle this argument about how we charge for international tours. Until recently, we had one set price for European tours that included round-trip airfare from New York City. Two things have changed. For one, some Europeans are wanting to take our tours, and they don't want to pay for airfare to the continent. For another, we would like to offer direct flights from other cities like Los Angeles; but then we have to charge more for the airfare. Here are the arguments.

Our computer analysts are telling us that we need to price the tour and the overseas flight separately. For instance, instead of one all-inclusive price of $3,500, we would have two prices, say $3,000 for the tour and $500 for the overseas airfare from NYC or $750 from LA.

Our accountants tell us that changing our long-held practice of single pricing is unnecessary, that they can easily deduct when no NYC-Europe airfare is involved and add back any other applicable airfare. So, if the accountants get their way, we will list a single price, $3,500. If you are in Europe, we will credit you $500 so your bill would read $3,500 less $500 for a total of $3,000. If you are in LA, your bill would read $3,500 less $500 plus $750 for a total of $3,750.

Personally, I think the whole thing is meant to justify making changes we don't need to the computer system! I say just consider each different airfare combination a different package and price it accordingly. So, for instance, the tour that starts in NYC would be package A for $3,500; the tour that starts in LA would be package B for $3,750; and the tour alone would be package C for $3,000.

Who's right?

Dear old pal:

Any of the alternatives you mentioned will work so far as pricing your tours go. However, general principles of good data design will help you avoid making more nasty changes to your computer systems in the future. I suggest you:

a. Listen to your computer people. If you don't, they will quit and leave you high and dry. Price the tour and the overseas flights separately.

b. Listen to your accountants: your computer people shouldn't be telling them how to do their business. Continue to include overseas airfare in the price. Give a credit if no airfare is charged; add a surcharge for cities other than New York.

c. Have some backbone! You are the boss. Develop a series of prices that include the tour and overseas air, depending on where the passenger will begin their tour.

Put a ticket for your next tour in the mail, and I will send you the correct answer. Happy to be of service.

First, let's figure out what would be right from a purely technical standpoint. I wouldn't pick option c. If they set up different packages for each of the different overseas airfare options, how would management then get total sales for a tour? It would be more difficult to determine total demand for a tour since there would be several different packages going to the same destinations. Giving credits or adding surcharges for the airfare from the rest of the tour (option b) would also be unnecessarily complicated. Both options b and c propose running the business based on a Derived Attribute and then working backwards to the Elemental Attributes. The accountants need to ask themselves, "Why are we spending a million on a new system that does everything the way we've always done it?" I suspect that the reason they are replacing their system has more to do with screwy practices like this one and less with the latest graphical user interface. Obviously the existing practice works, but billing becomes more complex. The boss needs to ask himself why he is paying people to develop systems if he himself is more qualified.

The analysts are pursuing a basic principle: keep the Predicates in their most elemental form. In this case, that means taking apart a Predicate like all-inclusive price of tour into its components, price of tour and price of overseas air. This option is better than the accountants' idea because it is simpler. Use the analysts' method, and price will always be calculated in the same way—by adding the components together. This procedure is not unlike the way you would add optional equipment to a car you might be purchasing. Since this analysis is being applied to a critical aspect of the system, I would counsel the analysts to fight this battle. (This scenario is based on a true story; in real life, the accountants got their way and the billing system became very complex.)

This example is intended as a counterpoint to the broader discussion emphasizing the need to pick your battles. The owners approach lawyers and accountants for advice: the owners tell them what they need, but then the owners step back and let those professionals do their jobs. If analysts want to be given license to do their jobs, they need to maintain relationships because owners will let only professionals they trust and respect make decisions for them. The analysts lost this battle not because of the merits of their argument on this important point but because they may be annoying everybody by arguing every point.

Too Much of a Good Thing

It is almost too trite to say, but here it is. You can drink too much water, breathe too much oxygen, and think about something way too deeply and for too long. Yet analysts often lose sight of the fact that the approach to modeling is based on an imperfect understanding of the way in which people organize information. You will run into many instances where it doesn't seem to quite work as advertised. Remember, a good model today is better than a perfect model tomorrow. The examples that follow all loosely fit into what we might term over-analysis, thinking about something beyond what has any practical impact on the ultimate goals of the project.

When It Becomes Too Real

The simplest Predicates are the most stable elements of your data model. Many Predicates represent characteristics that are as apparent as the nose on your face. Take, for example, the dimensions of a thing. The Predicate <u>length</u> was invented to serve some process; but the process is so universal that we just take <u>length</u> for granted.

Finding Predicates such as <u>length</u> in your information system analysis is very helpful. Because these Predicates are based on an external reality, they are inherently stable elements of the data model. A few more examples would include a <u>person's gender</u>, a <u>cylinder's capacity</u>, the <u>current exchange rate</u>, the <u>quantity of goods purchased</u>. Contrast these examples with other Predicates such as <u>marketing region</u> or <u>ethnic origin</u>, which rely on a shifting definition. If I didn't have a Marketing Department, I wouldn't need a region. If I don't have a clear purpose for <u>ethnic origin</u>, it becomes impossibly vague as is apparent by the current debate over distinctions among Caucasians or by various attempts to create multi-ethnic categories.

Do not fool yourself. The only reason to have even simple Predicates such as <u>length</u> in the database is to serve some process. You find Predicates not by inspecting objects but by asking people, "What do you do? What decisions do you make? What reports do you prepare?" Anything the system owners believe is relevant is a Predicate, whether that something is real or not. If you do find that your data model has a Predicate that is not used by some process, then get rid of it, regardless of how apparent it might be.

Still, you should beware of made-up Predicates. They must be defined internally as precisely as real Predicates are understood universally. Consider this excerpt from some project documentation: "When we do speak to the prospect, we describe our membership programs and indicate on our records a sense of whether we should pursue the prospect further." <u>A sense of whether we should pursue</u> is about as phony a Predicate as they come, yet it is central to the approach of this telemarketing company. If operators are writing down just anything that comes to mind, then that notation will be somewhat useful to that operator; however, it would not be useful to anybody else. The Predicate improves if the administrators set up a Domain for each operator to use, such as "1 being hot and 5 being cold"—but it would still be open to wide interpretation. There probably is no way to actually measure the likelihood that a prospect is going to buy, so this code is probably not ever going to get much better. In the end, your data model makes no distinction between real Predicates and any other Predicates. The only Predicates are the ones the owners demand. That owners often create Predicates that have limited utility is something we can counsel against, but an extra Predicate here and there is not a battle I would choose to fight.

What gives one Predicate stability while another Predicate might shift in meaning and cause rework? Why can one Predicate be broadly used across an information system while others have only limited applicability? Those Predicates that are understood by everyone inside and outside the scope of the information system, such as <u>length</u>, are the most stable and reusable. You can slide along a scale of decreasing consensus about the definition of a Predicate to a point at which the Predicate becomes very unstable. As the consensus breaks down, the power of the Predicate to communicate becomes more and more limited, and it becomes more susceptible to change.

Consider the following examples:

Quality of Predicate	Example Predicates	Comments
Stable & Useful	Height, Length, Width, Diameter	It is hard to imagine more widely understood or more elemental Predicates than these.
Stable within Reasonable Operating Limits	Weight, Color, Velocity	For business application, the definition is so standard that no one questions its meaning or applicability. True, when FedEx first ships to the moon, then they might wish that the Predicate weight were mass.
Relatively Stable & Useful	Universal Pricing Code (UPC), Area Code	Many codes and their meanings are managed by a standards committee. Should the organization decree that a change is needed, it will be implemented. However, a change would cause tremendous instability, and for that reason, the committees mostly discuss angels dancing on pins, renew friendships, and discuss the location of the next meeting.
Prone to Change & Less Useful	Region Code, Status, Account Code, Billing Flag	These are typical of the names given weak Predicates that have shifting meanings and limited use. Often they are found to have cross-purposes and poor accuracy, and may have fallen out of use.

While the above discussion advocates the pursuit of Predicates that have some meaning outside the information system, can you ever have enough Predicates to model every real-world circumstance? To answer this question, consider the story of a travel tour company that lived and died by its list of potential customers.

This coveted list had to fulfill two objectives. First, in order to save money while presenting a more personalized image, the company wanted to be sure to send only one copy of a mailing or to place only one phone call to a household. To accomplish this first requirement, the data model showed two Classes, INDIVIDUAL and HOUSEHOLD, and a Relationship, individuals belong to a HOUSEHOLD. Since the model recognized the household as well as the folks who lived there, a single letter could be sent to one address, containing information for everyone living there. Figure C-1 shows that a household is made up of one or more INDIVIDUAL.

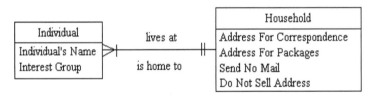

Figure C-1

The second objective required the travel company to keep track of multiple addresses for these households, because the company had an upscale clientele who would summer and winter like migratory birds. To accomplish this objective, the model had to be modified to show that each household could have many homes depending on the time of year.

Often, discussions about the most usual situations can deteriorate into fantastic imaginings fed by persons who want to prove that their jobs defy proceduralization and by data modelers who, like model train enthusiasts, cannot help themselves from adding a bit more detail. In the case of this travel tour company, such persons threw out questions such as "What if they have roommates who are not technically members of the family? What if individuals in the family each want their own mail? What if the wife lives in France by herself in the Winter but with her husband in New York in the Summer? What if they spend Fall and Spring in Boulder, the Winter and Summer in Paris? What are the valid postal codes in Antarctica?" You are not going to prove anything to anybody by creating Rube Goldberg data models that account for every bizarre thing that might happen in the real world. I believe the surrealist painter Salvador Dali once said something to the effect of "Isn't it amazing how many things that could possibly happen, don't?"

True, you can relatively easily begin to elaborate a model that accommodates any number of homes occupied at any time of the year by anybody. So you could create a model that could express everything, but you also need to consider how often such scenarios really happen. You also need to contemplate what real problems would arise if the model did not accommodate the situation. And you need to ask how much this is going to inflate the cost of this system. I am amazed that people who couldn't authorize the purchase of a box of pencils can demand enhancements to software costing tens of thousands. While you're at it, also ask who is going to keep up with all this data, how long a system owner will take to learn that these fantastic exceptions can be accounted for within the system, and just how all this data is going to be acquired in the first place. If after you raise all of these concerns, the owners insist that such scenarios happen enough, that the project is a full-stop without the requested feature, that they not only don't care how much it costs but that also you shouldn't worry about it, then you should quickly agree to the request. If all of those conditions are met, then this battle doesn't sound like a good one for you to fight.

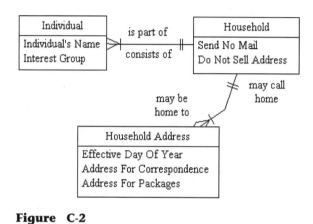

Figure C-2

Incidentally, the actual project on which this story is based settled for a model as you see in Figure C-2. The model was limited by its assumption that the family always stayed together and thus could have only a single address at any one time. The project team never disputed that a situation might arise in which the actual status of the family could not be correctly described in the system—even that it might mean tickets for a man and his mistress might get misdelivered again—only that the cost of providing for the ability to describe these rare instances was a bad investment. In this case, the analysts backed away from a fight; they gave up their desire for a perfect model; the relentless pursuit of the perfect model would have cost too much and been far too complicated.

Knowing Too Much

Consider another case. This time it is the story of an owner who has read a great deal about Data Modeling, but not quite enough.

Memo to the Project Team
From M. Puestos, Tax Manager

I have been reviewing our data model for mail-order sales. As was noted during our meetings, new laws require us to collect sales tax based on the address to which parcels are delivered.

From what I can gather, the Predicate <u>sales tax rate</u> should be replaced by the basic factors used to determine the applicable rate. We must pursue this question because the model as it stands requires that our operators know the sales tax.

<u>Sales tax rate</u> can be derived from the customer's address and by checking local statutes. Generally, sales taxes are the same for everyone in a given state; however, other taxing districts are commonly created to collect additional taxes for the operation of municipalities or other special needs such as redistributing income to football team owners. These districts are not necessarily drawn based on any other political scheme such as counties or zip codes. The numerous overlapping zones that are frequently changed make determining the proper sales tax for a given location very difficult, except on a case-by-case basis. Some other mail-order businesses use a single tax rate for each zip code. This is simple and generally, but not always, accurate. We would almost certainly pay some penalties for miscollected taxes when we are audited.

I'm sure some of you smart computer people should be able to figure something out.

What is the best way to resolve the concerns of the Tax Manager?

   a. Import into the system the data regarding boundaries and tax rates, which are Predicates of taxing authorities.

   b. Determine the tax rate for each customer and put it in the customer's records.

   c. Go ahead and use the customer's zip code to find out the tax rate.

When you are using a machine that can calculate a number to sixteen decimals, you are tempted to try to make every number absolutely accurate. However, at some point, the cost of accuracy is not redeemed; in the end everything is a question of economics.

Would it pay to create a system that could build the tax rate up from knowledge of the sales tax legislation? To accomplish this objective, you would set up a Class of taxing authorities whose boundaries and tax rates are Predicates (option a). Establishing the boundaries of the tax district and the proper tax amount at a point in time would be the easy part. Figuring out if a particular address fell within a taxing authority would be real work. Few projects would go this far to optimize the calculation of sales taxes. Some companies specialize in figuring out sales taxes precisely because it is so complicated and so common a problem. So the answer is yes, some one company has gone to these lengths and succeeded, but for a single company to pay for this development itself probably does not make economic sense.

What if you did determine the tax rate for each customer and put that information in the customer's records? This solution (option b) would create the result that many customers would have exactly the same tax rate copied into their files. That the rate is the same is no coincidence; very often customers who live near each other would enjoy the same rate of taxation. Usually, when my tax rate changes, all my neighbors up and down the block are also outraged. This fact proves that some more abstract Entity or Entities are setting the rates; the tax rate is therefore a Predicate of that abstraction, not the customer. Tax rate does not depend on the whole argument of a customer; even though a customer has but a single identifier, that identifier stands for more information than you need to know to determine tax rate. True, having each customer's tax rate as a field on each customer record would have the advantage of accuracy and of simplicity from the point of view of the computer; however, it places too much burden on the order-taker to determine and enter the correct rate. It becomes almost unworkable when you consider the difficulty of maintaining correct rates when the rates are changed. (Incidentally, this is typical of a Predicate that is not in Third Normal Form.) Although in the end this kind of decision has to be made by the tax department, the analyst should paint a picture of the implications behind requiring the business to enter the tax rate for each new customer address.

Despite the concerns of M. Puestos, using the customer's zip code to determine the tax rate (option c) is a standard practice. It has the great advantage of being simple. Because of his reading about Data Modeling, M. Puestos seems to have an understanding that a ZIP CODE Class with a tax rate Predicate would only approximate the way tax rates are established. A solution might be to let the system suggest or default a tax rate for a customer based on the zip code but to allow M. Puestos to change that rate as desired. You can bet that once M. Puestos has this ability, his department will never use it.

In the end, the problem of calculating sales tax is representative of modeling problems that are solvable but so complicated that they should just be left alone. You might call these problems the "black holes of analysis." Do not create complex data models of areas you know are not going to be constructed or will wind up being packaged solutions. Models are for construction, not for the pleasure of drawing them.

Looking for Trouble

Anticipating needs is one thing; inventing them is another. Analysts are fond of asking questions such as "Well, what if the customer will pay only in gold bars, then what?" Business people have a hard time saying "It'll never happen," because they are afraid of being hanged when it does. Computer systems will never be as flexible or adaptable as people. So you see how easily you can go too far trying to build the ultimately comprehensive data model.

Oftentimes, in the name of anticipating future needs or of being comprehensive, we find ourselves modeling fantastic scenarios, screwy transactions that happen once in fifty years. Some war-worn veteran will reminisce, "You don't remember when we had all that trouble, do you, Mr. Computer-Big-Shot? Maybe you don't go back far enough, but I do. Yeah, things were messed up for weeks. If this new-fangled computer can't handle that kind of thing, what good is it?" You can go on literally forever modeling increasingly unlikely scenarios.

Consider a typical meeting to discuss a Human Resources project. Eighty percent of the model is completed with little discussion. For instance, that there should be a Class INDIVIDUAL and that there should be a Relationship for their spouses is decided in five minutes (Figure C-3).

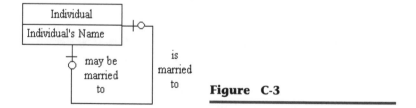

Figure   C-3

Another 19 percent of the cases are handled by a small elaboration allowing the model to account for someone to divorce and remarry without losing track of the first spouse in case of outstanding insurance claims (Figure C-4).

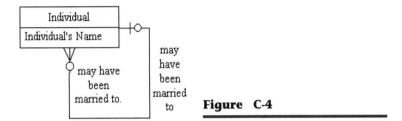

Figure C-4

The last one percent of possible cases stretches credibility, not to mention the patience of the owners. "What if a polygamist married another polygamist? What about someone who is celibate? What if they were both employees, but one...?" These kinds of discussions eat up eighty percent of the budget.

The bottom line is that no computer system will ever anticipate every possible situation. That's what the people are for. You should anticipate the unexpected and be sure that the system isn't so foolproof that it prevents the people from handling oddball situations.

Tip for Project Managers

The manager has to recognize two types of project team members that will go too far with modeling.

The first type are the visionaries who think they are always just one more Class and Relationship away from describing the entire universe of possibilities. They mean well; they simply overestimate the power of the computer and underestimate the complexity of business events. Rein them in.

The second type are the ones who were never on board anyway. These are the devious ones who will continue to feed the first type with ridiculous scenarios, pushing even more elaborate data models until the whole thing collapses under its own wait [sic]. Then they proclaim with great satisfaction, "See, I told you this was all poppycock."

Hard to Say

You cannot document every aspect of a company's business with a data model. For instance, data models do not express a sequence of events as does procedural logic. So, for example, you have no way to say "Put the lid on the jar before you shake it" in a data model. This is an intentional narrowing of the Data Modeling focus; Data Modeling gives you the things with which you work (lid, jar) but does not try to describe what you then do with them.

But the limitations of Data Modeling go much further than the intentional narrowing of scope just noted. Many rules about the interaction of data cannot be expressed in an Entity-Relationship Diagram (ERD) or in any other standard part of the data model. The following example of a group of reservations is just one of many types of rules that cannot be shown. Figure C-5 shows that a number of reservations may belong to a travel group and that a reservation is for a single departure (or trip). The grouping of reservations is intended to help reservationists make changes that affect everyone in the group. For instance, if a family is traveling together, Mama should not have to enumerate all the names of her children each time she calls. Yet nothing in the data model asserts the obvious rule that each Reservation within a Travel Group must be for the same Departure.

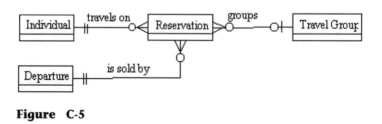

Figure   C-5

A common sense rule such as this one—that the members of a travel group should all travel together—is inherent in the idea of a travel group. It would be reasonable to put that rule into the model and in the database as we would do with the other rules, such as a reservation <u>must be for a</u> DEPARTURE. When it is in the database, it is much harder for somebody to foul things up.

Other rules about data are not so unchanging. "Take no order less than $50." A new Controller could easily change such a rule. There may be no minimum order, or minimum orders may depend on shipping weight or on the type of products. This kind of rule is implemented with both a user-defined parameter and software that implements it. Although in both cases, the rule needs to be documented during Analysis and implemented in Design, in neither case can you show this rule in standard Data Modeling notation.

Wet Noodle Syndrome

Systems owners cry "Flexibility!" when they fear they are going to forget something and never have the opportunity to fix the computer system again. Systems builders cry "Flexibility!" when they remember that the last time they went through this process the systems owners forgot a bunch of stuff, and it had to be added at the last minute.

What is meant by a flexible system? Analysts mean to say that you can do things with it that were not originally intended without additional programming. A flexible system is often said to be "parameter-driven," meaning that the software behaves differently, depending on what values the owners of the system put into parameters. An owner then could, for instance, put "10" in the pay commissions on day field, and the system would pay agents on the tenth of the month. If the owners change their minds, they can change the parameter. Let me go on record right now as totally in favor of running software off such parameters.

You can go to great lengths with such parameters. If you were writing a package for sale, you would want as many such parameters as you could imagine so that your software could be tailored to fit the greatest possible range of companies. When you are writing software for your own company and realize that parameter-driven software is trickier to write and much trickier to test, you might have parameters only for those processes that you guess might change. A highly parameter-driven system might be called generic since it suits many different installations.

There is another kind of flexibility, the special opportunity we all have to make a mess of the data. Consider the example illustrated in Figure C-6 in which the system owners insist on adding Relationships to the data model to provide flexibility but end up with disintegration. Sales agents are involved in Reservations in two ways: they receive a commission on sales and they get evaluated on their overall sales performance. Could we ever give a commission on a reservation but not count it towards an agent's overall sales goals? Or would we ever count something towards the sales goals but not give a commission? The owners of the actual project on which this example is based could not agree that this situation would never happen. In order to avoid the battle, the analysts modeled two Rela-

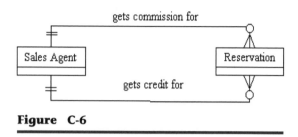

Figure   C-6

tionships. This is a kind of foolish flexibility. Unable to commit themselves to the simple idea that someone who made the commission will always also be given credit for the sale, the owners have taken upon themselves the responsibility of maintaining two independent Relationships between RESERVATION and SALES AGENT.

An ERD such as the one in Figure C-6 allows that a reservation could show on a sales agent's sales report but not be a part of that sales agent's commissions or vice versa. A reservation could even be on one agent's sales report but pay the commission to some other Agent. As I've already noted, this is a foolish flexibility.

Flexibility is one of those qualities that is difficult to oppose. The ultimately generic design is the blank page, the bare machine. Keeping things generic is sometimes an excuse to keep from having to think through the real needs. If I add a single Class and I declare it the set of all Entities, I have achieved a succinct model that is accurate and extremely generic. If I add a second Class, I have started down a slippery slope of having to explain to the world how I know an Entity belongs to one Class or the other. My design is less generic in that it places some constraints on the data. Obviously, I am exaggerating. A data model is a specification, a blueprint. It is not a machine or software that can be more or less flexible.

Intending to make a data model flexible, analysts instead make the model vague. Analysts will commonly declare in their data model "A Customer has many addresses" (Figure C-7). The analysts believe they are then finished with the issue of addresses no matter what requirement regarding locations an owner may toss their way: "I need a shipping address. I need a billing address. I need a location for legal correspondence." In each case, the analysts nod knowingly. When the owners are spent, the analysts might add, "You can have as many addresses as you could ever want, and you won't even have to call us up." The analysts have a generic model; the owners are delighted that they won't have to speak to the analysts anymore.

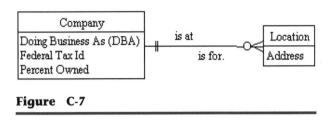

Figure C-7

Some will argue this approach makes for good software design, which it may. However, the weak semantic value of the Relationship <u>has</u> makes it a vague data model. It is non-specific so that it can accommodate anything, but if every requirement is met by this Relationship, then conversely it tells me nothing about the requirements of the owners. What happened to the billing, shipping, and legal addresses? Consider instead the very non-generic, that is specific, alternative illustrated in Figure C-8.

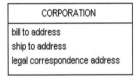

Figure C-8

This second model is easy for the owner to read and verify that all the requirements have been noted. The model is specific, but is it inflexible? The question is moot: the model cannot be inflexible or flexible in the way software can be. The data model cannot do anything at all; it is just a set of specifications. The specifications should not do anything other than what they are intended to do, which is to express the needs of the owners. The alternative shown in Figure C-8 does that.

This alternative model does require the analyst to think through each new address and document it, another good quality. An analyst might learn, for example, that the ship-to address cannot be a post office box, a fact that would elude an analyst who worked from the more generic model.

The first, generic, model is said to give the ability to owners to add addresses as they have need without any changes to the database. The phases of a structured methodology are intended to help the team divide the problem into manageable parts. The intent of Analysis is to focus narrowly on what the owners want the system to do; it very consciously omits any consideration of how these aims are to be achieved. Performance, capacity, security, audit, cost, uptime, and maintenance are among the issues that are reserved for later discussion during Design. But if you insist on dragging me into a conversation about software, the database that would be the natural transformations from Figure C-7 will not work. It will not work because there is no Predicate to tell me which address is to be used for what purpose. As soon as there is more than one address, there is no way for an owner or a program to choose between addresses. In effect, owners can add addresses but they don't know what to do with them.

So the second model in Figure C-8 is superior both in terms of the analysis it encourages and in terms of the database you would by default generate. Data models are not machines that need to be made parameter-driven. Data models are specifications: study the formation of the term SPECIFIC-ation.

Tip for System Analysts

Figure C-9 shows another alternative, which has adequate meaning but also makes the statement that one address may serve more than one purpose.

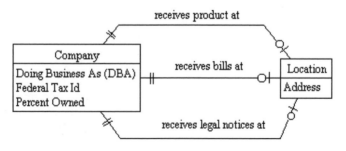

Figure C-9

In pursuit of ultimate flexibility, owners can get more expensive systems that probably still can't do the things they wanted. The proposed generic model in Figure C-7 does not allow for different rules about shipping addresses, adequate description of any address, or one address to serve multiple purposes.

Everyone applauds flexibility, but you should smell trouble when the analysts start down the road toward "keeping things open." Things were open when you started; the point of Analysis is to get some closure.

Don't allow the analysts to take up the challenge of a completely user-definable system; that's what the database and 4GLs are for. The completely user-definable system is a technical challenge and completely dodges the question "How should this application contribute to this business?"

This topic could also have been called "foolish economy." While building a data model, you often hear, "We need to have fewer Predicates!" Analysts will point out that the generic model has fewer data model objects. According to your estimating guidelines, the generic system appears cheaper to build. This appearance is the flaw in the estimating guidelines; they assume a certain type of data model. The generic system is much more expensive to write because many more of the business rules are written in software, as opposed to being controlled in a few statements that drive the behavior of all software. Further, the paths that the logic takes are exponentially greater causing software testing to become literally impossible. There is no reason to get by with fewer Predicates. On the contrary, the major deliverable of a data model is a complete set of Predicates.

Nothing is wrong with generic software, if that is what you were asked to develop. A data model should be specific. A very specific model is easily made into generic software; but the reverse is not true.

Lost in the House of Mirrors

The examples presented here all show how a modeler can go too far with the techniques. The real world is messier than anybody has time to model completely. Sometimes the argument (the unique key) that is just right to define a Predicate can be so difficult to determine that it is better to leave the model in a less than optimal state. Sometimes in trying to anticipate future needs, we lose sight of what is practical. Some of the legitimate things we discover cannot be easily expressed in the Data Modeling notation and should be documented in other forms. Finally, we can get so involved in our data model specifications that they seem to come alive, and we feel a need to make them flexible as if they were the software and not just the model from which the software gets built. If the first four parts of this book present what you should do with Data Modeling, then this last part is at least a partial list of some important things you should not do. On that subject, one more pitfall needs to be addressed: confusing meta-model and data model.

When I say that the car is owned by Dee, I am giving data about a car and a person. If I say that a car <u>may be owned by more than one</u> PERSON, then I am expressing an idea about data—data about data. Analysts often lose this distinction and begin to treat the data about data in the same way the data itself is treated. The result is a hybrid meta/data model that confuses both owners and analysts. At least the owners know they are confused.

The error I have most freely propagated in the models I have created to date is one in which I try to steal the name of the Predicate and treat this data about data as if it were some business data. To explain, let me return to the addresses I just discussed and add a bit to the model. The revised ERD—a work-around for an inadequately specific data model—is given in Figure C-10.

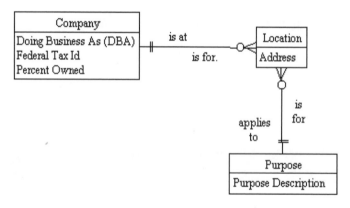

Figure   C-10

This new model eliminates the most important shortcoming of the flexible approach. The new Class PURPOSE is intended to have the address Entities such as "billing, shipping, and legal." This new Class supplies the missing meaning in the previously vague Predicate; taken together, the two Relationships spell out that a corporation <u>has an address for some one</u> PURPOSE. PURPOSE, however, is not a business Class; it is meta-data, because it tells me more about a Relationship, not more about some Entity in the world of the owners.

Why shouldn't I incorporate meta-data into the data model?

The data model is a document, an attempt to represent the things that the owners work with and the interrelationships among those things. Every document must have one audience; the narrower the audience, the easier it becomes to develop the document and the more expressive its content. When the model contains both a reflection of the needs of the owners and the design elements, the model loses its audience. The genius of the methodologies is the way all the tasks of software development have been organized into coherent phases with defined boundaries. In part, methodologies succeed by allowing us to divide the problem into manageable tasks. When the data model incorporates both requirements gathering and a design for owner-maintainability, we are biting off too much. You can always tell when you have slipped into Design—you begin to weigh various alternatives all of which provide the same information. On the other hand, defining requirements deepens your understanding of a Predicate—Figure C-9 defines the user requirements suggested by Figure C-8. Do not incorporate meta-data into your data model because it does not address either the audience or the basic concerns of Analysis.

PURPOSE is a part of the owners' model!

Yes, every Predicate in the model has a purpose. But if you begin to model the meta-data, why limit yourself to addresses? Are the purposes for which I keep phone numbers so different from the purposes for addresses? If I am concerned that the owners may want to have more addresses than I had anticipated, why not establish a model that would allow the owners to add any Predicate that I had not anticipated? There certainly will be new needs such as e-mail or Web site addresses. Would these be purposed with the phone numbers or the addresses; or would they have a different purpose altogether? Ultimately, a comprehensive model of data about data will result in a system to build systems, an end-user computer system. Stepping into the world of meta-data is a quicksand. A lattice of functional dependency holds the ERD together even when some of the Classes become quite conceptual. At the edges of the lattice, certain Classes anchor the ERD into concrete reality. Ultimately, the model of data is functionally dependent on some fact that is determined by inspection of objective fact. PURPOSE hangs on the edge of the model, but there is no basis for determining the functional dependency of any Predicate of PURPOSE. It is a concept alien to the data model—it is a visitor from another dimension, the meta-data.

Are you happy with your database, screen painters, query tools? They are the result of many thousands of hours of effort, the cost of which is being spread across hundreds of licensees. The database designers worked off a meta-model, whether it was documented as an ERD or some other schema. They anticipated that you would build an application, not another database engine. Their meta-model should not have contained any business data. Your data model should contain knowledge of the business only; it should not contain Classes that are intended for data about data. Classes in the data model are sets of business Entities, not system Entities. The ERD in Figure C-10 draws meta-data into the same diagram as the data model and is therefore improper.

Here's what you should have learned from studying this part:

- Predicates are the central element of the information model.
- Predicates based on the nature of a thing are more stable than Predicates that are invented to suit a particular purpose; but many essential Predicates are invented by the owners.
- All Predicates must be useful to some process.
- The real world is more complex than your information system needs to be.
- Some analysts, not satisfied with the complexity of the task at hand, will try to invent even greater complexity.
- Data Modeling notation cannot express every rule.
- The data model is a specification of user needs; it is not meant to be generic in the way we hope our software to be.
- The data model is a representation of the business needs; it should not contain Classes of Entities that describe data (that is the meta-data).

If I Had More Time...
I'd Have Written Less

A CIO once turned to me in the middle of a top-to-bottom analysis of his company and said, "Ten years ago I wrote this whole system without your methodology. Then it seemed easy. When did everything get so complicated?" Team members working on their first data model have to understand the business of the owners just as before, but they also have to learn new techniques. More to the point, the technique draws out more about the business and does so more quickly than just getting in and coding. Coding is relatively concrete; Analysis is abstract. Data Modeling does unveil the complication early for everyone to see rather than allowing each team member to work through a little each day in isolation.

Data Modeling cannot make the business any more complicated; the business is what it is. Data Modeling can give you a way to cut through to the requirements and to organize them for verification, cost estimation, and preparation for design. Allowing the team to see the whole problem leads to business process improvement, smarter software, simpler user interfaces, higher quality, more controllable projects, and a more easily maintained finished product.

That's a value proposition worth the work. To get it, you have to face an assumption that is behind every class and every text on Data Modeling; that is, something called Data Modeling really exists. If each team member interprets what is meant by Data Modeling differently, then no such thing really exists. What must be true is that Data Modeling is a set of principles akin to Algebra. Data Modeling is not an art like creative writing. Otherwise, how can two modelers study the same problem and arrive at the same answer? And if these modelers cannot do so, then how can the owners have any confidence that we analysts are progressing in some predictable way towards giving them what they want? How can a team of people work on the same problem without spending too much time arguing about how to model? How can models developed in different areas or at different times be reconciled and assembled together? The answer is that none of these things are possible unless one consistent and widely accepted approach to Data Modeling exists. The answer is that all the benefits of Data Modeling are real to the extent that the modelers work together with a single understanding of the principles involved.

The one right way to develop models is not a standard that everyone simply agrees to follow. Just as Foucault demonstrated that the earth spins, the right way to model data is outside the reach of our standard-setting bodies. It is a natural fact. The one approach to model data for CASE must have its roots in the instinctual way we organize data in our heads. The nine concepts central to this book comprise a model of the human way of organizing data that works for thousands of simple and complex data storage problems.

At this point, you deserve to turn around and look back on all the territory you have covered. Many words ago, you began this study of information with three basic ideas. First, we gauge our experiences: each sensation is placed on some scale. For example, one thing is more salty than another, farther away, or harder to move. We extend these basic Domains into a conceptual world; we can say that a statement is more likely, an index is up, a document is wordy. Second, we name things. Perhaps we begin with basic names, such as "Jacob's son" or "Roddemacher," and then extend the idea to anything that we might want to refer to later, "Nile" or "asset #444." And finally, we apply our measures to the things we measure: "Jacob's son is down by the Nile; The Dow Jones is up." These three concepts stand apart from everything else you have studied in that they are foundational; all the other essential parts of an information system build on these three.

The Predicate is the key to all information system analysis. It is the nexus of three concepts, a Domain, some Named thing, and some kind of relevance we attach to that measurement. So we take a Domain like distance, apply it to a thing like the Nile, and then give it significance as in its width. This might yield a fact such as "The Nile is 400 feet wide." Capturing facts in this form, as the owners require of us, is the unambiguous aim of software development. If an owner tells me that he wants to keep track of how many miles a car has been driven, then I am left with few questions—except, what else do you want to track?

From this point, we create the other concepts by connecting Predicates. An Entity is the one set of all Predicates that describe the same thing. A State is some subset of an Entity's Predicates that is necessary for some process. We can create sets of States to show how States sometimes interact.

Once we have connected Predicates into Entities and States, we can group Entities into Classes. A Class is the one set of all Entities with all the same Predicates. A Superclass is the set of all Entities that share certain Predicates as may be needed for a particular process. A selection is a set of all Entities based on the values of the Predicates, not the Predicates themselves. The following table (which first appeared in the Introduction) might help to summarize these latter concepts. For instance, the first row reads, "The concept Entity is a group of Predicates based on having the same argument which results in each Predicate pertaining to one and only one Entity. The concept is implemented as a record."

Concept	is a group of	based on having	which results in	Concept becomes a
Entity	Predicates	the same argument	each Predicate pertaining to one and only one Entity.	record
State	Predicates	the same argument and relevance to a process	any Predicate pertaining to any number of States.	projection of some fields of a record. Software encapsulates validation rules.
Class	Entities	the same set of Predicates	each Entity pertaining to one and only one Class.	table
Superclass	Entities	the same Predicates and relevance to a process	any Entity pertaining to any number of Superclasses.	projection of some fields and a union of records having those fields
Selection	Entities	the same value in some Predicate(s) and relevance to a process	any Entity pertaining to any number of selections.	select statement

Although this text has been presented as a set of examples either of the way we speak about the information we keep or actual circumstances that arise on a project, the organization of the material has been based on the progression from basic parts to the various ways those parts can be aggregated. The solutions to the examples made sense to the extent that they were consistent with the formal definitions of each of the Data Modeling concepts. The formal constructs explained in this book can be applied to all basic communication. The constructs taken together give rise to a model that we can all use today to develop better systems, so that over time we may even come to a better understanding of all the ways we reason about our surroundings.

Appendix

This text provides you with hundreds of examples of Classes, Relationships, Attributes, and Domains. Most of these examples are taken from one particularly rich data model developed for a company that organized worldwide group tours. The Analysis covered the entire business from tour planning, marketing, sales, reservations management, post-tour evaluation, accounting, and purchasing. You will find many parts of the data model used throughout the body of the text. You can more easily understand a part of a data model if you can see how it relates to the rest of the model; for this reason, the entire data model is reproduced in this Appendix and provided on the enclosed CD-ROM as a SILVERRUN data model.

This model was developed over six months, consuming a minimum of five person-years. The model describes a highly complex business through its information content and activities in such a way that an effective computer system could be built. It is not the consensus of a group of thinkers in an office park: it is the consensus of the business persons who held a stake in the success of the project.

I see no point in creating something that would take five person-years for you to get through. Some simplifications have been made when similar data structures can be found in other parts of the model. The model states, for instance, an individual may pay for her tour with discount coupons, cash, or through a travel agent, but the model assumes that the fictitious travel company accepts no credit cards. The various forms of payment shown exhibit enough complexity that a student should be able to infer how a credit card transaction should be modeled. A number of common data structures like this repeat over and over again in any data model. Rather than try for a world's record number of examples, this text attempts to exhibit an extremely wide variety of different structures you might encounter on a project without being repetitive. So, for example, you will find examples of all ten possible Relationships. You will find Classes as common as INDIVIDUAL and as rare as SCALAR RESPONSE. The models cover enough ground that you should be able to find starting points for your own models.

The examples chosen are not contrived to prove that the techniques work. Instead, they represent the best solution to real problems. The problems posed in the case and these solutions are not simple—neither are the challenges that you face on your project. I have no interest in graduating analysts with dreams of an invoice <u>has</u> INVOICE LINE dancing in their heads as they walk in to discuss a new system for managing space station logistics. This text and the techniques it promotes grew out of a team's best efforts to solve the problems of a real business. Because of that, you find no technique that was not required of us; we never set out to come up with a lot of clever things to do while developing a computer system.

True stories often have unexpected endings and don't seem to progress the way a script would. In the same way, this case study does not build from one made-up situation to another. The reader will find simple and complex situations side by side. If you are not already familiar with data modeling, I recommend that you begin with the explanations as presented in the main body of this text. Once you are familiar with the concepts, roam the model until you find something that challenges you.

I hope that the case study contains enough detail to be comprehensible. And I also hope that the really interesting parts of the case study aren't obscured by its breadth.

Each Class in the model is represented in its own diagram together with all the other Classes that are directly related. All diagrams are courtesy of SILVERRUN Technologies, Inc.

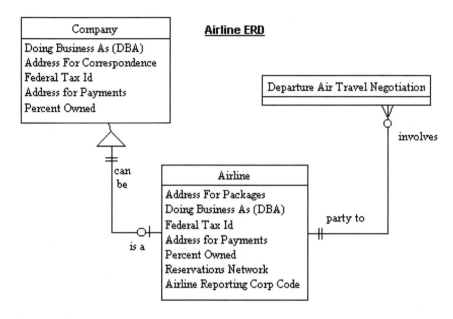

Figure   A-1

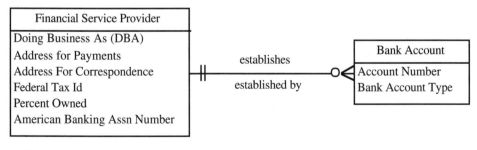

Figure   A-2

Bounty Coupon ERD

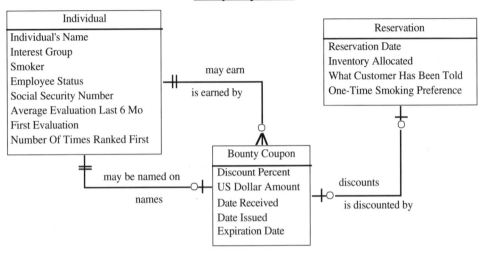

Figure   A-3

Cabin ERD

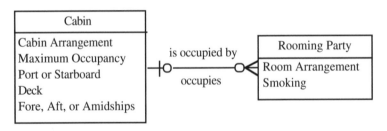

Figure   A-4

Car ERD

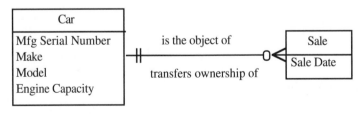

Figure   A-5

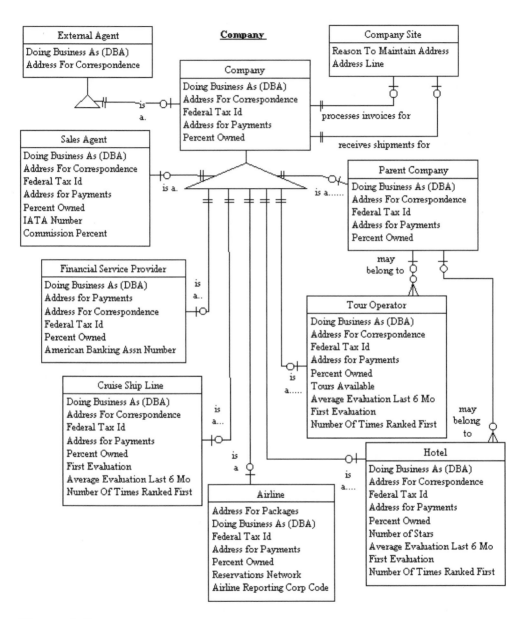

Figure A-6

Country Currency ERD

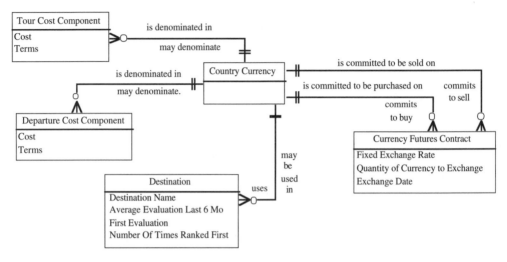

Figure   A-7

Cruise Ship Line ERD

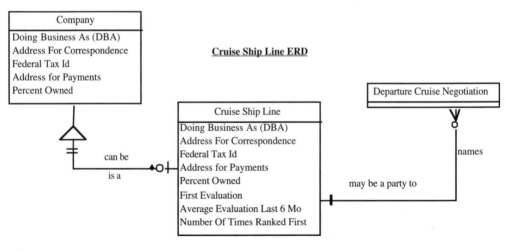

Figure   A-8

Currency Future Contract ERD

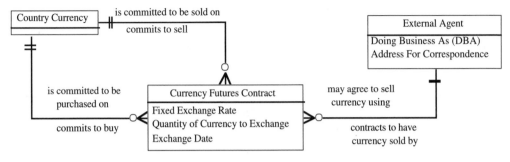

Figure   A-9

Departure Cost Component ERD

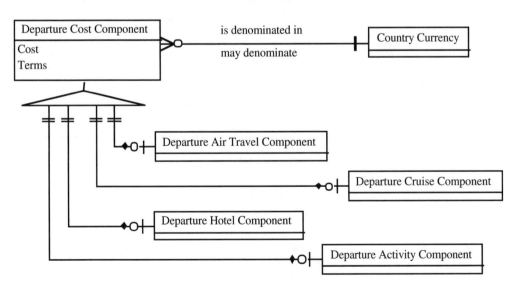

Figure   A-10

Departure ERD

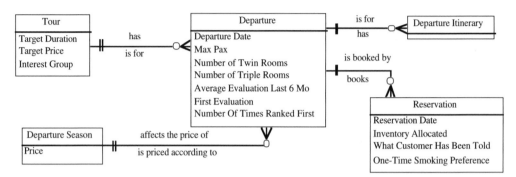

Figure   A-11

Departure Itinerary ERD

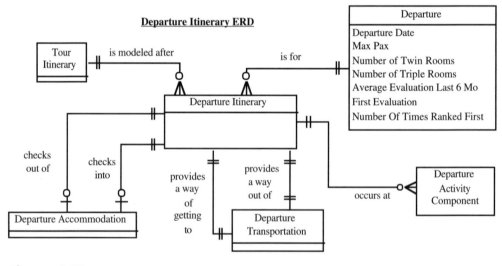

Figure   A-12

Destination ERD

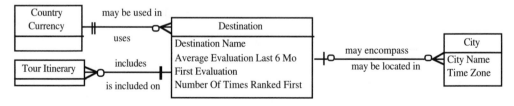

Figure   A-13

External Agent ERD

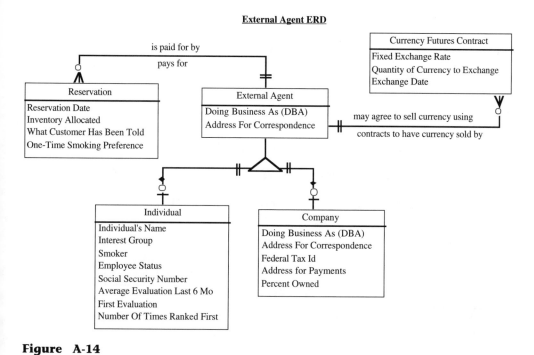

Figure   A-14

Financial Service Provider ERD

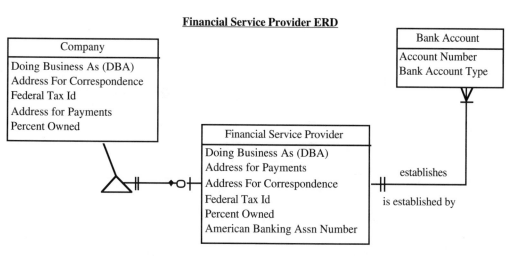

Figure   A-15

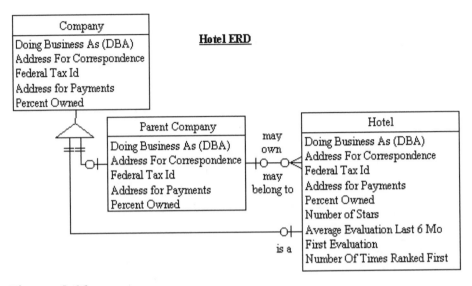

Figure   A-16

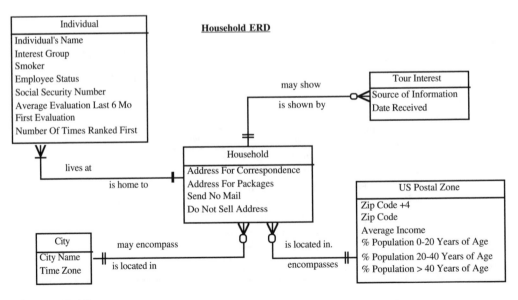

Figure   A-17

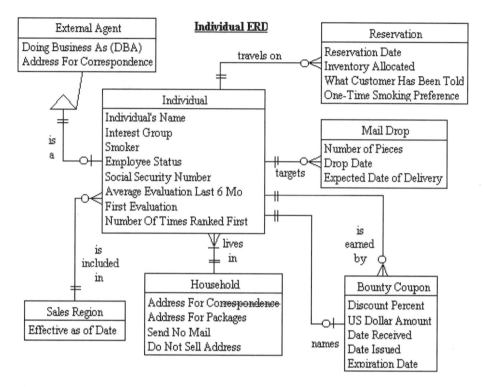

Individual ERD

Figure   A-18

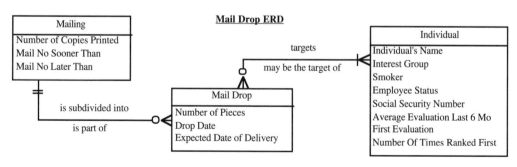

Mail Drop ERD

Figure   A-19

Object of Evaluation ERD

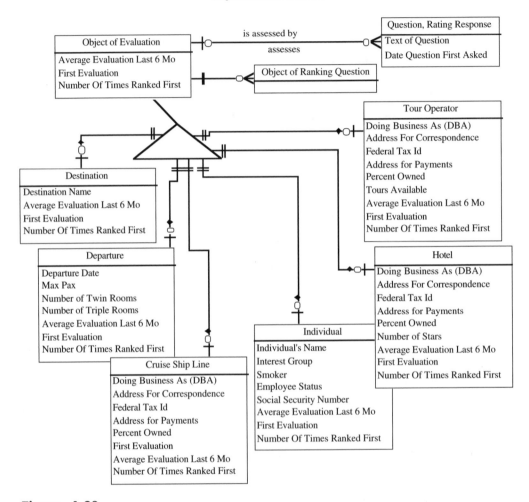

Figure   A-20

Parent Company ERD

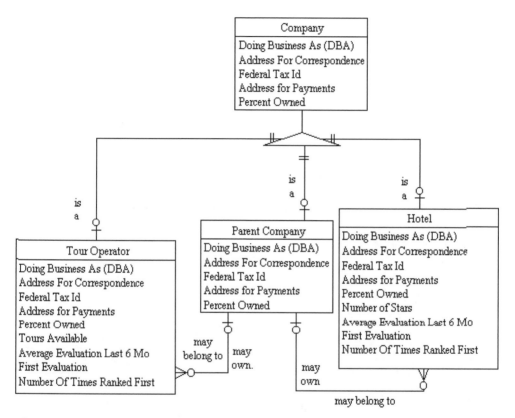

Figure   A-21

Question, Rating Response ERD

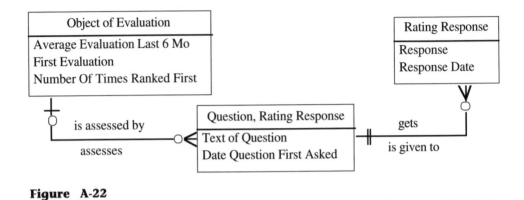

Figure   A-22

Rank Answer ERD

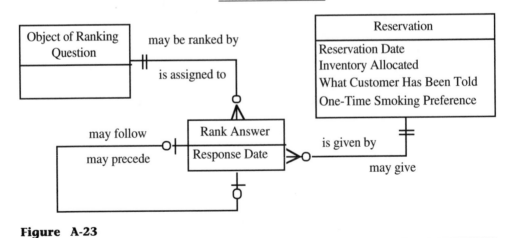

Figure   A-23

Rating Response ERD

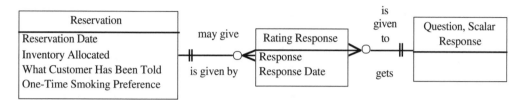

Figure   A-24

Refund ERD

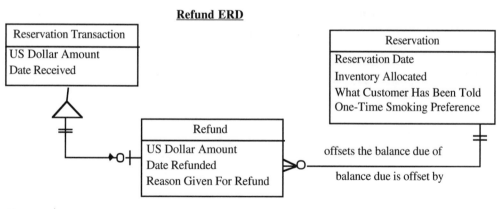

Figure   A-25

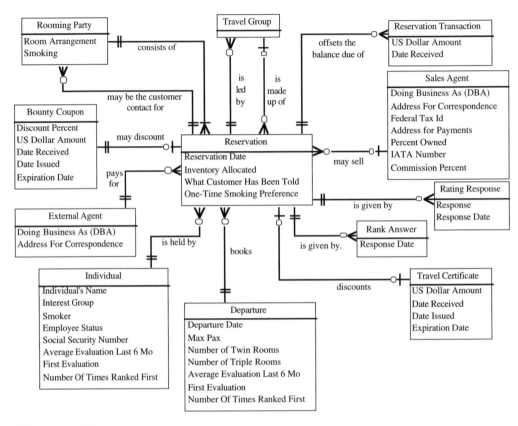

Figure   A-26

Reservation Receipt ERD

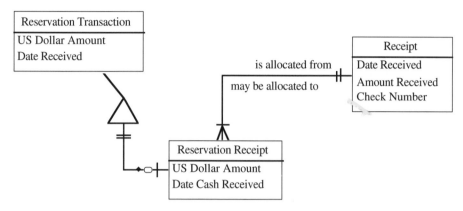

Figure   A-27

Reservation Transaction ERD

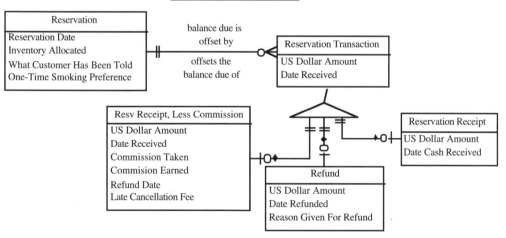

Figure   A-28

Resv Rcpt, Less Commission ERD

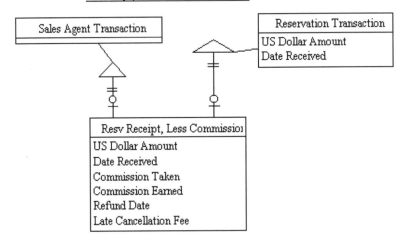

Figure   A-29

Rooming Party ERD

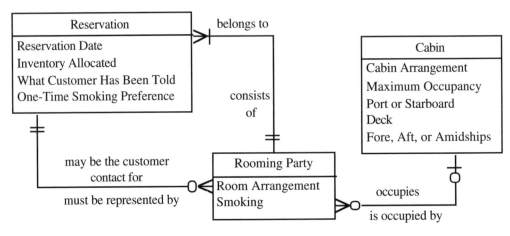

Figure   A-30

Sales Agent Agreement ERD

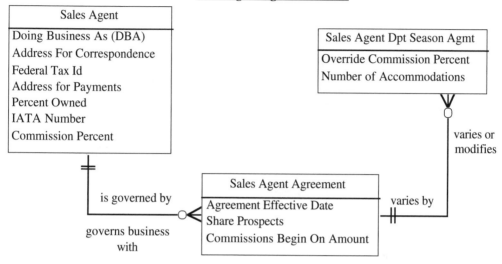

Figure   A-31

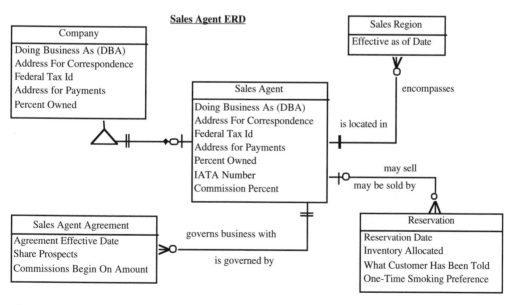

Sales Agent ERD

Figure   A-32

Sales Agent Transaction ERD

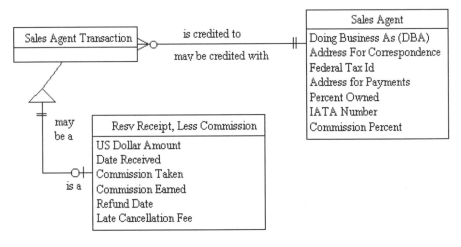

Figure   A-33

Sales Region ERD

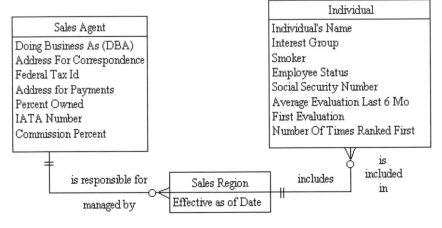

Figure   A-34

Tour Accommodation ERD

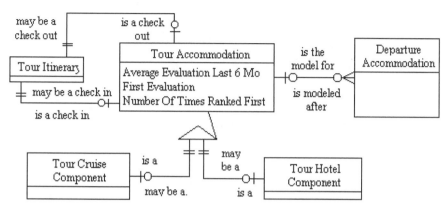

Figure   A-35

Tour Cost Component ERD

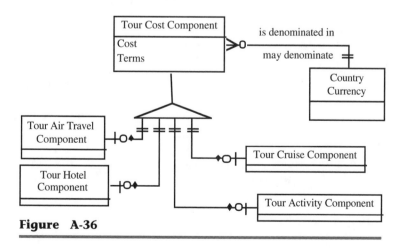

Figure   A-36

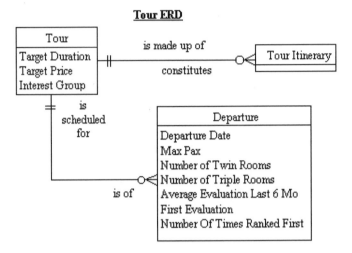

Figure   A-37

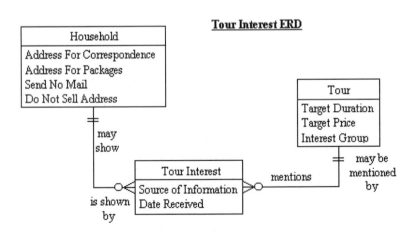

Figure   A-38

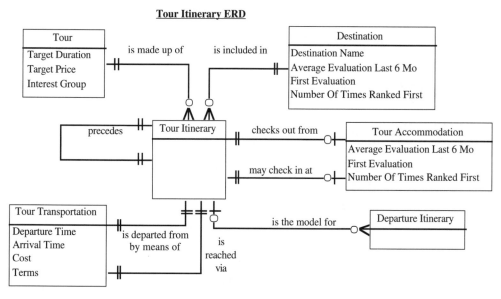

Tour Itinerary ERD

Figure A-39

Tour Operator ERD

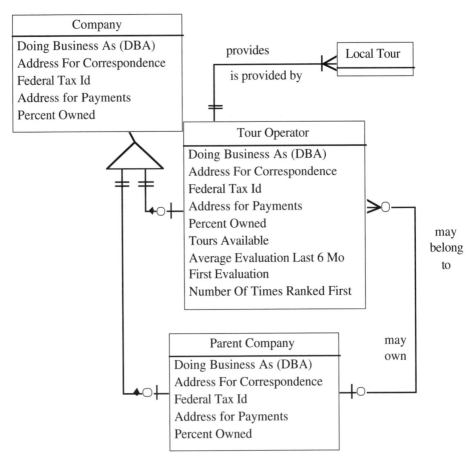

Figure   A-40

Tour Transportation ERD

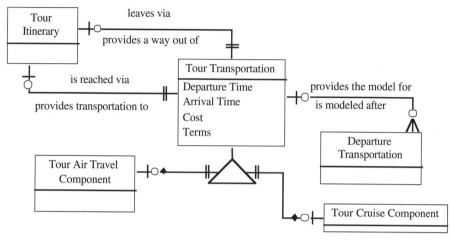

Figure   A-41

Travel Certificate ERD

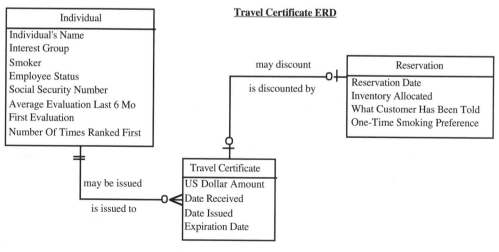

Figure   A-42

Travel Group ERD

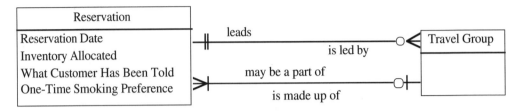

Figure   A-43

Index

D

E

U

V

W

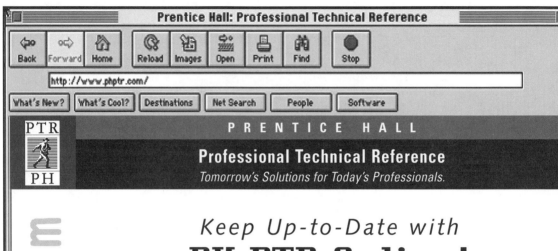

LICENSE AGREEMENT AND LIMITED WARRANTY

READ THE FOLLOWING TERMS AND CONDITIONS CAREFULLY BEFORE OPENING THIS SOFTWARE MEDIA PACKAGE. THIS LEGAL DOCUMENT IS AN AGREEMENT BETWEEN YOU AND PRENTICE-HALL, INC. (THE "COMPANY"). BY OPENING THIS SEALED SOFTWARE MEDIA PACKAGE, YOU ARE AGREEING TO BE BOUND BY THESE TERMS AND CONDITIONS. IF YOU DO NOT AGREE WITH THESE TERMS AND CONDITIONS, DO NOT OPEN THE SOFTWARE MEDIA PACKAGE. PROMPTLY RETURN THE UNOPENED PACKAGE AND ALL ACCOMPANYING ITEMS TO THE PLACE YOU OBTAINED THEM FOR A FULL REFUND OF ANY SUMS YOU HAVE PAID.

1.   **GRANT OF LICENSE:** In consideration of your payment of the license fee, which is part of the price you paid for this product, and your agreement to abide by the terms and conditions of this Agreement, the Company grants to you a nonexclusive right to use and display the copy of the enclosed software program (hereinafter the "SOFTWARE") on a single computer (i.e., with a single CPU) at a single location so long as you comply with the terms of this Agreement. The Company reserves all rights not expressly granted to you under this Agreement.

2.   **OWNERSHIP OF SOFTWARE:** You own only the magnetic or physical media (the enclosed CD-ROM) on which the SOFTWARE is recorded or fixed, but the Company retains all the rights, title, and ownership to the SOFTWARE recorded on the original CD-ROM copy(ies) and all subsequent copies of the SOFTWARE, regardless of the form or media on which the original or other copies may exist. This license is not a sale of the original SOFTWARE or any copy to you.

3.   **COPY RESTRICTIONS:** This SOFTWARE and the accompanying printed materials and user manual (the "Documentation") are the subject of copyright. You may not copy the Documentation or the SOFTWARE, except that you may make a single copy of the SOFTWARE for backup or archival purposes only. You may be held legally responsible for any copying or copyright infringement which is caused or encouraged by your failure to abide by the terms of this restriction.

4.   **USE RESTRICTIONS:** You may not network the SOFTWARE or otherwise use it on more than one computer or computer terminal at the same time. You may physically transfer the SOFTWARE from one computer to another provided that the SOFTWARE is used on only one computer at a time. You may not distribute copies of the SOFTWARE or Documentation to others. You may not reverse engineer, disassemble, decompile, modify, adapt, translate, or create derivative works based on the SOFTWARE or the Documentation without the prior written consent of the Company.

5.   **TRANSFER RESTRICTIONS:** The enclosed SOFTWARE is licensed only to you and may not be transferred to any one else without the prior written consent of the Company. Any unauthorized transfer of the SOFTWARE shall result in the immediate termination of this Agreement.

6.   **TERMINATION:** This license is effective until terminated. This license will terminate automatically without notice from the Company and become null and void if you fail to comply with any provisions or limitations of this license. Upon termination, you shall destroy the Documentation and all copies of the SOFTWARE. All provisions of this Agreement as to warranties, limitation of liability, remedies or damages, and our ownership rights shall survive termination.

7.   **MISCELLANEOUS:** This Agreement shall be construed in accordance with the laws of the United States of America and the State of New York and shall benefit the Company, its affiliates, and assignees.

8.   **LIMITED WARRANTY AND DISCLAIMER OF WARRANTY:** The Company warrants that the SOFTWARE, when properly used in accordance with the Documentation, will operate in substantial conformity with the description of the SOFTWARE set forth in the Documentation. The Company does not warrant that the SOFTWARE will meet your requirements or that the operation of the SOFTWARE will be uninterrupted or error-free. The Company warrants that the

media on which the SOFTWARE is delivered shall be free from defects in materials and workmanship under normal use for a period of thirty (30) days from the date of your purchase. Your only remedy and the Company's only obligation under these limited warranties is, at the Company's option, return of the warranted item for a refund of any amounts paid by you or replacement of the item. Any replacement of SOFTWARE or media under the warranties shall not extend the original warranty period. The limited warranty set forth above shall not apply to any SOFTWARE which the Company determines in good faith has been subject to misuse, neglect, improper installation, repair, alteration, or damage by you. EXCEPT FOR THE EXPRESSED WARRANTIES SET FORTH ABOVE, THE COMPANY DISCLAIMS ALL WARRANTIES, EXPRESS OR IMPLIED, INCLUDING WITHOUT LIMITATION, THE IMPLIED WARRANTIES OF MERCHANTABILITY AND FITNESS FOR A PARTICULAR PURPOSE. EXCEPT FOR THE EXPRESS WARRANTY SET FORTH ABOVE, THE COMPANY DOES NOT WARRANT, GUARANTEE, OR MAKE ANY REPRESENTATION REGARDING THE USE OR THE RESULTS OF THE USE OF THE SOFTWARE IN TERMS OF ITS CORRECTNESS, ACCURACY, RELIABILITY, CURRENTNESS, OR OTHERWISE.

IN NO EVENT, SHALL THE COMPANY OR ITS EMPLOYEES, AGENTS, SUPPLIERS, OR CONTRACTORS BE LIABLE FOR ANY INCIDENTAL, INDIRECT, SPECIAL, OR CONSEQUENTIAL DAMAGES ARISING OUT OF OR IN CONNECTION WITH THE LICENSE GRANTED UNDER THIS AGREEMENT, OR FOR LOSS OF USE, LOSS OF DATA, LOSS OF INCOME OR PROFIT, OR OTHER LOSSES, SUSTAINED AS A RESULT OF INJURY TO ANY PERSON, OR LOSS OF OR DAMAGE TO PROPERTY, OR CLAIMS OF THIRD PARTIES, EVEN IF THE COMPANY OR AN AUTHORIZED REPRESENTATIVE OF THE COMPANY HAS BEEN ADVISED OF THE POSSIBILITY OF SUCH DAMAGES. IN NO EVENT SHALL LIABILITY OF THE COMPANY FOR DAMAGES WITH RESPECT TO THE SOFTWARE EXCEED THE AMOUNTS ACTUALLY PAID BY YOU, IF ANY, FOR THE SOFTWARE.

SOME JURISDICTIONS DO NOT ALLOW THE LIMITATION OF IMPLIED WARRANTIES OR LIABILITY FOR INCIDENTAL, INDIRECT, SPECIAL, OR CONSEQUENTIAL DAMAGES, SO THE ABOVE LIMITATIONS MAY NOT ALWAYS APPLY. THE WARRANTIES IN THIS AGREEMENT GIVE YOU SPECIFIC LEGAL RIGHTS AND YOU MAY ALSO HAVE OTHER RIGHTS WHICH VARY IN ACCORDANCE WITH LOCAL LAW.

ACKNOWLEDGMENT

YOU ACKNOWLEDGE THAT YOU HAVE READ THIS AGREEMENT, UNDERSTAND IT, AND AGREE TO BE BOUND BY ITS TERMS AND CONDITIONS. YOU ALSO AGREE THAT THIS AGREEMENT IS THE COMPLETE AND EXCLUSIVE STATEMENT OF THE AGREEMENT BETWEEN YOU AND THE COMPANY AND SUPERSEDES ALL PROPOSALS OR PRIOR AGREEMENTS, ORAL, OR WRITTEN, AND ANY OTHER COMMUNICATIONS BETWEEN YOU AND THE COMPANY OR ANY REPRESENTATIVE OF THE COMPANY RELATING TO THE SUBJECT MATTER OF THIS AGREEMENT.

Should you have any questions concerning this Agreement or if you wish to contact the Company for any reason, please contact in writing at the address below.

Robin Short
Prentice Hall PTR
One Lake Street
Upper Saddle River, New Jersey 07458

What's on This CD

Find two full-function CASE repositories containing the illustrations in *Data Modeling for Information Professionals*. These are not just static images. Use these working data models to save time and to give you a head start on your own analysis projects.

These data models were developed over the course of a complete business process redesign of a world-wide travel tour company. Because the project was high-profile, managed by a leading big-six consultancy and closely supported by executive management, the work is excellent. The model is real-world and extensive, not contrived to support some theory. Travl_dm.rdm is the project repository. Figures.rdm contains all other data models shown in the text.

To launch these repositories, the CD-ROM at the back of this book also contains the following fully functional demo and evaluation copies from the SILVERRUN suite of data modeling tools provided by SILVERRUN Technologies, Inc.

- SILVERRUN Relational Data Modeler (RDM), the feature-rich data modeling tool used to create the data models and diagrams used in this book. With SILVERRUN RDM, you may view and modify the data models that are contained in this book....or you may create your own data models.
- SILVERRUN Business Process Modeler (BPM), which you can use to identify data required to support business processes. You can also use SILVERRUN BPM, along with SILVERRUN RDM and ERX, to create conceptual, logical, and physical data models that truly support the business.
- SILVERRUN Entity Relational Modeler (ERX), which you can use to define and normalize conceptual data models. SILVERRUN ERX includes an imbedded expert system that enables you to create third normal form data models from data structures, existing file definitions, and business rules.

Call SILVERRUN at 800-537-4262 (US and Canada) or 01-201-391-6500 from outside those countries. Or click to WWW.SILVERRUN.COM.

Also included on the CD-ROM is a demo copy of Infostructor, an interactive education in data modeling. Infostructor aka CASE Essence is the original work from which *Data Modeling for Information Professionals* was drawn. Contact agpw about Infostructor at 800-795-7953 (US and Canada), 01-314-361-5224, or WWW.AGPW.COM.

To enable you to use the documentation, this CD also contains Adobe Acrobat Reader and Microsoft® Internet Explorer. Microsoft is a registered trademark in the United States and other countries and the Microsoft Internet Explorer Logo is a trademark of Microsoft Corporation.

To install the above software, you need the following:

Windows =>	3.x	95	NT 3.51	NT 4
Minimum Processor (type/speed)	386/33	486 DX/33	486 DX/33	486 DX2/66
Recommended Processor (type/speed)	486 DX/33	486 DX2/66	486 DX2/66	Pentium 133
Minimum RAM	8 Mb	8 Mb	24 Mb	32 Mb
Recommended RAM	8 Mb	16 Mb	32 Mb	32 Mb
Disk Space	100 Mb	100 Mb	100 Mb	100 Mb

To install any of these programs, launch the appropriate set up program. RDM and Infostructor may be run directly from the CD by clicking twice quickly on their respective icons. A more detailed description of the above along with installation instructions may be found in the ReadMe file on the root directory of the CD-ROM.

NOTE: SO THAT YOU CAN LAUNCH SILVERRUN AS QUICKLY AS POSSIBLE, A DEMO VERSION OF SILVERRUN RDM IS PRE-INSTALLED ON THE CD. RUNNING RDM FROM THE CD IS NOT OPTIMAL; FOR EXAMPLE, YOU MAY HAVE DIFFICULTY WITH THE HELP FUNCTION. TO FULLY APPRECIATE THE CAPABILITIES OF SILVERRUN INSTALL IT TO YOUR HARD DRIVE USING THE INCLUDED INSTALLER SETUP.EXE FOUND IN THE RDM_NSTL FOLDER/DISK 1.

Prentice Hall does not offer technical support for this software. However, if there is a problem with the CD, you may obtain a replacement copy by emailing us with your problem at: discexchange@phptr.com

You can obtain commercial support and consulting from the vendors as identified above.